RENEWALS 458-4574
DATE DUE

GAYLORD			PRINTED IN U.S.A.

From Protagoras to Aristotle ～

From Protagoras to Aristotle ~

ESSAYS IN ANCIENT MORAL PHILOSOPHY

Heda Segvic ~

Edited by

Myles Burnyeat
With an Introduction by Charles Brittain

PRINCETON UNIVERSITY PRESS • PRINCETON AND OXFORD

Published by Princeton University Press, 41 William Street, Princeton New Jersey 08540

In the United Kingdom: Princeton University Press, 6 Oxford Street, Woodstock, Oxfordshire OX20 1TW

Library of Congress Cataloging-in-Publication Data

Segvic, Heda, 1957–
    From Protagoras to Aristotle : essays in ancient moral philosophy / Heda Segvic; edited by Myles Burnyeat; with an introduction by Charles Brittain.
        p.   cm.
    Includes bibliographical references and index.
    ISBN   978-0-691-13123-8 (hardcover : alk. paper)   1. Ethics—History.
I. Burnyeat, Myles.   II. Title.
    BJ101.S44   2008
    170.938—dc22   2008016967

British Library Cataloging-in-Publication Data are available

This book has been composed in Goudy

Printed on acid-free paper. ∞
press.princeton.edu

Printed in the United States of America

10 9 8 7 6 5 4 3 2 1

Contents ~

Acknowledgments ∼

These essays originally appeared in the publications listed below. Permission from the publishers to reprint them is gratefully acknowledged.

1. "Protagoras' Political Art" in *Rhizai: A Journal for Ancient Philosophy and Science* 2 (2004): 7–34. Sofia, Bulgaria: East-West Publishing House.

2. "Homer in Plato's *Protagoras*" in *Classical Philology* 101 (2006): 247–262. Chicago: University of Chicago Press.

3. "No One Errs Willingly: The Meaning of Socratic Intellectualism" in *Oxford Studies in Ancient Philosophy* 19 (2000): 1–45. Oxford University Press.

4. "Aristotle on the Varieties of Goodness" in *Apeiron: A Journal for Ancient Philosophy and Science* 37 (2004): 151–176. Kelowna, B.C., Canada: Academic Publishing and Printing.

5. "Aristotle's Metaphysics of Action" in *Philosophiegeschichte und logische Analyse / Logical Analysis and History of Philosophy* 5 (2002): 23–53. Mentis-Verlag, Paderborn, Germany.

6. "Deliberation and Choice in Aristotle" in *Moral Psychology and Human Action in Aristotle*, ed. Giles Pearson and Michael Pakaluk (Oxford: Oxford University Press, 2008).

7. "Aristotle, *Nicomachean Ethics*, trans. Roger Crisp" in *Utilitas* 14 (2002): 408–412. Cambridge: Cambridge University Press.

8. "Two or Three Things We Know about Socrates" in *Stanford Agora: An Online Journal of Legal Perspectives* 1 (2004): 47–50.

Introduction ～

*H*eda Segvic died on March 12, 2003, at the age of forty-five. Her unexpected death meant the loss of an intensely loyal friend for those who knew her, and the end of the passionate philosophical engagement her friendship implied. She had published little, because she saw her role as a historian of ancient philosophy as one that required more than precise reconstructions of historical arguments through careful scholarship: she wanted to achieve a real understanding of what she took to be a still urgent set of questions about practical reason. At the time of her death, she had made public only a brilliant reevaluation of Socratic intellectualism and a provocative defense of Aristotle's theory of action—enough to make clear to those who did not know her the intensity and originality of her thought, but no more.

Since then, however, four of her papers have been published posthumously, so that it is now possible to present a representative selection of her work on ancient ethics. The six essays on Protagoras, Socrates, and Aristotle and two shorter pieces collected here were not intended as contributions to a single project. (Heda had plans for a book on Socratic intellectualism and a monograph on Aristotle's theory of practical knowledge.) But they are unified by their intense focus on a distinctive set of concerns about practical reason and an overarching historical thesis that lay behind much of her thinking about ancient ethics: Aristotle was the philosophical heir of Protagoras, as well as of Socrates. The essays develop this historical thesis indirectly through the analysis of the competing conceptions of the nature and function of practical reason in the two earlier philosophers (essays 1–3), and the elucidation of three topics in Aristotle's moral theory that reflect his revision and integration of their views (essays 4–6). The result is inevitably incomplete both as a historical thesis and as a philosophical investigation of practical reason. But the collection reveals Heda as a striking thinker—and writer—whose work merits, and rewards, further philosophical engagement.

～

Heda's unconventional work was the product of a complicated life. She was born on the 24th of April, 1957, in Split, in Croatia, where she had the benefit of a classical education of a rigor long since abandoned in the noncommunist world. After a brief spell at Zagreb University in Croatia, she took her undergraduate degree in Belgrade (1977–82), the capital city of her country, Yugoslavia. There she began her lifelong study of Aristotle and formed the interests in Nietzsche and Kant that later informed her teaching on ancient philosophy. In 1982 she moved to the United States to pursue a graduate degree in philosophy, initially at the University of California, Los Angeles, but eventually at Princeton (1984–92). In Princeton, she studied widely in the history of ancient philosophy, though with a special focus on Stoic ethics, before switching to work on Aristotle's ethics for her dissertation, which she began with Michael Frede and completed under the supervision of John Cooper.[1]

The influence of her teachers (and later friends) at Princeton on her work on ancient philosophy is evident from the topics she pursued through the rest of her life—Socratic intellectualism, the development of a notion of the will, and Aristotelian practical reason—and in her determination to derive philosophically rich results from the close study of ancient texts in their original languages. (Harry Frankfurt, whose work on the will became a contemporary standard against which to test her reflections on its early history, should also be listed among her mentors.) Her own influence on her fellow students at the time—certainly in her last three years at Princeton, when I came to know her—was just as strong: she shone out for her kindness and loyalty, no less than her philosophical brilliance and intensity, in a highly competitive environment.

Her life at Princeton was complicated, however, by two catastrophes: the breakup of her marriage to a philosopher and historian of philosophy who inspired her, Raymond Geuss, and the civil war in Yugoslavia, which saw her country torn apart, threatened her family, and lost her the only 'home' she ever owned—a flat in Belgrade expropriated by the new Serbian authorities. Despite all her joy in the company of friends and in the enjoyment of beauty—especially the complex and passionate beauty of classical opera— Heda did not fully recover from the long exile from Europe and emotional insecurity caused by these events until the final six months of her life.

In 1992, she took a position at the University of California, Santa Barbara. She was exhilarated by the natural beauty of the ocean and the hills, but felt cut off from Europe and the community of ancient philosophy. An initial remedy was a visiting position at Stanford (1993–94), where she benefited from the philosophical company of Julius Moravscik. But she needed a permanent community. She thought she had found it in 1995, when she took a position in the Department of Philosophy at the University of Pittsburgh. At Pittsburgh, she gained much, especially from her colleagues John McDowell and James Allen (the influence of the former on her understanding of Aristotelian ethics is clear in her essays). But in the end she lost first her faith in academic institutions, then her health, and finally her life.

[1]The degree was awarded in 1995.

Her gradual disillusionment with the department at Pittsburgh—and her increasing ill health—was alleviated by her joy in teaching Socrates, Aristotle, the Stoics, and Nietzsche, and the discovery of a series of local cafés incorporated within bookshops. (This was in the now distant era in which the pleasures of a twentieth-century European intellectual—reading or discussion, eating pastries and drinking coffee, and smoking—could still be licitly combined in public in some parts of the United States.) It was also punctuated by productive visiting fellowships at Clare Hall in Cambridge, in 1996, and at the Center for Human Values at Princeton, in 2000–2001. The latter visit had spurred Heda to publish some of her work despite her now customary ill health, and by the summer of 2001, when I last saw her, she had regained her intellectual balance, and was burning with eagerness to complete her projects on Socrates and Aristotle.

The following summer, however, her ill health suddenly overwhelmed her. She became completely incapacitated as she was attempting to escape—or 'elope', as her last letter to me put it—to Europe. She was denied medical leave and, subsequently, tenure by her university, and had to be rescued by Myles Burnyeat, whom she had come to know through his visiting appointments in the Pittsburgh department. Myles took her to England, cared for her through the extraordinary pain of her illness, and finally allowed her to find the happiness that had eluded her in America. (They were married in the winter of 2002.) She died in Cambridge in the early spring of 2003.[2]

~

The papers in this collection can be read as independent essays on some of the central questions in Greek ethics, with Heda's brilliant and original essays on Socratic intellectualism and Aristotelian deliberation (essays 3 and 6) forming their philosophical core. Reading the collection as a whole, however, is rewarding because the resonances between the essays are indicative of a distinctive understanding of the development of ancient ethical theory from Protagoras to Aristotle. I can perhaps best show the direction and ambition of Heda's work by giving a more precise sketch of her overarching historical thesis about Aristotle's debts to Protagoras and noting its effect on the treatment of two striking themes in her work on the Socratic and Aristotelian theories.

The historical thesis is that Aristotle's elaboration and defense of the antirelativist ethical tradition he inherited from Socrates and Plato draws directly on some of the central Protagorean insights that Socratic 'intellectualism' was intended to replace. The vital consequence of this thesis is that Heda is able to explain Aristotle's explicit and critical revision of Socratic views in, e.g., *EN*

---

[2] The cause of her death was chronic inflammatory demyelinating polyneuropathy, a disease of the nervous system, compounded by undiagnosed multiple sclerosis.

III. 1–5 and VII. 1–10 as part of a broader response to his 'intellectualism' which rests on deeper objections to it than those that Plato had developed in the *Republic* and later dialogues. And a corollary is that it yields an interpretation of Aristotle's ethical theory that is quite distinct from its Platonic antecedent (the first attempt to temper Socratic rationalism without sacrificing the objectivity of goodness).

The basis for Heda's historical thesis is set out in her original and sympathetic reconstruction of Protagoras in essay 1. She presents him as the proponent of a theory of civic virtue as a form of imaginative self-expression, crafting subjective values into a coherent life within a relativist framework of societal norms. Her thesis relies on four connected features in her interpretation of Protagoras: (1) his bottom-up approach to goodness, which derives it from the subjective appearances of value that constitute the 'moral facts'; (2) his consequent emphasis on the diversity of goods, not least the good of social recognition; (3) his stress on the subjectivity and cultural relativity of virtue and happiness; and (4) his emphasis on the necessity of rational reflection on the variety of ethical theories and societal norms for constructing a rich conception of happiness.[3] (This is why Protagoras, and the Sophists generally, posed such a threat to the conservative societies of the late fifth century BC.)

The first part of the collection, essays 1–3, presents Heda's forceful interpretation of Socrates' rejection of this approach to ethics: his fundamental disagreement with Protagoras' reliance on our corrupt social institutions (essay 1); the rhetorical strategies that he uses in the *Protagoras* to undermine the bewitching allure of Protagoras' views on their contemporaries (essay 2); and the objectivist theory he developed to supplant sophistic ethics (essay 3). The second part of the collection, essays 4–6, shows the application of the historical thesis in her treatment of Aristotle's views about goodness, the psychology of action, and deliberation. These essays suggest that some of the most distinctively Aristotelian elements of the moral theory set out in the *Ethics* are revisions of the four Protagorean claims outlined above. Aristotle's theory is one that starts from the facts, that is, the evaluative stands that even our nonrational desires involve (essay 5); and, in explicit opposition to Platonic and Academic theories of a unitary good, it aims to reconcile the evident existence of a diversity of *per se* goods—including pleasure and social recognition—with a rationally unified life, through the agent's overarching conception of happiness (essay 4). It is also a theory in which the agent's conception of happiness is subjective in crucial respects: first, because it is not

---

[3] Heda's reconstruction of Protagoras does not give a precise account of the nature of his relativism. Essays 1 and 6 suggest that she understood its historical form to have been on the lines of the social and moral relativism set out in Plato's *Protagoras* (and thus saw Plato rather than Protagoras as the source of the universal agent-centered relativism refuted in the *Theaetetus*).

complete at any one time, but rather the product of an ongoing negotiation between the agent's current conception and desires, mediated through rational deliberation; and, secondly, because there are no external standards for deliberation or for the kind of life we should choose—the standard for correctness is the practically wise *agent*, rather than an elusive science of the good (essay 6). Lastly, Aristotle's *Ethics* are theoretical rather than practical works because they are intended to encourage rational reflection on ethical theories and norms in their readers, in order to enrich their conceptions of happiness (essay 6).

A schematic overview of this sort, however, gives little sense of the heuristic value and philosophical fertility of the historical thesis in Heda's essays. So I will supplement it with more concrete examples, using two of the most striking themes in the collection. The first is Heda's identification of the Socratic model of ethical knowledge in Plato's *Gorgias* and the Aristotelian model of deliberation in the *Ethics* as both formative and integral parts of the history of the concept of the 'will'. The central idea of Heda's reevaluation of Socratic intellectualism in essay 3 is her controversial thesis that Socrates takes genuinely rational desire (*boulêsis*) to be a factive response to recognized goodness, which is possible only when the agent is in possession of systematic knowledge. (On her view a Socratic rational desire is thus neither a *de re* desire for something good nor a *de dicto* desire grounded on a merely true belief that something is good—although she does not deny that all Socratic agents have such true beliefs.) Heda argues that if we understand Socrates' conception of rational desire in this way, we should recognize that his presentation of virtue as the only reliable form of *power* constitutes the introduction of a theory of the will. Virtue, the epistemic and desiderative disposition of an agent capable of genuine rational desire, is power, Socrates claims, because it is necessarily strong enough to determine the agent's action in every case. But a disposition that determines that all action is right action is a prototype theory of 'the good will', which we can also identify in the Stoics and find explicitly in Christian philosophers from Augustine onwards.

Heda's claim that Socrates introduced a conception of 'will' was part of an ongoing study of that complex notion or set of notions.[4] She is careful to stress that the Socratic 'will' is more concerned with what we might consider psychological 'freedom' than its metaphysical descendents. It involves neither the context of determinism or providence that was central to later discussions

---

[4] Heda's views on the history of the concept of the 'will' were shaped by her long-standing debate on this issue with Michael Frede. Michael argued in his Sather Lectures that this concept is the product of a series of metaphysical assumptions that did not arise before the first century AD, some of which we, like Aristotle, are better off without. But Heda intended to show that in its vital form—the expression of practical reason—it is something that ethics and ethical agency cannot do without.

of 'free will', nor a distinct faculty—it is rather the virtuous state of the unitary faculty of 'reason'. The Socratic notion is nevertheless a conception of will, she argues, since it describes a model for the rational determination of action, and a form of psychological power, which is also an ideal of freedom—the freedom of the perfectly rational agent from the constraints of false belief and ignorance. And it does so using a set of lexical items that helped to shape the concept's history over the next thousand years (*boulêsis* ['rational desire'] and *hekôn* ['willingly']).

In essay 6, Heda argues that Aristotle's model of deliberation—a central element in his response to Socrates in *EN* III and VII—provides the second stage in the history of the 'will', since Aristotelian 'choice' (*prohairesis*) is a naturalization of Socratic rational desire. She construes Aristotelian choice—i.e., the kind of rational desire (*boulêsis*) that is the product of an ordinary agent's deliberation about how to act—as a special form of 'wishing' that constitutes the effective rational determination of desire. In Aristotle's theory, however, an agent's rational choice of a course of action does not always determine even her immediate action, far less all her actions, as it did in Socrates' model, since nonrational motivations may disable or bypass her rational agency.[5] Nevertheless, Heda argues, a rational choice still constitutes an act of 'willing' since it amounts to a preparedness to act, grounded on the agent's (sometimes implicit) awareness that she can determine her own action through rational desire mediated by deliberation.[6] Aristotelian choices are thus ordinary acts of reason that shape the agent's initial or first-order desires in accordance with her reflective goals. Heda does not argue explicitly that this transmutation of the Socratic virtue of 'the good will' into something closer to 'willings' in a more contemporary sense is a direct debt to Protagoras. But her wider discussion of Aristotle's theory of deliberation in essay 6 suggests that it was his Protagorean sympathies that led him to loosen 'choice' from its Socratic anchoring in the factive perception of an objective good, as the historical thesis predicts.

A second example of the application of the historical thesis in these essays is Heda's treatment of the ideal of the rational integration of one's desiderative (and cognitive) states in Socratic and Aristotelian ethics. Essay 3 argues that Socrates' paradoxical theses about virtue—that it is unitary, constituted by knowledge, and sufficient to eliminate moral error—support a theory that is far

[5] The essays do not present Heda's interpretation of Aristotle's theory of emotion and 'weakness of will' (*acrasia*). She intended to defend his conception of the interaction between rational and nonrational desire and cognition in the *Rhetoric* and *EN* II–VII in her monograph on practical knowledge.

[6] Heda derives the constraint on the agent's awareness from Aristotle's emphatic narrowing of the scope of *prohairesis* to deliberated rational desire for something within the agent's general capacity to bring about in *EN* III. 3 and *EE* iii. 10.

richer than the historical reception of 'Socratic intellectualism' suggests. Socrates' demand for moral knowledge did not undervalue the role of emotion in our lives; nor, she argues, did his proto-cognitivist theory of emotion deny the heterogeneity and irreducibility of our experience. His intention was rather to argue that desires and desiderative states are constitutive parts of reason, and hence, in the ideal case, constituents of moral knowledge. By linking the way in which we conceive or represent value with the nature of our desire, Socrates proposed to show that the particular 'appearances of goodness' basic to our ordinary experience are fundamental *activities* of reason—and hence subject to rational determination in accordance with our general or universal beliefs. Since we use 'the whole of our soul' in all our experience, moral knowledge or virtue is a disposition that characterizes all of it, or none. (Heda's beautiful study of the erotic power of wisdom in the narrative of Plato's *Protagoras* in essay 2 should be seen as a dramatization of her interpretation of Socrates' theory no less than an examination of Plato's dramatic representation of his character.)

Socratic virtue represents a model for the perfect integration of our desiderative (and cognitive) states. Heda's historical thesis suggests that we should read essays 4–6 as presenting her argument that Aristotle retained the Socratic drive for psychological integration, but regarded it as an unrealizable ideal. She identifies two Protagorean limitations on the ability of Aristotelian agents to achieve the Socratic ideal. The first is Aristotle's acceptance of nonrational appearances of value, and of nonrational desires, as presenting us with irreducible 'moral facts' about the diversity of goods.[7] One consequence is that even in the case of a virtuous person, the best we can hope for is that her nonrational desiderative or cognitive states will be *shaped* by reason: they remain irreducibly discrete—and perhaps inherently unstable—states.[8] Another consequence is that the integration of our desires in the form of a happy life is an ongoing process of negotiation between discrete goals; but since the successful realization of some of our goals is contingent on external events, their integration requires continual adjustment and is never complete (essays 4 and 5). The second limitation is that the Aristotelian mechanism of integration—his theory of deliberation—depends on the agent's subjective understanding of her final goal. But, Heda argues, our conceptions of happiness are always only

---

[7] Essay 5 gives an interpretation and philosophical defense of Aristotle's theory of intentional action that identifies the appearance of goodness under some description as its fundamental trigger. Essay 4 examines his recognition of 'external' *per se* goods, and its impact on his views on deliberation and the way we conceive of happiness.

[8] The essays do not assert the view that even virtuous Aristotelian agents are permanently liable to 'weakness of will' (*acrasia*); nor do they advance the weaker thesis that the ability of such virtuous agents to resist aberrant nonrational desires always requires their active attention. But Heda's Protagorean interpretation of Aristotle perhaps suggests something along these lines.

partially explicit, vague in some respects, gappy, and developing in the face of
new situations, new considerations produced by past deliberation, and reflection on other agents' actions and motivations (essay 6). Hence, the problem of
integration is one that we can never perfectly resolve.

These Protagorean limitations on the Socratic ideal do not undermine
Aristotle's adaptation of it, as Heda construes it, since his aim was precisely to
refashion it into a form realizable by human agents. Aristotelian virtue, on her
reading, is constituted, as it is in its Socratic model, primarily by the agent's
set of actual desires and desiderative states, when they have been shaped by
reason through deliberation. A virtuous action is thus one that is in accordance with the agent's choice in the sense that it derives from a sensitivity to
the salient moral features of the situation, which in turn derives ultimately
from deliberation. But Aristotle's recognition of nonrational desiderative and
cognitive states means that this sort of sensitivity is not immediately a matter
of having the correct general beliefs about actions, even in the ideal case: it
consists in the immediate, often nonrational appearances generated by the
agent's overall disposition. As a result, Heda argues, chosen, and hence virtuous, action is not always or even usually the consequence of a process of calculation or so-called practical reasoning—though in such a case, it remains
the *expression*, if not a direct act, of the agent's reason. So Aristotelian virtuous action is produced by 'the whole soul', too, despite its discrete forms of
representation and motivation.

~

A reading of the collection as a whole of the sort sketched above shows, I
hope, something of its ambitious scope and philosophical richness. The
achievement of the historical thesis uniting Heda's independently forceful
essays is that it yields a brilliantly original and suggestive view of ancient
ethics—if one that is inevitably incomplete as a systematic interpretation of
its Socratic or Aristotelian forms. Heda's premature death forestalled her
plans to elaborate the consequences of her reappraisal of sophistic ethics, Socratic intellectualism, and her distinctively Protagorean view of Aristotle's revision of his Socratic inheritance. But a second achievement of the collection
is to have outlined a series of vital historical and philosophical questions for
further research. The most significant historical question is perhaps the task
of identifying in more detail how Aristotle's response to relativism differs from
Plato's. Heda locates the difference in Aristotle's recognition that nonrational
appearances aim at genuine goods, his specification of the practical function
of rationality through the theory of deliberation, and his advocacy of a form
of objectivity that does not require one to ignore situational or societal difference. She did not have time to show why Plato did not take this approach, or,
perhaps, the extent to which we can see that his later work pointed towards it.

The most pressing question, however, in Heda's view, was a philosophical one: can an Aristotelian theory—or her Protagorean interpretation of Aristotle's own theory—ultimately leave room for the objectivity of goodness that Aristotle was concerned to defend? She was confident that it can; and she intended to show that in Aristotle's case it did, by defending the objective conception of rationality that underlies it.[9] The posing of such questions, and the opportunity to resolve them, is her bequest to the reader.

A third achievement of the collection is that the set of individual essays reveals not just a powerful and original thinker, but an approach to the practice of ancient philosophy that justifies the enterprise as a search for real understanding. The complexity of her essays, their precise attention to linguistic detail, and the remarkable elegance of their English (Heda's third language) are the result of her intense reading of the texts in their original languages under the stimulus of a passionate search for philosophical insight.[10] She had a rare talent, of a sort we perhaps do not cherish sufficiently in our scholastic age.

Charles Brittain

ὁ μακάριος δὴ φίλων τοιούτων δεήσεται (EN 1170a 2).

---

[9] She intended to defend this position in her monograph on practical knowledge by a detailed study of Aristotle's dialectical method in the Ethics, and perhaps of its epistemological and metaphysical underpinnings in his other works.

[10] Her exceptional sensitivity to English nuance was itself the result of an intense reading and study of English literature, of a sort that is increasingly rare among native speakers in our philosophical community. Essays 2, 7, and 8 are brilliant demonstrations of its value, the first in capturing the literary enchantment of the Protagoras, the second in comparing three translations of the Nicomachean Ethics, and the third in explaining our evidence for Socrates to a lay audience.

Part One

One ~

Protagoras' Political Art

Protagoras' Art of Living

*I*n a number of Plato's dialogues Socrates is shown eager to create the impression that he is not in the same business as the Sophists. Yet there are some striking overlaps. Socrates goes around Athens discussing the nature of virtue and the question of how best to live one's life, while the Sophists—most notably, Protagoras—go all over Greece discussing, among other things, the same topics. In Plato's *Protagoras* Protagoras makes a point of saying that he does not, like the other Sophists, burden his student with subjects such as arithmetic, geometry, astronomy, or music. He will teach Hippocrates precisely what he has come to learn, how to deliberate well in both his private and his public life (*Prot.* 318d 7–319a 2). It is practical matters concerning the conduct of life that Protagoras focuses upon—much like Socrates.

When Protagoras says that those who associate themselves with him will become better (*Prot.* 316c 9–d 1, 318a 6–9), this is really another way of saying that his concern is with virtue, ἀρετή.[1] Apart from the focus on human virtue, Socrates and Protagoras seem to share the following, more specific, views. To begin with, they both appear to assume that there is such a thing as doing well or ill in life, and that humans generally want to do well in life. As far as Socrates is concerned, see for instance his words at *Prot.* 313a 6–9: '. . . but when it comes to something you value more than your body, namely your soul, and when everything concerning whether you do well or ill in your life depends on whether this becomes worthy or worthless. . . .'. 'Doing well' translates εὖ πράττειν. To do well in life is the same thing as to attain

---

[1] The Greek ἀρετή designates the highest, or a very high, level of some praiseworthy quality. This noun is related to the superlative ἄριστος, the best. In everyday speech all sorts of desirable qualities, such as physical beauty, physical fitness, wit, or charm, can be designated by the term ἀρετή. Living things and inanimate objects alike are described as having virtues, or, as the word is sometimes translated, excellences. The scope of ἀρετή Socrates and Protagoras are interested in is in fact narrower than this, but is still broader than that of the English term 'virtue'. For instance, cleverness, an ἀρετή, is not usually designated in English by 'virtue'. With regard to the connection between ἀρετή—as a term related to ἄριστος, best—and εὐδαιμονία, note that εὖ in εὐδαιμονία, and in εὖ πράττειν, means 'good' or 'well'.

εὐδαιμονία—, rendered usually as 'happiness' or 'the good life'. Protagoras for his part acknowledges, for instance at 351b 3–4, in response to
Socrates, that some people live badly and others well. It seems to go without
saying that he thinks that they all want to live well. (The discussion that follows upon 351в presupposes this.) Socrates and Protagoras are thus in agreement that there is such a thing as εὐδαιμονία, and that humans in general
want to attain it. Further, they agree that having ἀρετή leads to doing well in
life. Given how far-ranging the term ἀρετή is, this second claim is more open-
ended than it might at first sight appear to be. If one can hit upon the good
life by one's own effort, it is some combination of admirable qualities called
'virtue', whatever this may turn out to be, that enables one to do so.

In addition, Socrates and Protagoras both use the term τέχνη in order to
throw light on the connection they envisage between virtue and the good life.
The role played by Socrates' frequent references to τέχνη in the early dialogues is the following. A particular art or craft leads to success in some specific domain of practice: for instance, the knowledge of medicine enables this
particular person, a doctor, to be reliably successful in curing people. Now if it
is possible to achieve success, or some measure of success, in restricted domains of practice—in curing people, sailing, building houses or tables—by
employing a relevant body of practical knowledge, might it not be possible to
achieve success, or some measure of success, in living one's life by employing
an appropriate body of practical knowledge? The question thus is whether
there exists a counterpart to the established arts and crafts (carpentry, archi-
tecture, medicine, navigation) which, if one had it, would enable one to live
well. This art, if it existed or if it could be developed, would appropriately be
called an art of living.[2]

A τέχνη is practical knowledge or expertise. For Plato, as for Aristotle (EN
VI. 3 1139b 14–7, 1140a 23) and Greek philosophers generally, this is in the
first place a set of capacities a person has. It is something that belongs to the
person's soul; only secondarily is it a set of abstract rules, or a set of established
practices that constitute the exercise of a profession. The human soul is what
makes us live; if the soul had the art of living, it would be in good shape and
well-equipped to make us live well.

As we shall see shortly, when Protagoras comes to formulate his own
μάθημα, teaching, his words on the face of it suggest that such an art is possible. Under one reading of his formulation at any rate, what he professes to
teach is, precisely, an art that enables his students to lead a good life. After he
has given his formulation, he will agree with Socrates that it is 'political art' or
'civic art', πολιτικὴ τέχνη, that he professes to teach. When he speaks of political virtue, πολιτικὴ ἀρετή, he treats it as identical with political art.

---

[2] The term itself—'the art of living'—is attested only in Hellenistic writers. The concern, however, goes back to Socrates.

Virtue and art are not obviously identical, since virtue need not be thought of as an expertise of the sort I have just described. However, Socrates appears to identify the two, and he is not alone in this. Protagoras appears to do pretty much the same. (I say 'pretty much', because part of what Protagoras has in mind when he claims that he has the πολιτικὴ τέχνη is that he can *make* other people have virtue. He need not take virtue in every variety to *be* a τέχνη. His view, judging from the speech he makes as a whole, might be that virtue in its highest form, as possessed by a teacher of virtue, is a τέχνη.) Socrates will question Protagoras' claim to be a teacher of virtue. Against Protagoras, he will argue—at any rate, to begin with—that virtue is not teachable, or more generally that it cannot be deliberately and reliably transmitted through any human practice.[3]

Keeping this general framework in mind, let us look at the issues more closely. What is it exactly that Protagoras professes to teach? When he says that his students will be improved by their studies with him, what kind of virtue does he have in mind? Does this correspond to virtue as Socrates understands it?

Prodded by Socrates (318d 5 ff.), Protagoras becomes more specific about his teaching. At 318e 5–319a 2, he offers the following:

> What I teach (τὸ μάθημα) is sound deliberation (or good judgement: εὐβουλία), both in domestic matters (τὰ οἰκεῖα), so as to best manage one's household, and in the affairs of the polis (τὰ τῆς πόλεως), so as to become most capable (or most competent, δυνατώτατος)[4] in word and deed in such affairs.

Two readings immediately suggest themselves of the characterization Protagoras gives here of his own teaching. First, one can think of a 'pragmatic' reading of his words, according to which he teaches how to manage best one's household affairs—handling things like household finances, slaves, etc.—and also how to speak well in public, and how to be conventionally speaking successful in politics or public life. On the second reading, τὰ οἰκεῖα or domestic affairs include one's own affairs in a broader sense. The relevant questions here are how one should treat the members of one's family or household, how one should deal with whatever problems arise in one's household, and more generally, how one should arrange one's own affairs so as to live one's life in the best way. As for τὰ τῆς πόλεως, the affairs of the polis, these would cover issues such as how to be a good citizen, how to participate well in public life both in speech and in action, and perhaps also how best to run the city. In the context of the second reading, political or civic art should be construed

---

[3] To be more precise, he is arguing that the sort of virtue Protagoras aims to impart is not teachable. I shall return to this point below.

[4] The superlative δυνατώτατςς indicates possession of the highest, or a very high, degree of some δύναμις—power, capacity, or competence.

broadly: the art of being a good πολίτης, citizen, can be seen as including the art of being a good husband, good father, good head of household, and in general a good human being. For in response to Protagoras' characterization of his teaching, Socrates says that this seems to him to be the πολιτικὴ τέχνη, political art, or the art of making people good citizens (319a 3–5), and Protagoras agrees. Socrates thus includes the running of one's own affairs in the art of politics, and Protagoras goes along with it.

If the virtue that Protagoras professes to teach is understood in the second way, the virtue that he aims at imparting to his students looks a lot like the sort of virtue which Socrates, according for instance to the account we find in Plato's *Apology*, spends his days debating with his fellow citizens. On this reading, the convergence between Socrates and Protagoras is great, but may still not be complete, since Socrates as presented by Plato never professed to have an art of this sort, or to teach virtue. As Socrates stresses in the *Apology*, he has never been anyone's teacher. Leaving this difference aside for a moment, let us focus upon the virtue which Protagoras professes to teach.

Socrates appears to think that the virtue Protagoras believes himself capable of imparting is not the same as that virtue the nature of which he himself is at such pains to discover in all his conversations. He imputes, in his habitually indirect way, something far more pragmatic to Protagoras—something much more along the lines of the first reading of Protagoras' teaching outlined above. In order to find out about this, he proceeds with his inquiry. As a way of challenging Protagoras, he claims that the virtue the Sophist professes to teach cannot be taught, or transmitted to others through a reliable human practice.

Socrates argues, at 319a 8–320c 1, that what Protagoras professes to teach is not—on the face of it at least—teachable or learnable. He brings up two observations about his fellow Athenians. (i) Whereas in technical matters people seek advice from specialists, in public affairs (political affairs, affairs of the polis) everybody deliberates, makes decisions, and gives counsel to others; (ii) in private, the wisest and best citizens, such as the statesman Pericles—a striking example of someone of remarkable political virtue—fail to impart their virtue to their sons and others around them. So they either try to teach virtue and fail, or they do not even try, knowing that this cannot be done. The two observations suggest, according to Socrates, that Athenians do not think that virtue can be taught. Socrates is offering them in support of his own view (as professed here) that the virtue in question cannot be taught.

In this argument, Socrates assumes that the beliefs underlying the Athenian practices of deliberating political issues in the assembly are true—otherwise (i) would not support the conclusion he is arguing for here, that virtue is not teachable. The assumption is deliberate. He makes it explicit by declaring at the outset that in his own opinion and that of the rest of the Greek world Athenians are wise (319b 3–4). But why is he assuming this? He appears to think that Protagoras will take as true what the majority of Athenians take to be true of themselves.[5] Protagoras might do so because of his own democratic leanings, or because he tends to side with the opinion of the majority, or in order to ingratiate himself with those whose city he is currently visiting. Or, Protagoras could be taking as true what the majority of Athenians think to be true because of his own view that what *appears* to a person or a community *is* so for that person or that community. The relativist tenet that Plato attributes to Protagoras in the *Cratylus* and *Theaetetus* is not explicitly mentioned in the *Protagoras*, but the possibility that it lies behind some of the arguments must be borne in mind.

The belief that Socrates imputes to the Athenians—namely, that virtue is not teachable—is presented by him as something that justifies Athenian democratic political practices, such as their willingness to keep the floor open during discussions and deliberations in the assembly. If the belief in question plays this role, a supporter of democracy would find it hard to disagree with. But Protagoras' own credibility as a teacher of political virtue demands that he disagree with this opinion. Socrates appears to have set up a test, and possibly a trap, for Protagoras. As he has constructed the argument, either the reputation of the Athenians as wise has to go, or Protagoras' own reputation as a teacher of virtue has to go. Protagoras is free to step out of the trap. Whatever he does, Socrates' two prima facie arguments are set up so as to test the man himself—his sincerity as a supporter of democracy, his integrity as a self-styled teacher of virtue—and not merely his professed beliefs. Protagoras' standing as a teacher of virtue is at stake here, but no less so is the thing he wishes to impart to others—his own virtue.

Protagoras' Anthropogonic Myth

Protagoras gives his answer to Socrates' challenge in a long speech (320c 8–328d 2). I shall look in this section at the first part of his speech, in which Protagoras tells a myth about the creation by gods of mortal races, and their endowment upon the creation (320c 8–322d 5). It is the endowment of human beings that the myth is focused upon.

Protagoras' myth can be read as a story about human δυνάμεις—the capacities, powers or competences that human beings possess. These capacities fall into three different categories. The myth conjoins this difference in kind between the capacities with their temporal accession: upon creation by gods, human beings are *first* given a bunch of capacities, *then* another bunch, and *at*

---

[5] When Socrates says, with some irony, that he and the rest of the Greek world think that Athenians are wise, he is referring primarily to what many Athenians believe of themselves. Will Protagoras dissent?

the end yet another. Epimetheus, The One Who Thinks After The Fact, pre-
vailing upon his brother Prometheus, The One Who Has Foresight, to let him
distribute capacities to mortal races, is said to have 'used up' all the powers
and abilities he had at his disposal on the non-reasoning animals (321c 1),
leaving the human race 'naked, unshod, unbedded and unarmed' (c 5–6). The
powers that Epimetheus set out to distribute were all of a certain sort, and
there was nothing more left *of that sort*. When Prometheus afterwards gives
human beings fire, he gives them something different in kind from the powers
that non-human animals had received.

Desperate to find a means of survival for the human race after Epimetheus'
blunder, Prometheus steals fire on behalf of humans, taking it from the house
where Athena and Hephaestus, the patrons of arts and crafts, practice their
arts. Prometheus' gift to humans is, however, not just fire, but something
larger: a whole set of practical abilities that make humans go about things in
a way that is different from the way non-reasoning animals go about things.
As Protagoras puts it at 321d 1, together with fire humans receive from
Prometheus ἡ ἔντεχνος σοφία—technical wisdom, or wisdom in the arts or
crafts. (Later, at 321e 1–2, the theft is described as that of 'the art of fire',
which belongs to Hephaestus, and another, Athena's, art.) As a result of this
gift, humans go on and—by themselves—invent houses, clothes, blankets,
etc., develop articulated speech, and start founding cities (322a–b).

The last part of the myth (322a 3–d 5) describes humans being destroyed
by wild beasts, and attributes this to human beings not having the art of war,
which is part of the political art. They try to band together and form cities,
but not being able to abstain from attacking one another, they have to dis-
band, falling prey again to wild animals. Zeus, fearing that the human race
might be all wiped out, sends his messenger Hermes to give humans αἰδώς
and δίκη—shame and justice—so that they may live peacefully together under bonds of friendship (δεσμοὶ φιλίας, 322c 3) in the cities they had started
to form. He decides that, unlike the particular arts or crafts they had already
received, shame and justice will be distributed not just to some human beings,
but to all. He lays down the law that those who cannot partake of shame and
justice should be killed as a 'disease (νόσος) to the city'.

By receiving technical wisdom along with fire, human beings receive an
ability to make for themselves precisely the sort of things Epimetheus forgot to
give them. It is in virtue of a certain use of reason—the kind of reason that
finds its use in arts and crafts—that humans can now do things for themselves,
namely, take care of themselves by themselves. In acquiring reason—the technical sort of reason—humans do not just acquire some one extra thing, unre-
lated to the endowments they had received before, but a capacity that changes
the way in which they use their basic, animal-type, capacities.

There is a symbolism in the hierarchical choice of the gift-givers, which
matches the hierarchy of the endowments that are bestowed upon human

beings. The first gift-giver, Epimetheus, the one who thinks after the fact, is succeeded by Prometheus, the one who has forethought. The capacities Epimetheus bestowed are for the most part used after the fact. When attacked, one runs, or uses bodily strength to counter the attack. Prometheus' gift is of the abilities that embody and exercise foresight. Anticipating their future needs and the situations that may arise, human beings use technical arts to provide for their needs in the anticipated situations. The highest and most valuable gift is bestowed upon human beings by the most powerful among the gods, Zeus, who acts through his messenger Hermes. Zeus is the god that governs the whole realm of mortals and immortals, and the gift he gives to human beings enables them to govern their mutual intercourse, and themselves. The precise role of δίκη and αἰδώς is not specified, but δίκη or justice is the component that primarily governs mutual intercourse among human beings, enabling them to live peacefully together; αἰδώς or shame the component that enables each to govern himself in his conduct toward other human beings. Δίκη and αἰδώς are treated as belonging together, as if forming a unity. When present, they jointly ensure the right attitude of humans toward gods.

In his explanatory 'postscript' to the myth (322d 5–323a 4), Protagoras professes that the Athenians and others (presumably, citizens of democratically run cities) rightly accept advice from everyone when the debate concerns political excellence because they correctly assume that everyone has a share in political virtue, or else 'there would not be any cities'. The myth is presented as giving a certain kind of account or representation of this 'because' (see αἰτία at 323a 4).

Protagoras has not made it clear what kind of virtue humans—all humans—get from Zeus. In the myth he refers to Zeus's gift as being that of αἰδώς and δίκη, shame and justice; in the postscript he speaks of advice being taken from all concerning πολιτικὴ ἀρετή, political or civic virtue. He thus appears to take πολιτικὴ ἀρετή as covering the ground that the language of the myth expresses as αἰδώς and δίκη. Since political virtue is just what he had previously himself professed to teach, he must see the myth as connected with the characterization he had previously given of his own expertise. Political or civic virtue, he also says in the postscript, must entirely proceed from justice, δικαιοσύνη, and temperance, σωφροσύνη (323a 1–2). σωφροσύνη now seems to pick up the role of αἰδώς,[6] and δικαιοσύνη that of δίκη. The link between the latter two is straightforward; the two words are often used as variants. As for αἰδώς and σωφροσύνη, it is the government of oneself, which finds its expression especially in imposing limits on oneself, that seems to underlie the two notions.

---

[6] Recall Charmides' characterization of σωφροσύνη as αἰδώς. A traditional link between the two seems to stand behind this, as well as behind Protagoras' linking of the two in his postscript to the myth.

However, Protagoras himself has not taken trouble to make clear the relationship between the various virtue terms he uses, relying on some kind of conventional, shared, understanding of them. That he has not bothered to make clear the nature of each of these virtues, and their mutual relationship, will be of importance later on, at 329c 2 ff., when Socrates turns to the question whether the particular virtues—justice, piety, temperance, courage, and so on—are really distinct, or whether they all amount to the same thing. Protagoras has implicitly spoken of them as a unity; the roles of 'shame and justice' have not been differentiated, but whatever their specific assignments, they have come implicitly together in the virtue that is the domain of Protagoras' expertise, political virtue. Does Protagoras' expertise embrace the whole virtue of a man, or some part of it, roughly covered by the 'shame and justice' of the myth? Is courage, the virtue Socrates will give his account of at the end of the dialogue, to be included in Protagoras' expertise? His speech as a whole does not tell us, and Socrates will therefore, reasonably, try to get Protagoras to be more specific about the relationship of these supposedly distinct virtues and their place in the virtue of a man as a whole.

'Shame and justice' is itself a traditional formula,[7] which Protagoras has appropriated here, but has not spelled out. He evidently wants to use the formula to flesh out through the expressive resources of his myth the content of the 'political virtue' which he had specified before as the thing that he imparts to his students. One of the lessons of the myth is the function that shame and justice serve. Like the other capacities and competences that have been bestowed upon the human race upon their creation, shame and justice ensure the σωτηρία of the human beings, their preservation. One could complain, and Socrates probably would, that shame and justice have been made into something purely instrumental. They are in place merely to preserve the human race from extinction. Protagoras' emphasis on the art of war as the part of the political art that was needed to keep the humans in existence can add fuel to this reading. But although the function of preserving the human race is stressed throughout the myth, a far more sympathetic reading is available.

The same term, σωτηρία, will be used later by Socrates as he argues against the commonly shared assumption that weakness of the will exists. As used by him, the word σωτηρία clearly does not indicate mere preservation from extinction; he has in mind something like salvation. The working assumption here is that the human good is pleasure. If in such circumstances human beings had the art of measuring pleasures, their possession of the art would constitute their salvation in life. They would, in other words, calculate correctly what makes life worth living and hit upon it, thus finding their own well-being. There is no reason to bar Protagoras from this usage, even if he has not said much in the myth to draw attention to it. The hallowed origin of shame

---

[7] Found, for instance, in Hesiod, *Works and Days* 192.

and justice, the fact that they come as a gift from the highest god, makes humans partake in the divine. They will surely partake in it at least as much as they are said to be able to partake in the divine through Prometheus' gift of fire and technical wisdom (322a 3). When they received the new Promethean arts, human beings became something different from the other, ἄλογα or non-rational, animals. From then on, their fulfillment in life started to depend on the exercise of their newly acquired, providential, expertise. Resourcefulness (εὐπορία) comes along with it, together with cunning, ingenuity and other propensities of practical intelligence. Similarly, αἰδώς and δίκη come to capture what makes human beings into the creatures they are.

Αἰδώς, shame, is best characterized as that feature of the human soul that restrains it from πανουργία. Πανουργία is the 'doing of everything'. A πανουργός stops at nothing; a person who has shame will not take whatever expedient at his disposal will enable him to achieve what he wants to achieve. Technical reason is concerned with the provident manipulation of whatever lies about ready to be used and harnessed to some purpose. It chooses and rejects in accordance with its own standards of how to achieve the desired goal. Αἰδώς puts restraint to the technical use of reason, when this counsels something that is inappropriate on grounds that go beyond anything prescribable on technical grounds. Αἰδώς thus restrains and governs the previously acquired, Promethean, level of competences. Shame chooses and rejects in accordance with a new set of standards. Shame can restrain a person not only from taking particular means to a goal but also from the pursuit of certain goals. Something else seems to be in place now, distinct from the ability to find means for the fulfillment of one's immediate needs.

As a force in human action, shame is only apparently negative. Shame avoids what is αἰσχρόν, ugly, ignoble or disgraceful. This framework presupposes the presence of something that is its opposite, the καλόν, something that is beautiful, respectable or admirable. Similarly, δίκη is exemplified in doing not only what is just in the narrow sense, thus refraining from harming others, but also in doing what is generally speaking right.

However more precisely Protagoras wants to construe 'shame and justice', in his myth he has tied them very closely to life in political communities. He has emphasized the instrumental value of shame and justice in the preservation of human life, but has not cut himself off from a line of thought that sees in these features a source for a new way of life, and a certain new kind of σωτηρία, that has now, in consequence of Zeus' gift, become possible for human beings. When he turns to the more argumentative mode of discourse following the myth, Protagoras will say that those who do not partake of justice [and the rest of political virtue, see 323b 2] in any way at all are not 'among human beings' (323c 1–2). They do not, or ought not to, count as human. This sounds like something more than mere survival.

Ancient Sophistry and Protagoras as Educator

In his first long speech in the dialogue (316c–317c) Protagoras invokes the famous wise men of old and claims that they were Sophists in disguise. There
can be little doubt that he means to be legitimizing his own, sophistic, art.
Socrates will later (in the excursus about Spartan and Cretan wisdom, at 342a
6–343b 3) parody this attempt. But Protagoras' claims about Sophists in disguise should not be seen as a mere ploy.[8] Given what we learn about Protagoras later in the dialogue, something other than sheer name-dropping seems to
be going on in his self-introduction.

When Protagoras represents the various wise men of old as Sophists *in disguise*, he is going beyond the claim that they were intellectuals of one sort or
another. While relying on the traditional connotations of the word 'Sophist',
he also has in mind something more specific.

Poets, musicians and founders of mystery rites were generally regarded as
wise, and often claimed wisdom for themselves. But not every kind of wisdom
would create the sort of enmity Protagoras is speaking of. Why should these
men in his view have had to 'take cover' under music, or mystery rites and oracles, professing admitted and acceptable forms of wisdom? In what way is this
taking of cover to be understood? The common view was that to be a poet is
to be a wise person of one kind, and that to be an expert in mystery rites is to
have wisdom of another kind. Poetry and expertise in mystery rites so understood are no cover, but simply examples of wisdom. Protagoras, however, is
presenting the situation differently. As he has it, Homer's, Hesiod's or Simonides' expertise in poetry, Orpheus' and Musaeus' in mystery rites and oracles, and even in some cases expertise in gymnastics, were a cover for some
other kind of wisdom.

Protagoras sees the old 'Sophists' as more intimately sharing his own educational enterprise. To begin with, we should note that he claims, later on in
the dialogue, that understanding poetry is the greatest part of a man's education (338e 6–339a 6). This is a preface to his proposal that he and Socrates
should interpret a poem by the sixth century BC poet Simonides, the *Ode to
Scopas*. Given what Protagoras had said about himself in the very beginning,
that he admits openly to being a Sophist and educating people, the claim that
understanding poetry is the greatest part of a man's education is likely to reveal something about his conception of the sophistic enterprise. He suggests
that his expertise can be exhibited in a substantive way through evaluating,
analyzing, and giving an account of, say, a poem by Simonides.

---

[8] This is so quite apart from the fact, stressed especially by George Grote, that in naming these
wise men 'Sophists', he is not departing from traditional uses of this word.

We don't get to hear Protagoras expound on the *Ode to Scopas*, since it is Socrates' turn to speak. However, Protagoras no doubt hopes, just as Hippias does (see 347a 6–b 2), that he will have a chance to show his own under-standing of the poem he has selected for discussion. He alleges a contradiction in the poem as soon as he sets the task of interpreting it to Socrates (339b 9–d 9), clearly displaying an interest in having a chance to say some more about it. Protagoras takes himself to be on his own territory here; his expertise in part consists in interpreting ancient wisdom.

Protagoras imputes the *same* sort of wisdom to himself and to the poets and religious experts of old. What he must have in mind, in the first place, is that the men he mentions, Simonides and Orpheus included, were experts, like himself, in political or civic virtue. Poetry and expertise in mystery rites and oracles are the shape in which the old Sophists couched their thoughts about how to live a life, as a private person and as a citizen.

Some reports about the historical Protagoras square well with the assump-tion that his own approach to myth and poetry was rationalizing, and possibly allegorical. According to Eusebius and Diogenes Laertius, Protagoras wrote a treatise *On Gods* which started as follows: 'Concerning gods, I have no means of knowing either that they exist or that they do not exist, or what form they might have, for there is much preventing one's knowing: the non-evident na-ture of the subject (ἥ τ' ἀδηλότης), and the shortness of human life'. (Eus., *PE* XIV. 3.7, Diog. Laert. IX. 51, 54; alluded to at Pl. *Theaet.* 162d–e) Walter Burkert offers an interesting comment on this sentence: 'it is a mystery what else he could have written to fill a book on gods after this beginning'.[9] How-ever, Protagoras could easily have gone on at great length after the sentence quoted. He could have described and interpreted a variety of myths about gods. The opening sentence would simply be a warning to his readers that he is not committing himself to the literal truth of the myths he reports on and interprets.

In the *Protagoras*, Protagoras himself ventures—in quasi-Orphic fashion—an anthropogonic myth. The myth, as he tells it, is strikingly allegorical in character. It is told in a way that invites us to cash out its meaning in non-mythical terms. When human beings are represented as being given one bunch of capacities and then a following bunch, the temporal succession can be readily understood as indicating the difference in kind among the capaci-ties themselves. Protagoras will proceed to unpack the myth himself, follow-ing it with a discursive account of what he had set out to say in the myth.

---

[9] Burkert (1987), 466, n. 13, ad p. 313. Kurt von Fritz (1957, 920) had denied the existence of the treatise *On Gods* on the ground that there was nothing that Protagoras could have said about the topic of gods after this alleged first sentence. I suppose that Burkert's remark indicates his en-dorsement of von Fritz's puzzlement, even though he is not himself tempted by the conclusion that there was no such treatise.

Before embarking on the myth, he even offers his audience the option of hearing what he has to say concerning the question whether virtue is teachable—his ἐπίδειξις that virtue is teachable—either in the form of a myth or in the form of a more discursive argument, λόγος (*Prot.* 320c 2–4). Protagoras appears to assume that he can make the same point equally well in either medium. To tell them a myth will be more graceful or pleasing (χαριέστερον, 320c 6–7).

Since Protagoras does not know whether the gods exist and what shape they have, he presumably does not know about their actions either. It makes sense to think that in telling his myth he is setting out a story which he does not take to be literally true. We can now understand his claim that Orpheus and Musaeus were really Sophists in disguise. Protagoras sought to interpret the meaning of the old myths about the gods told by poets and religious figures such as Orpheus and Musaeus in a way that presents these poets as speaking in code. Like Socrates in the *Phaedo* (69c), Protagoras would then be claiming that Orpheus (as one of the founders of mysteries) was speaking 'in riddles', namely, telling a story the meaning of which is not to be found on the surface, but has to be decoded. If Protagoras assumes that the 'Sophists of old' were, like himself, agnostic about the existence of the gods, we can readily see why their wisdom would be the same as his, and why it would be of the sort to invite φθόνος, envy and resentment. To express openly views of this sort could easily land a person in trouble.[10] In this way Protagoras would have provided the men he regards as ancient Sophists with something they might well have wanted to hide. It is also easy to see why Protagoras' strategy of coming out and openly declaring himself to be a Sophist who 'educates people' would be seen by him as an entirely new departure. Among the things that Protagoras presumably does not hide is his agnosticism about the gods.

Both Protagoras' imputation of a *secret* wisdom of some kind to the ancient wise men, and his claim that they were Sophists—engaged in the same project he is engaged in—make excellent sense if he assumed that these wise men, like him, were not committed to the literal truth of the stories they told about various gods and heroes, without however letting this on. By imputing a secret wisdom to them, Protagoras seems to be saying that the authors in question were deliberately presenting their insights about the human condition in allegorical garb. When Hesiod spoke, for instance, about Prometheus giving humans the gift of fire, he could have been using Prometheus merely as a symbol of powers that human beings at some point acquired for themselves. To speak of Prometheus' intentions for humanity would then be to express in a symbolic fashion the significance that the discovery and use of the technical arts had for human beings.

---

[10] Whether or not the stories about Protagoras' prosecution are true, his views apparently did earn him the nickname ἄθεος. The charge of ἀσέβεια, impiety, was a serious one.

The suggestion that some of Protagoras' interpretive practices were rationalizing and allegorical[11] makes it easier to appreciate not only what he says about ancient sophistry, but also Socrates' parody of these practices later in the dialogue (342a 6 ff.). Socrates could reasonably complain that the views Protagoras imputes to the cultural heroes he associates himself with are quite unlikely to have been their own. When he rejects Protagoras' proposal to investigate virtue by looking into the poetry of, for instance, Simonides, Socrates need not have been dismissing every practice of interpreting poetry. He need not have thought that every such practice involved reading one's own thoughts into the verses of the poets. Rather, Socrates might have found Protagoras' way of interpreting poets and ancient religious authorities to be arbitrary and tendentious, and wanted to steer clear of it. Socrates' own approach to poetry in the *Protagoras* is strikingly different: he prefers to address the issue at hand in its own terms, philosophically, while making abundant use of contextually relevant poetic metaphors and allusions.[12]

When Protagoras at 323a 5 switches from his myth to a logos—namely, to a more discursive treatment of the issues discussed in the myth[13]—he strikingly abandons any mention of the gods. The talk is now explicitly about what οἱ ἄνθρωποι, human beings, think about issues to do with political virtue (see 323a 5–6). (Later on, the views and practices of Athenians, which Socrates has questioned, are given special attention.) In the myth itself, the gods are addressed from the point of view of the contribution they make to humanity; it is easy to think of these gods as simply mythical representatives of humans' own accomplishment. What the myth tells us about human beings is that two types of δυνάμεις, capacities, competences or powers, distinguish humanity from other animals.

First, human beings have the technical ingenuity that enables them to make for themselves precisely the things they perceive themselves as lacking (what Epimetheus 'forgot' to give them). This art embodies practical resourcefulness (εὐπορία), which enables humans to take care of themselves by themselves. It is humans' own προμήθεια, their forethought on their own behalf, that they celebrate as Prometheus' gift. The origin of articulated language belongs here (322a 6), since the original purpose of language is the communication of human needs. Zeus' gift stands for what makes human beings distinctively human:

---

[11] Allegorising interpretation of myth and poetry is at least as old as Theagenes of Rhegium (*fl.* C. 525 BC). And compare Hippias as an interpreter of Orpheus and Musaeus (DK 86B 6) or Prodicus' rationalizing of the gods (DK 84B 5).

[12] For illustration and discussion of some of these poetic allusions see my 'Homer in Plato's *Protagoras*', chap. 2 below.

[13] This happens earlier than Protagoras himself announces. The logos part of Protagoras' speech is 323a 5–328d 2; he announces leaving μῦθος for λόγος at 324d 6–7.

their morality, which enables them to live peacefully in cities. The gods as mythical givers are a symbol of humanity's own cultural achievement.

At this point we must remind ourselves of Protagoras' most famous pronouncement, that the human being is measure of all things. Plato in the *Theaetetus* presents Protagoras as applying his dictum to perceptual qualities, and—the case that interests us here—values. What he might be saying in his myth is in keeping with this: human beings construct their values. To say that human values are a construct is not to say that human beings can shed them. They can shed them no more than they can shed another human construct, language. Creation of values is unique to human beings, and is their highest cultural achievement (therefore, mythically, a gift from the highest god). It is what makes human beings fully human. (Recall *Prot.* 323b 7–c 2). Technical expertise expresses human forethought on behalf of themselves as individual members of the species, political virtue their forethought on behalf of their fellow citizens (recall the bonds of friendship that draw the citizens of a polis together: δεσμοὶ φιλίας συναγωγοί, 322c 3).[14]

If this is what Protagoras has in mind, what sense can we give to his claim that he is making his students better? In the first place, Protagoras could have pointed out that his view, according to which values are human constructs, empowers humanity. When he says that he goes to foreign cities and 'persuades the best among young men to abandon their associations with others, relatives and acquaintances, young and old alike, and to associate with him instead, on the grounds that they will become better through association with him' (316c 7–d 1), he has in mind something that goes beyond his role as principal educator of the young men in question. Judging from the first sentence of his treatise *On Gods*, Protagoras has something to teach his student that will indeed pull the student away from the way of thinking he has been raised in. The stories that the young man has heard about the gods will assume a new meaning. The set of values the young man has been brought up in will come to appear as one among many sets of different values that human beings guide their lives by. A study of a range of different cultural traditions, including interpretations of poets and religious experts, will prepare the student for embracing those values that seem to him upon critical examination to do best the job which morality is meant to serve in a human society.

Many views that the student has in the past accepted at face value will thus be shed. He will no longer believe that there is a single moral truth, and that his family and friends showed him the way to it. He will, however, take seriously the appearances of value he encounters. He stands to learn a lot from traditional beliefs, which embody insight concerning humanity. What he will

---

[14] Political art, however, comprises also the art of war, and thus a τέχνη concerned with the destruction of hostile human beings, or at least those the polis decides to regard as hostile.

lose in the process of Protagorean education is the conviction that traditional
moral and religious beliefs have the status of objective moral truth.

'Most Powerful in Word and Deed'

ποιήσαντες ἐκκλησίαν οἱ Ἀθηναῖοι γνώμας σφίσιν αὐτοῖς προυτίθεσαν ...
καί παριόντες
ἄλλοι τε πολλοί ἔλεγον ... καί παρελθὼν
Περικλῆς ὁ Ξανθίππου, ἀνὴρ κατ'
ἐκεῖνον χρόνον
πρῶτος Ἀθηναίων, λέγειν τε καί πράσσειν
δυνατώτατος, παρήνει τοιάδε.

Whereupon the Athenians called an assembly and gave their citizens an opportunity to express their opinions [. . .] And many others came forward and spoke
[. . .] and finally Pericles son of Xanthippus came forward, the foremost man
among the Athenians at the time, most powerful both in word and in deed, and
advised them as follows. (Thucydides, History I. 139)

When Protagoras says, at *Prot.* 319a 1–2, that his teaching is how to become δυνατώτατος in word and in deed with regard to the affairs of the polis, he might not have in mind only becoming most capable of handling such
affairs, or most competent in handling them. He might have in mind becoming very powerful in running them. 'Power' is a straightforward rendition of
the Greek noun δύναμις, while 'powerful' and 'most [or very] powerful' likewise straightforwardly translate the adjective δυνατός and its superlative
δυνατώτατος. To say that Protagoras aims at making people politically powerful adds a new dimension to the understanding of his educational goals; the
two possible lines of interpretation sketched in the first section of this paper
have not prepared us for this reading.

To talk of capacities alone is too tame to express the meaning of Protagoras'
μάθημα. Δυνάμεις or powers in the sense of capacities or abilities, and competences, remain of course highly relevant to his expertise. On the proposal I am
now making, Protagoras' promise to his students is that they will acquire new inner powers, and by employing them, will be able to attain positions of power in
the polis. Among those present in Callias' house we find Critias, Charmides and
Alcibiades. These men will play a considerable role in the political future of
Athens. The lag of several decades between the dramatic date of the dialogue
(the late 430s BC: 433 or 431 have been mentioned as the possible dates) and
the date of its composition and publication (uncertain, but the dialogue most
probably belongs to the early period of Plato's career) allowed Plato to depict
people whose future—brilliant, problematic, and in some cases fateful—
political (and other) careers were well known to his readers. The presence of

future politicians in Callias' house is not an accident. The 'political virtue' that Protagoras professes to teach is, on this reading, something that qualifies a person to become above all a political leader.

When Socrates says at 316b 10–c 2 that Hippocrates would like to become ἐλλόγιμος in the city and believes that Protagoras is the best person to bring this about, he may have in mind not merely that the young man would like to become well-known or famous, but more specifically that he would like to become prominent in running the life of the polis. Socrates' formulation is not sufficiently specific to enable us to decide what it is that he takes Hippocrates to want, and Hippocrates himself is presented as not having too clear a conception of what he wants. Protagoras, however, promises to teach Hippocrates exactly what he came to learn; he might thus be imputing to Hippocrates a desire to become a person of influence in political affairs of the city.

A corresponding use of δυνατώτατος, and of δύναμις, is found in Thucydides. He in fact uses a phrase that is a nearly identical match to Protagoras' δυνατώτατος καὶ πράττειν καὶ λέγειν in Plato's *Protagoras*, and he undoubtedly has in mind political power. Thucydides applies the phrase to the political leadership of Pericles, at a momentous point in his *History* (I. 139). The Athenian statesman is about to embark on a speech that will help precipitate the Peloponnesian war. Athenians have gathered in the assembly to discuss how to respond to the ultimatum that had been delivered to them by the Spartan ambassadors. Many had already spoken up in front of the assembly, some in favor of war, some against, when Pericles came forward to deliver a decisive speech in favor of plunging into war with the Spartans. In introducing the speech, Thucydides describes Pericles as 'the foremost (πρῶτος) among the Athenians of his time,' and λέγειν τε καὶ πράσσειν δυνατώτατος, 'most powerful in word and deed'.

It is not Pericles' outstanding abilities as a speaker and man of action that Thucydides is directly referring to here, but the actual power he wields through his speech and action, underwritten of course by his outstanding abilities. The power of his speech is itself connected with power—it has to do with his ability to influence others. The speech which Thucydides will put into his mouth at I. 140–44, immediately following the words quoted, has great persuasive force.[15] At I. 145 we will learn how effective Pericles' speech

[15] The speeches Thucydides puts into the mouth of historical figures do not closely correspond to what the speakers probably said on the occasion in question. By his own account, Thucydides strove to provide the general purport of the actual speeches, although on occasion he supplied what in his view the speaker would have been most likely to say (I. 22). There is reason to think that from the very beginning of the war he took notes on speeches he was present at. Historians tend to be rather critical of Thucydides' practice of composing the speeches, although they play an important role in his account of the historical events he describes. See de Ste. Croix (1972), 7–16; Brunt (1993), 150–153.

in fact was. But the effectiveness of this speech, its ability to influence action, hangs also on the statesman's own prior effectiveness in action. Much of his argument in the speech turns on Athens being a great naval power, which he claims gives it a decisive edge over Sparta in an eventual future war. Pericles' own proven successes in commanding the Athenian fleet, which Thucydides registers at I. 111, 114, and 116–117, conspire with his gifts as a speaker to help him persuade the audience that he is a competent judge of what he is speaking about, and that he can bring off the successes he predicts. Thus his reliably successful prior leadership underwrites the power he wields through his speech, and the power he will soon wield through his action.

As further support for this reading of δυνατώτατος in Thucydides, let me say a few words about a crucial role that δύναμις plays in his History. Power is one of the driving forces of historical events as Thucydides sees them. A telling sign of this is his conjecture that it was in fact Agamemnon's preeminence in power (he is described as τῶν τότε δυνάμει προύχων) that enabled him to assemble the Greek fleet and initiate the war against Troy, not the oath that Helen's suitors had supposedly made to Tindareus (I. 9). It is Agamemnon's actual power, backed by his wealth and conjoined with his ambition, that Thucydides sees as playing the decisive role in the outbreak of the legendary Trojan war. The putting down of the oath, which according to some ancient accounts played an important role in the outbreak of the war, is characteristic of Thucydides' way of seeing historical events. If Helen's suitors had made such an oath, this could have had a role to play in the events that followed. Yet the oath in Thucydides' view would hardly have been decisive. It is the ambitions of political leaders and the realities of power that, in his opinion, are far more likely than oaths to play a decisive role in precipitating a major war.

Thucydides speaks here (in I. 9) of long-past events, about which he cannot have had any direct evidence, or any testimony that by his lights would have been reliable. He is thus applying to these distant events his understanding of the forces at work in the events which he has in part himself witnessed, or for which he had sought as direct testimony as he could get. Pericles and other contemporary Greek politicians must be looming large in his mind, not Agamemnon. When Thucydides describes Agamemnon at I.9 as τῶν τότε δυνάμει προύχων, 'the most pre-eminent in power among the men of his day', he has in mind much the same thing as when he describes Pericles in I. 127 as δυνατώτατος τῶν καθ᾽ ἑαυτόν, 'the most powerful man of his day'. The δυνατώτατος in I. 139, in the phrase that interests us, λέγειν τε καὶ πράσσειν δυνατώτατος, reflects the same usage. These expressions all draw on the same conception of the role that power plays in historical events.

Now Plato is writing for an audience which is familiar with Thucydides, as his parody of Pericles' funeral oration in the Menexenus shows. We cannot be certain whether he wants his readers to recognize the phrase, as used by Thucydides of Pericles at a very memorable point in his presentation of the events that led to the outbreak of the Peloponnesian war. However, in view of this connection, 'most powerful' as a meaning of δυνατώτατος has to be very seriously considered—along with the usual rendition of the word as 'most capable'—when we are looking at Protagoras' characterization of his teaching. Let me therefore pause briefly to explore the relationship between Plato's use of the phrase and the use of the closely matching phrase in Thucydides I. 139.[16]

The dramatic date of the *Protagoras* most probably falls somewhere between the years 433 and 431 BC. Pericles delivered the speech which Thucydides reports in 432 BC. The two 'dramatic dates' could well coincide. If Plato is referring to Thucydides' phrase and wants his readers to think of Thucydides' characterization of Pericles as 'most powerful in word and deed', he would show Protagoras on a visit to Athens promising to teach his students how to become most capable in political speech and action at almost exactly the same time as the most prominent Athenian statesman, 'most powerful in word and deed', was shaping the course of history by one of his speeches. The thought that Protagoras is promising to turn his student into a Pericles, his abilities permitting, would be very strong indeed.

Furthermore, it is after Protagoras has given the characterization of his teaching in terms of δυνατώτατος that Socrates raises his two *prima facie* objections to Protagoras' assumption that virtue can be taught. He himself brings up Pericles. Two issues, as we have seen, were raised: first, the practice Athenians follow, when deliberating in the assembly, of listening to everyone who wants to speak on a non-technical issue, and second, the fact, or presumed fact, that Pericles did not impart his own virtue to his sons. That he could not teach his sons the political excellence he himself possessed does raise a *prima facie* question whether one could transmit this kind of excellence through teaching. If Pericles could not do it himself, what qualifications does Protagoras have that would enable him to do so?[17] As for the practice of letting anyone speak in the assembly, Athenians may permit anyone to speak in the assembly, but the advice they followed on the particular occasion in Thucydides when they started the war came from someone they in fact believed had practical expertise in the conduct of war. If the Athenians are wise, and such advice is to be followed, are they wise in letting themselves be influenced by those who do not have knowledge about the issues discussed in the assembly? (Given the Athenian debacle in the war, known to Plato's original readers, a question arises also about the wisdom of Pericles' advice.)

[16] The affinities between some views of Thucydides and the views of the Sophists have prompted the opinion that Thucydides was himself influenced by the Sophists. This remains a speculation. I should point out, however, that it is not the question of direct influence I am primarily interested in here. It is the relationship between the ideas expressed in Plato and other writers of this time.

[17] Pericles' two sons are among the members of Protagoras' entourage at *Prot.* 315a (cf. 320a).

The issue whether Plato wants the reader to have the Thucydidean phrase in mind cannot be decided with certainty.[18] Yet the fact remains that Plato represents Protagoras as using the phrase 'most capable/competent/powerful in word and deed with regard to political affairs' somewhere around 433 and 431 BC in Athens. The phrase is bound to call Pericles to mind. That Thucydides could use it to describe Pericles, in his characteristically apt and pregnant way, underscores this point. If Plato did want the reader to have in mind Thucydides' description of Pericles, Socrates' two objections, especially his reference to the way Athenians deliberate in an assembly, become far better motivated.

It would be wrong to think, however, that the possible reference to Thucydides' phrase gives any support for the view that Protagoras is a democratic thinker, an ideologue of Periclean Athens.[19] If Plato did make Protagoras employ the Thucydidean phrase, the meaning of that phrase in the original context—something Plato is very attuned to[20]—would have to be taken into account. When using his nearly identical phrase, Thucydides almost certainly had in mind the political influence Pericles enjoyed among the Athenians in 432 BC. Protagoras offers to teach his prospective student how to live a successful life, both privately and publicly. If Plato uses the Thucydidean phrase, political power would undoubtedly be a part of what Protagoras wants to convey by using the phrase δυνατώτατος καὶ πράττειν καὶ λέγειν in the summary of his teaching.

Protagoras then, who is in Athens, and is considering taking on an Athenian Hippocrates as a student, promises to make him a man of Periclean influence, most powerful in word and deed in political matters, should his capacities permit it. This, however, tells us nothing about what promise he might make to a youth from an oligarchic city. Plato was undoubtedly preoccupied with the thought that the Sophists' conception of the good life gave pride of place to power. Socrates' overall argument in the Gorgias—directed against the Sophist Gorgias and two interlocutors who inherit his argument, Polus and Callicles—is intended as a challenge to the notion that power, including especially political power, is a central component of the good life.[21] It is power, not Pericles as such, that is at the center of his concern.

---

[18] Neil O'Sullivan (1995, 15–3) reports a TLG search which showed that Plato's phrase is uniquely matched to the Thucydidean original and votes for deliberate allusion.

[19] See, for example, Farrar (1988), 77 ff., opening with the claim that 'Protagoras was, so far as we know, the first democratic political theorist in the history of the world'.

[20] So I argue in chap. 2 below.

[21] See the first two sections of chap. 3 below. This is not to say that the exercise of unrestrained power of the sort advocated by Callicles is Protagoras' ideal. Rather, on this reading of his μάθημα, Protagoras sees human happiness in its full form as discharging the competence for ruling which he cultivates in his student.

Protagoras believes that the principles of Athenian democratic political
life—such as universal participation of citizens in the deliberations in the
assembly—are sound, since every citizen of a law-governed state has the ability
to form a judgement about the common good, and has a contribution to make
to the consensus that defines the good of the community. Yet this consensus
can take many forms. Nothing Protagoras says in our dialogue commits him to
the view that a citizen of, say, an oligarchic polis cannot meaningfully contribute to the very different kind of consensus that governs their community.
Protagoras' emphasis on the variety and plurality of human values might make
him especially sympathetic to Athenian democracy; it does not, however, commit him to democracy as the correct political arrangement. However attractive
it may be for us to construe him as an ideologue of Athenian democracy, to do
so is to go well beyond what his speech in the *Protagoras* entitles us to.

The ambiguities in Protagoras' δυνατώτατος phrase may well provoke
Socrates' suspicion. What does Protagoras have in mind by this phrase? Does
he have in mind someone who has the competence to speak about things political, give advice and carry through with the relevant action, or does he
have in mind someone who wields political influence? Pericles could be an instance of both.

Given the strikingly negative attitude Socrates has toward Protagoras'
teaching, it is tempting to construe his view of Protagoras' teaching in the following way. Protagoras' wisdom is a ticket to power. When promising to make
his students 'δυνατώτατο[ι] in word and deed in the affairs of the polis', he is
promising to help them attain political power. They will learn how to get on in
life. Managing one's household well probably comes down to amassing wealth,
whereas becoming δυνατώτατος in the affairs of the polis is a matter of acquiring power.[22] When Protagoras says that he will teach his students precisely
what they have come to learn, this is what he really has in mind. He assumes
that his students crave power to begin with, and he offers himself as the person
uniquely suited to teach them how to satisfy their craving. Protagoras' 'political art' so understood would stand in sharp contrast with the political art as
Socrates thinks of it, which is a matter of making people good citizens.

As understood by Socrates, πολιτικὴ τέχνη is best rendered as 'civic art'.
When he says that what Protagoras promises to teach seems to him to be
πολιτικὴ τέχνη, and glosses this as the art of 'making people good citizens',
this is a bona fide characterization of πολιτικὴ τέχνη as Socrates himself understands it. But he clearly does not believe that Protagoras makes his pupils
good people and good citizens. He pleads, as we know, with Hippocrates to
consider with care the threat to which he might expose his soul if he became

---

[22] In the *Republic*, Adeimantus counts wealth as a form of power. He speaks of vicious people who
have 'wealth and other forms of power' (πλουσίους καὶ ἄλλας δυνάμεις, 364a 6) and are generally thought to be living happily (εὐδαιμονίζειν, 364a 7).

Protagoras' student. Now if Socrates thinks that Protagoras offers his students instruction on how to acquire political power while claiming to make them good citizens, then he could easily present Protagoras as engaged in a deceptive practice. 'Shame and justice', as Socrates would understand these virtues,[23] have nothing to do with the wielding of political power. Moreover, Protagoras' would be deceptive regardless of how Socrates thinks of these matters. Protagoras implicitly identified political virtue with 'shame and justice' and explicitly agreed that his goal is to teach his students how to become good citizens. If all he in fact aimed at was to help his students satisfy their naked political ambition, his description of his educational goals would be deceptive.

We do not have direct evidence that this is how Socrates understands Protagoras' account of his teaching. It is our task to unpack his assumptions and insinuations in order to examine them. We know that Socrates thinks the Sophist might well deceive the student in what he sells. The deceptive strategy I have made explicit above is *one* way in which Socrates' warning to Hippocrates can be fleshed out.[24]

Socrates' take on Protagoras is undoubtedly presented as strongly unfavourable. He appears throughout to be suspicious of Protagoras' motives. None the less, even as a view of what Socrates might think of Protagoras, I am not certain that this is the best reading. And it would certainly be wrong to think that Plato himself has portrayed the Sophist Protagoras in this dialogue as deceptive. The impression one gets from Protagoras' own words as represented by Plato points to a different picture of his intentions. The picture seems to me to be the following.

Protagoras wants to empower his students, and especially so in the political sphere. For all the emphasis he puts on the link between the traditional forms of wisdom and his own wisdom, he sees himself as providing a new and higher kind of education. His enterprise is intellectual. It aims at widening and enhancing his students' understanding of their own affairs and of public affairs. A broader cultural education, which involves a critical

---

[23] The terminology is not Socratic. If Socrates were to count 'shame and justice' as virtues, the terms he would use for them would be σωφροσύνη and δικαιοσύνη—the same as those used by Protagoras later in the more discursive part of his speech (323a 1–2).

[24] The interpretation I have sketched corresponds to a not uncommon understanding of what the Sophists were actually up to, an understanding that has undoubtedly emerged from the reading of Platonic dialogues. Since the *Protagoras* must be a prominent source, it is worth our while to consider how this picture arises. As an understanding of the actual practice of the Sophists, the view just outlined is extremely problematic. Socrates' take on Protagoras' μάθημα is not made explicit: he might well have had something of the sort in mind. However, I sketch below what seems to me a more interesting picture of what Socrates might see as deceptive in Protagoras' announcement to his student.

examination of the views of the traditional bearers of wisdom, especially of poets, helps to provide such an understanding. But the ultimate goal of the education Protagoras offers is practice, including especially political practice. When he says that he will teach his students what they have come to learn, what he has in mind is that he will make them men of action, who will be qualified, if they so wish and if their capacities permit, to take high political office.

When Protagoras uses δυνατώτατος in the statement about the goals of his teaching, he appears to have in mind not power and influence alone, but power and influence backed by competence.[25] He thinks of himself as above all imparting virtue to his students. Like Socrates, he takes virtue to be competence of some sort. Virtue is what enables the person reliably to achieve success in the conduct of life. Where Protagoras seems to differ from Socrates is in his understanding of what success in life amounts to. We have no reason to attribute to him a crassly materialistic conception of a successful life. Likewise, his view need not be that successful participation in the life of the polis simply boils down to acquiring power. Although his conception of the good life is not fully fleshed out, his speech indicates that his understanding of success in life accords more with traditional Greek ways of thinking about these matters than the Socratic conception does.

Social recognition plays an important role in the Protagorean conception of the good life. To do well in life is to achieve the sort of success that is acknowledged by one's fellow citizens. Protagoras sees himself as someone who has run his life well. He is highly regarded, tends to fascinate people and attract followers. It is clear from his self-introduction, as well as from the way he presents himself in the rest of the dialogue, that he thinks he deserves the respect he gets. He wants to make his students outstanding people, who will, like Protagoras himself, deserve the recognition and reputation they are aspiring to, and the office they will fill. Someone who is highly competent in political affairs and who has achieved the success he aims for has δύναμις in the full sense of the word. A pinnacle of success for a young man who wants to play a prominent role in the life of the polis and who has the abilities to match would be to become a statesman of Pericles' stature.

Socrates might well see this as a dangerous playing with the different senses of δυνατώτατος. Yet to accuse Protagoras of equivocation on this score, and of deceptiveness in his approach to the objectives of his teaching, would not be fair. Protagoras wants to cultivate the abilities of his students, and help them become good deliberators in private and public life. The goal of his education, however, is competence that discharges itself in practice. The field in which the relevant practical competence plays itself out is ex-

---

[25] As I use the word 'competence', it is significantly stronger than 'capacity'. The term 'success' is here used very broadly, not to refer to whatever may pass as successful in a given community.

plicitly conceived as social and political; moreover, the standards for the successful discharge of the practice are social as well. Social recognition is in part constitutive of the successful discharge of the deliberative and decision-making competence that Protagoras aims to impart. Having a position of influence in the polis provides room for a broad exercise of this competence. To suspect Protagoras of disregarding everything but recognition and external forms of success is not warranted by what we find him saying in the dialogue. It is likely, however, judging by the formulation he gives of his teaching here, that being in a position to shape the social and political life of one's time is the highest achievement Protagoras had in mind for his student.

Protagoras' approach could be seen as trusting. Provided that the polis is set up in a right way, there does not seem to be anything wrong with a person of abilities seeking a position of influence. Socrates' basic assumptions are, however, entirely different. He appears to be suspicious of the very thing Protagoras regards as a hallmark of a successful life—one's social standing and reputation, $\delta\acute{o}\xi\alpha$, as well as power, $\delta\acute{v}\nu\alpha\mu\iota\varsigma$, when this is understood as the ability to do whatever one may wish to do. At any rate, if these are set as the goals of life, Socrates would see them as not only hollow but potentially dangerous. If Athens is in fact not run well—if it is corrupt, or if its political institutions are seriously flawed—following the Protagorean goals of playing a prominent role in the affairs of the city will lead the person to do harm rather than good, and to harm himself as well as others. If the art of living is one's professed expertise, Socrates would probably argue, one cannot afford to have Protagoras' trusting attitude. One of the first things a person who possesses this expertise should be able to judge is whether the polis is run well or not. To have standards by which to judge such issues is essential to having the deliberative excellence Protagoras speaks of.

$E\mathring{v}\beta o\nu\lambda\acute{\iota}a$ is the disposition to deliberate well. For Socrates, to deliberate well is to do so in a way that is conducive to making correct choices. But Protagoras' eyes, in Socrates' view, are not turned in the direction of ethical correctness. Protagoras makes it look as if he is in possession of the standards of ethical evaluation and judgment, yet there is no evidence that he has any concern for ethical correctness. If one thinks, as Socrates does, that living well is a matter of doing what is right, and deliberative excellence is specifically an ability to reach correct choices, someone who claims to be able to impart this excellence to others, but shows no concern with ethical correctness, would be, in his view, engaged in a practice that is inherently deceptive.

Socrates' stance toward Protagoras—his worry about the risk Hippocrates runs in studying with the Sophist—might be closely linked to Protagoras' being an ethical relativist. If Protagoras believes that what appears to the citizens of Athens is generally speaking so for the citizens of Athens,[26] he would not be in a position to exercise the sort of critical judgement that Socrates thinks is fundamental to Protogoras' professed expertise. If relativism is at stake here as I believe, Socrates would not be seeing Protagoras as merely oblivious to the critical judgment on which the ability to make correct decisions hangs. He would see him as not entitled to critical judgment at all.

Socrates would, of course, need to support this charge by argument. He would have to show that the view according to which there is a plurality of correct standards, where the standard is relative to a given community, is untenable. In the *Theaetetus*, we find Socrates developing an argument to the effect that Protagorean relativism is a self-defeating position. We know enough about Socrates' view on these matters to make sense of his negative attitude toward Protagoras' professed expertise, and to understand why he considers it dangerous.

If Socrates has this in mind, he does not disclose it in the *Protagoras*. I have proposed that his dissatisfaction with Protagoras' position is likely to turn upon Protagoras' uncritical attitude toward 'appearances', and especially upon the received or socially accepted standards of goodness. Knowing what we do about Plato's portrayal of Socrates' attitude toward this Sophist in other Platonic dialogues, the possibility that Protagoras' relativism is lurking behind the views he expresses in the *Protagoras*, and that it is the underlying source of Socrates' strikingly agonistic stance toward the Sophist, must be taken very seriously.

What this part of the dialogue does reveal is that the interpretation of Protagoras' educational goals which I earlier labelled, roughly, 'pragmatic' does not seem to capture adequately what he stands for. It is not, moreover, my impression that the Socrates of the *Protagoras* regards Protagoras' educational practices as just a smoke screen for unscrupulous money and power grabbing. What seems far more certain is that even if that is how we want to interpret Socrates' attitude toward Protagoras, Plato writes the dialogue in a way that gives the reader plenty of opportunity not to concur with this understanding of the Sophist.

If we attend to Protagoras' own characterization of his own teaching, as given by Plato, this Sophist is most reasonably seen as the advocate of an art of living. His notions about what the good life for a human being is, and how one can be guided toward it, are quite different from Socrates'. Socrates has put a question mark over Protagoras' ability to deal with the fundamental ethical

---

[26] 'Generally speaking', because the exact purport of this kind of relativism would have to be specified more precisely if the position were to be properly examined. Not every belief by every Athenian citizen need count; some kind of consensus may be what would matter to Protagoras. We do not have the details of the picture. What we can be sure of is that any variant of relativism would be unacceptable to Socrates.

issues which he ought to be capable of handling if he is to be credited with the expertise which he claims for himself. However, Socrates does not show in the remainder of the dialogue that Protagoras' substantive assumptions about the good life are unwarranted. The importance Protagoras attaches to social recognition remains unexamined and unchallenged by Socrates.

Protagoras emerges as a serious contender to Socrates, and a genuine intellectual rival. By the end of the dialogue we shall find Socrates committed to the view that virtue is knowledge, and that it can be taught. Protagoras' own claim that virtue can be taught has been defeated, and he is now—dialectically speaking—committed to the view that virtue cannot be taught. But Protagoras' position has not been fully examined by Socrates, or conclusively defeated. Protagoras has a rival conception of moral learning, and of the sort of teaching and training which helps bring about political and civic virtue. Some elements of this rival conception will emerge in Plato's *Republic*. Protagoras' conception of the good life, and of the path to it, has also left a deep trace on Aristotle, whose views on these matters were shaped by the dispute between Socrates and the Sophists, especially Protagoras.[27] It was for good reasons that the dialectical outcome of the *Protagoras* did not put an end to that dispute.

Bibliography

Brunt, P. A. (1993), *Studies in Greek History and Thought*, Clarendon Press, Oxford.

Burkert, W. (1987), *Greek Religion*, Harvard University Press, Cambridge MA.

de Ste. Croix, G.E.M. (1972), *The Origins of the Peloponnesian War*, Duckworth, London.

Farrar, C. (1988) *The Origins of Democratic Thinking: The invention of politics in classical Athens*, Cambridge University Press, Cambridge.

O'Sullivan, N. (1995), 'Pericles and Protagoras', *Greece and Rome* 42, 15–23.

Segvic, H. (2000), 'No One Errs Willingly: The Meaning of Socratic Intellectualism', *Oxford Studies in Ancient Philosophy* 19, 1–45.

Von Fritz, K. (1957), 'Protagoras', *RE* 45, 920.

---

[27] I discuss this in chap. 4 below. We have evidence that Aristotle read, and was engaged with, Plato's *Protagoras*.

Two ～

Homer in Plato's *Protagoras*

> We should notice when the subject-matter of an allusion is at one with the impulse that underlies the making of allusions at all, because it is characteristic of art to find energy and delight in an enacting of what it is saying, and to be rendered vigilant by a consciousness of metaphors and analogies which relate its literary practices to the great world.
> —Christopher Ricks, "Allusion: the poet as heir"

"*I*n his dialogue the *Protagoras*," says Wilamowitz, "the youthful Plato created a masterpiece. [. . .] It took him a long time to reach again such a high literary level, and in a sense one can say that he attained something he would never accomplish again."[1] Among the dialogue's most memorable achievements is the opening sequence, where Socrates tells an unnamed friend the narrative of how he was woken before dawn by the young Athenian Hippocrates banging on the door of his house to demand an introduction to Protagoras (309a–314c), followed by the scene in the house of Callias when eventually they gain entry to meet Protagoras and other Sophists (314e–317e). My purpose here is to discuss the literary allusions which are threaded through these two passages. For they contribute dimensions of meaning which have either not been noted or not fully elucidated.

Socrates' opening words in the dialogue quote Book 10 of the *Odyssey*. Two short quotations from Book 11 follow, transferring the events Socrates will narrate into a Homeric context. Socrates appropriates two connected Homeric stories in order to tell his own. The two stories turn the ensuing philosophical contest between himself and Protagoras, the most famous of the fifth-century Greek Sophists, into a Homeric encounter.[2]

The epigraph is taken from Christopher Ricks, "Allusion: the poet as heir", in R. F. Brissendon and J. C. Eade, eds., *Studies in the Eighteenth Century*, vol. 3 (Canberra & Toronto, 1976), 209.

[1] U. von Wilamowitz-Moellendorf, *Plato: Sein Leben und Werke*, vol. 1[5] (Berlin, 1959), 104.

[2] The role of the first quotation from the *Odyssey* is little explored in the literature. Indeed, it is sometimes taken to be a quotation of an identical line in the *Iliad*. (So J. Labarbe, *L'Homère de Platon*, Bibliothèque de la Faculté de la Philosophie et Lettres de l'Université de Liège, Fascicule 117 (Liège, 1949), p. 260 (on the grounds that Plato often cites *Iliad* 20!) and the note *ad* 309ab

Plato goes beyond mere quotation. He writes in prose that deliberately echoes a poetic original, using Homeric language in Socrates' own narration. He makes the stories from *Odyssey* 10 and 11 run as an undercurrent to the encounter related by Socrates, providing a symbolic matrix for the characters in the events reported by him and for his subsequent philosophical argument with Protagoras.

Although I do not engage in a general discussion of the role poetic quotation and allusion play in Plato, the analysis that follows of the intertextual links in the opening part of the *Protagoras* will lead us far from the view, expressed recently by Stephen Halliwell, that Plato typically displays little interest in the meaning of a poetic quotation in its original context.[3] The quotations from Books 10 and 11 of the *Odyssey* in the *Protagoras* are heavily context-laden.[4] They are by no means isolated incursions into the text of the dialogue. They serve as external markers of a deeper symbolic engagement with the epic text.

The literary and the philosophical cannot be prized apart in Plato. The Homeric interplay in the opening scenes of the *Protagoras* is much more than a diverting prelude to the serious philosophic discussion that follows. Symbolic

---

in M. Ostwald's revision of Jowett's translation of the *Protagoras*, ed. G. Vlastos (Indianapolis-New York, 1956). An honorable exception is A. Capra, ᾽Αγὼν λόγων: Il «Protagora» di Platone tra eristica e commedia (Milan, 2001), 132, who also has the fullest discussion (pp. 67–71) of the two quotations from the *Nekyia* in Book 11 that follow. The latter are briefly discussed by S. Bernadette, *The Argument of the Action: Essays in Greek Poetry and Philosophy* (Chicago and London, 2000), 186–7. Jacqueline de Romilly notes the same pair of quotations from the *Nekyia*, but remarks that this "may be just a nice game of learned allusion". She observes, however, that the atmosphere created is remarkable (J. de Romilly, *Magic and Rhetoric in Ancient Greece* [Cambridge, Mass., 1975], p. 97, n. 16).

[3] Stephen Halliwell, "The Subjection of Muthos to Logos: Plato's Citations of the Poets," *CQ* 50 (2000): 94–112. Although context-free quotations do occur in Plato, when quoting from Homer and other poets he is usually quite engaged with the context of their work. Andrea Nightingale has convincingly shown the extent of this engagement in Plato's use of Euripides' *Antiope* in the *Gorgias* (A. Nightingale, *Genres in Dialogue: Plato and the Construct of Philosophy* [Cambridge, 1995], 67–92). Halliwell mentions Nightingale's analysis (p. 100, n. 22), but does not draw appropriate conclusions from it.

[4] Halliwell, "Plato's Citations", 96–7, treats the *Odyssey* 11 citations as "parodic clips" that enrich the irony of Socrates' description of the Sophists' gathering and thereby display the speaker's conversational finesse; similarly, W. J. Verdenius, "Bemerkungen zur Einleitung des > Protagoras<", in K. Döring & W. Kullmann (eds.), *Studia Platonica: Festschrift für Hermann Gundert* (Amsterdam 1974), 46: "Platon wollte die Sophisten nicht als Schatten darstellen . . . sondern das Zitat dient nur zur Belebung der Erzählung". By contrast, Ingo Klär, "Die Schatten im Höhlengleichnis und die Sophisten im Homerischen Hades", *Archiv für Geschichte der Philosophie* 51 (1969), 225–259 at 254–259, while fully appreciating that the Sophists *are* represented as shades of the dead, treats the scene as an early sketch of the metaphysics implied by the Cave simile we read in the *Republic*; this makes it as irrelevant to the *Protagoras* as the author claims the Cave is to the *Republic*.

conjunctions established in this early part of the dialogue introduce the philosophical themes explored in later, more argumentative, parts. The literary
crosses over into the philosophical not only within this dialogue, but afterwards as well. For the characterization of the Sophist Protagoras as a sorcerer,
which in the *Protagoras* appears only as a part of the literary symbolism, will in
Plato's later dialogue the *Sophist* enter into a complex philosophical characterization of the figure of the Sophist in general (234c 5, 235a 1, 235a 8, 241b 7).

1. Homer and Eros in the *Protagoras*

Eros steps into the *Protagoras* at the very outset. Socrates' unnamed interlocutor alludes to Socrates' attraction to Alcibiades. He describes the younger man
as "still" (ἔτι) beautiful. A beautiful man he is, however—not a boy—as his
beard is "already" (ἤδη) filling out. The interlocutor is dropping a hint that
Alcibiades is beyond his prime (309a 1–5). He is thus challenging the young
man's beauty—the very thing that is supposed to attract an older lover.
Socrates comes to Alcibiades' rescue, as a lover would, reporting in turn how
Alcibiades had come to his rescue when he himself was under attack earlier in
the day (309b 5–7; cf. 336bd, 347b).

Socrates immediately appeals to the interlocutor's admiration for Homer,
and proceeds to quote from the poet a line which says that youth is most
charming when the beard is first blooming (309bl).[5] He firmly defends his presumed beloved, leaping to his defense at a mere hint of disparagement. Characteristically indirect, his intervention is none the less remarkably effective.

The words are Homer's; Socrates has done no more than point them up. It
almost looks as if the job of defending Alcibiades has been done by Homer
himself—or by the interlocutor, through the admiration for Homer that
Socrates has attributed to him. And if the interlocutor's admiration for Homer
were itself an expression of eros, the vindication of Alcibiades would look like
Eros' own work.

Later, at 316a 4–5, Socrates will reintroduce Alcibiades, and bring him
into his own narration, with the words: "Alcibiades the Beautiful, as you [the
anonymous interlocutor] say, and I don't argue," aligning himself with Alcibiades in the same relaxed, hands-off, way. Presumably, he has reason to acqui-
esce in the role of lover that the unnamed interlocutor had assigned to him,
even as his words indicate a certain distance from the younger man.

---

[5] *Od.* 10.279. Burnet's OCT follows Hirschig in adding πρῶτον to the Platonic text. In their edition of 1893 Adam and Adam leave the reader to supply the word by memory. Labarbe,
L'Homère de Platon, 260–61, argues that Plato deliberately omits the word because Alcibiades is
too old for it to fit. Verdenius, "Bemerkungen", 42, cites Lucian, *Sacr.* 11 and Photius ὑπηνήτης·
ἄρτι γενειῶν to show that πρῶτον is redundant.

"The charm of youth is greatest," Socrates says quoting Homer, in a young man with "the first down upon his chin" (*Prot.* 309b 1). It is the context that makes these Homeric words memorable. In the line of the *Odyssey* from which Socrates is quoting, 10.279, the "first down" graces the chin not of a human being, but of an apparition.[6]

Odysseus is on the island of Aeaea, in dire straits. Half his companions have disappeared in the house, as he is told, of a "woman or goddess" (10.255) who beguiled them with her sweet song. It was, in fact, Circe "of many poisons" (πολυφάρμακος, 10.276) who bewitched them. She turned them into boars by giving them a potion spiked with baneful drugs (φάρμακα λύγρα, 236). Odysseus is on his way to Circe's house—alone, deeply troubled, on a quest to save his companions which has little chance of success—when a god appears to him in the shape of a young man, "the first down upon his chin".

The god is Hermes. Plucking a herb (φάρμακον) from the earth, which the gods call μῶλυ, he gives it to Odysseus. This good and potent drug (φάρμακον ἐσθλόν, 287, 292) will counteract the noxious drugs the sorceress has administered. The very look of the herb suggests its power: black at the root, it is topped by milky-white petals (304). With such power to aid him, Odysseus will not fall under Circe's spell. Hermes instructs him how to thwart Circe's further actions: when she waves her magic wand, he will draw his sword, and frighten her. He will then make her swear a great oath, so that she may not harm him, stripping him of his "courage and manhood" (301).

Odysseus, reluctant yet determined, reaches Circe's house and follows Hermes' instructions. The sorceress's drug has no effect. Amazed that he has not become bewitched (οὐ . . . ἐθέλχθης, 326), Circe says: "the mind in your breast is not one to be put under a spell" (σοὶ δέ τις ἐν στήθεσσιν ἀκήλητος νόος ἐστίν, 329). She invites him to her bed. Having sworn the great oath, as Odysseus bids her, she no longer plots against him.

When Socrates defends Alcibiades' beauty with words borrowed from this Homeric episode, he conjures up the image of a god, who, assuming the shape of a young man of enchanting beauty, protects by providing an antidote to magic charm. In a line of the *Iliad* (24.348) identical to the one Plato is quoting, Hermes appears in the same youthful shape kindly to accompany, and help, Priam on his way to the Greek ships in an attempt to recover the body of his dead son. It is Hermes as a helper and guide, then, who, without being mentioned by name, is invoked by Socrates as he speaks his first words in the dialogue.

In presenting Hermes as a youth, Homer strayed from the normal archaic representation of him as bearded.[7] Plato in turn provided a living image of the Homeric youthful Hermes in Socrates' beloved, Alcibiades. The world evoked

[6] See νεηνίη ἀνδρὶ ἐοικώς at *Od.* 10.278 (similarly *Il.* 24.347–8: κούρῳ αἰσυμνητῆρι ἐοικώς).
[7] See A. Heubeck and A. Hoekstra, *A Commentary on Homer's Odyssey*, vol. 2: *Books 9–16* (Oxford, 1989) ad 10.274–9.

by Plato's literary references will have been vividly present to the mind of his original readers, even if they often escape their modern successors. Curiously, Clement of Alexandria reports that statues of Hermes in Athens bore a resemblance to Alcibiades.[8] If what Clement reports is true, the beginning of Plato's *Protagoras* could be responsible for this.

The Homeric image turns Socrates' words about Alcibiades' beauty into a strikingly effective defense of his presumed beloved. But the literary allusion plays a wider role in the dialogue. It places the philosophical debate Socrates and Protagoras will have about virtue into the larger world of Greek myth, religion and culture. To begin with, a divine world is conjured up by these words, gods that bewitch and harm (Circe), and gods that protect (Hermes). Socrates' invocation of Hermes foretokens in mythical terms the real situation he found himself in earlier that day, which he will shortly proceed to describe. For he encountered magical powers that lead astray. He was, as his invocation appears to indicate, in need of a powerful and benevolent guide. Socrates will also soon descend, symbolically, into the underworld (see Section 3 below), where Hermes is a guide.

Plato makes Socrates designate his interlocutor an admirer of Homer in the very opening of the dialogue, in the same sentence in which he invokes Hermes. By doing so, he appears to signal to the reader that Homer and the world of myth have a role to play in the events and conversations that will unfold.

Quoting from Homer is in keeping with the role that Socrates has quietly assumed. He conveys the impression of being well-educated, as the more mature lover is supposed to be. Later in the dialogue he will reinforce this impression by further skillfully chosen quotations from Homer, and by his thorough familiarity with a poem of Simonides which Protagoras will bring up for discussion, apparently out of the blue.

The competitive side of the encounter from which Socrates has just returned is brought out when he describes Alcibiades as having said much on his behalf and having come to his rescue ($\beta o\eta\vartheta\tilde{\omega}\nu\ \dot{\epsilon}\mu o\dot{\iota}$, 309b 6). Socrates makes out that he was embattled and in need of rescue earlier in the day. He was in fact not so embattled as to need Alcibiades' help, but the situation was highly agonistic, hence of the sort in which a beloved or lover would be inclined, and perhaps expected, to intervene.

2. Socrates' Narration: Hippocrates and Protagoras

We do not know who the man is that Socrates is speaking with at the beginning of the dialogue. His designation in our editions as $\dot{\epsilon}\tau a\tilde{\iota}\varrho o\varsigma$, a friend,

---

[8] [. . .] ὥσπερ αὖ καὶ οἱ λιθοξόοι τοὺς Ἑρμᾶς Ἀθήνησι πρὸς Ἀλκιβιάδην ἀπείκαζον(Protr. 53, 6).

is not part of the text as written by Plato. The rest of the dialogue is a story
told by Socrates to this unnamed man. A slave is present (310a 3–4). Besides him and the unnamed acquaintance no one else need be listening, although ἡμεῖς at 310a 6 allows for other persons to be present too. The effect
created is that of Plato's readers, an indeterminate lot, listening in on a conversation.

As Socrates tells them, the events of the day have a glow of remembrance.
This is a recent remembrance, told by a narrator keen to tell an audience keen
to hear.[9] We hear Socrates' story as told to a person who has vividly in mind
the places the narration will take us to, and the characters we shall there encounter. The unnamed interlocutor is well acquainted with Socrates and his
companions, and with the locale. We can conclude from the words Socrates
initially addresses to him that he understands intimately the cultural life in
which the story he will hear is embedded.[10]

A young Athenian, Hippocrates, sets in motion the events of the day. It is
with him that Socrates' narration, which takes up the rest of the dialogue,
begins.

Hippocrates rushes to Socrates' house before dawn, bangs his stick on the
door with great force, and when it is opened to him, makes his way quickly to
Socrates' bed, shouting: "Socrates, are you asleep or awake?" As Socrates tells
it: " 'Protagoras has arrived,' [Hippocrates] said, as he stepped near me (στὰς
παρ' ἐμοί)." The words στὰς παρ' ἐμοί echo Homer,[11] especially ἡ δέ μευ
ἄγχι στᾶσα προσηύδα δῖα θεάων, "Then the lustrous goddess came close
to me and said," *Odyssey* 10.400 and 455.[12] (The goddess is Circe.) Bursting
into a person's house before daybreak and coming to sit on his bed, in the
dark, close to him, while possessed with the most intense desire to speak to,
and become close to, someone else, makes for a peculiar situation. Hippocrates is too excited to notice the peculiarity. In the pre-dawn darkness,
Socrates, intrigued, examines the young man about the reasons for his
excitement.

---

[9] At 310a5 Socrates indicates that it would be a favor to him if his audience would listen, and his
interlocutor replies that it would be a favor to those listening if Socrates would speak (ἐὰν
λέγῃς, a6). Socrates initiates this ritual of politeness. He disregards such rituals, or engages in
them ironically, when that suits his purpose.

[10] Since the dialogue has important things to say about human culture, and culture is located
in memory, the tone of remembrance struck in the beginning of the dialogue is very
apt. Protagoras' "memory" will stretch far back, to Homer and beyond, to the pre-Homeric
figure of Orpheus (316d), and, in the myth he tells, to the very beginning of the human
race.

[11] "Πρωταγόρας", ἔφη, "ἥκει", στὰς παρ' ἐμοί has a striking poetic rhythm of its own, situat-
ing Hippocrates between Protagoras and Socrates.

[12] For the formula, see also *Od.* 4.370, 6.56; cp. *Od.* 10.377.

Socrates' narration takes us from the modest bed in his still dark room[13] to the splendor of one of the richest houses of Athenian society, from the easy and immediate familiarity of two people accustomed to conversing with each other[14]—one lying in bed, the other sitting at his feet—to the speeches and conversations that take place in a gathering that has brought together under one roof some of the best minds of Greece and some of their most ardent admirers. Hippocrates vividly recalls for Socrates how he learned from his brother, the night before, that Protagoras was in town, speaking as one does when one remembers a momentous event. Since it was late at night, he had to force himself not to run to Socrates' house right away. He rushed over as soon as he woke up, arriving before dawn (310c 5–d 2).

The style of writing Plato adopts throughout this narration shows him bent on pursuing the Homeric parallel. Hippocrates uses Homeric language to describe his awakening at 310c 8–d 1: [ἐπειδὴ δὲ τάχιστά με . . .] ὁ ὕπνος ἀνῆκεν [. . .], "[but as soon as] sleep released me [and took away my tiredness, I got up and came here]". Compare ὕπνος ἀνῆκεν in Odyssey 7.289, 18.199, 19.551, 24.440; Iliad 2.71.[15]

Socrates, recalling Hippocrates' words, reports how he recognized the young man's "manliness (ἀνδρείαν) and excitement (πτοίησιν)" (310d 2–3). Ἀνδρεία is a word for courage, but its connotations range wide. Here it appears to relate to Hippocrates' being so passionately after something, and his readiness to do whatever it will take for him to get what he wants. When later in the dialogue the virtue of ἀνδρεία becomes the topic of discussion, the courageous person will be described as ἴτης—ready to go for something, poised to act.[16] Hippocrates is poised for action. He is all set to pursue the object of his desire. That object is Protagoras.

As Hippocrates declares what has brought him over at such an hour, telling Socrates, while drawing close to him, that Protagoras is in town (310b 7–8), he displays strikingly different attitudes toward the two men. He is close to

[13] The σκίμπους on which Hippocrates finds Socrates is apparently a light bed used by the poor and on military campaigns. See G. Rodenwaldt, 'skimpous', RE 3 A 1 (1927): 527–9. Cp. Ar. Nub., 254, 709.

[14] Socrates recognizes Hippocrates' voice (καὶ ἐγὼ τὴν φωνὴν γνοὺς αὐτοῦ, 310b4) in the dark. Hippocrates relates the incident of his slave running away the day before as one he would already have told Socrates about had something not distracted him (310c 3–5).

[15] Halliwell, "Plato's Citations", 95 n. 4, rightly treats Hippocrates' phrase as a Homeric allusion, but does not note that it reinforces other Homeric elements in the opening of the dialogue.

[16] The description is much emphasized: introduced by Protagoras at 349e 3, it is recalled by Socrates at 359c 1, again mentioned by Socrates at 359c 3 and d 1, and implicitly connected with the tendency of the brave to "go after" something (ἔρχονται ἐπί) at 359c 5–6 and d 1–2. Aristotle describes the courageous as spirited, θυμοειδεῖς, and observes that θυμός, spirit, is most keen to go for, ἰτητικώτατον, dangers (Eth. Nic. III.8 1116b 25–7).

Socrates and at ease with him. He has never seen Protagoras or heard him lecture (310e 4), but having heard everyone praise him as a most clever speaker (σοφώτατον εἶναι λέγειν, 310e 6–7), he stands in awe of the man.

His excitement, πτοίησις, is at the same time trepidation. Πτοίησις and the corresponding verb are often used of erotic desire.[17] The object of Hippocrates' fascination is the wisdom Protagoras is reputed to have. Hippocrates wants it for himself. As he puts it a moment later: "he [Protagoras] alone is wise (μόνος ἐστὶ σοφός), and is not making me so" (310d 5–6). Hippocrates is anxious to become Protagoras' student. As for Socrates, Hippocrates knows enough to assume that among his acquaintances he is the right person to turn to for the favor of being put in touch with Protagoras. He wants Socrates to be his conduit to Protagoras.

As a reader familiar with Plato's *Apology* will recall, Socrates has some claim to wisdom. It is an unusual claim. Quite early in his speech of defense, Socrates boldly summons no less a witness than "the god at Delphi" (*Ap.* 20e 3–8). He recalls how one of his companions, Chaerephon, had the daring (ἐτόλμησε) to go to Delphi and ask the oracle there if anyone was wiser (σοφώτερος) than Socrates. The Pythia replied that no one was. For Socrates, the reply is an enigma. Well aware that he does not possess wisdom about any important matter—either concerning the kosmos, which he does not investigate, or concerning human affairs, which he does—Socrates observes that he differs from those who are reputed to be wise by realizing that he is ignorant (21d 2–7). He decides that this is what Apollo must have had in mind in his enigmatic reply to Chaerephon: Socrates is wiser than anyone else because he does not think that he knows what he doesn't know. This is wisdom of a sort. Socrates had previously called it a human kind of wisdom (20d 6–e 3). It is the only kind he claims for himself. He is wiser than others to that tiny extent (σμικρῷ τινι αὐτῷ τούτῳ of not thinking he knows what he is ignorant of (21d 6–7). Beyond the *Apology*, Plato will consistently present Socrates as someone who denies having wisdom about human affairs.

Hippocrates, however, is not linking Socrates to wisdom in any way. He is not taking in Socrates at all, except as a man who will put him in touch with Protagoras. This is so as he steps close to Socrates (310b 7–8), as he feels around in the dark for his bed and sits down at his feet (310c 1–2), and as he says, a moment later, that Protagoras alone is wise (310d 5–6). His words deny wisdom to Socrates.

Hippocrates is a victim of erotic contagion. Since he has never seen Protagoras or heard him speak, he must have picked up the attraction from some

---

[17] See Sappho 31.5–6, τό μ' ἦ μὰν καρδίαν ἐν στήθεσιν ἐπτόαισιν, "Truly that sets my heart trembling in my breast" (Campbell's translation). In *Rep.* 4.439d 6–7 Plato uses the verb to describe the appetitive part of the soul: the non-rational and appetitive part of the soul lusts, thirsts, hungers, and "feels the flutter of other desires," περὶ τὰς ἄλλας ἐπιθυμίας ἐπτόηται.

of those who have. Socrates himself, as he starts the conversation with the
unnamed acquaintance, pretends to be among those smitten by Protagoras.
He has just been with Alcibiades, he says, but something strange happened:
he paid no attention to him, and often forgot about him altogether, having met someone far more beautiful, "the wisest man alive" (σοφωτάτῳ μὲν
οὖν δήπου τῶν γε νῦν, 309d 1). Socrates is ironic when he describes Protagoras as the wisest man alive—as the rest of his sentence hints: "if you think
(εἴ σοι δοκεῖ) that Protagoras is the wisest" (309d 1–2).

The irony is not expressive of cynical detachment. Socrates is genuinely
excited by the conversation he reports, as he reveals by his eagerness to tell
the story. But this is not because he is himself taken with Protagoras as 'the
wisest'. He is quoting the reputation Protagoras enjoys, and alluding to Hippocrates' uncritical acceptance of it. Socrates for his part will proceed in
the rest of the dialogue to put this reputation into question.

By the end of the dialogue we find the situation considerably changed. The
makings of an erotic reversal are firmly in place, following the outcome of the
dialectical contest between Socrates and Protagoras. Protagoras is the one who
moves to put an end to the conversation. Tactfully, he does it with a word of
praise for Socrates:

> "Socrates, I commend your eagerness for arguments and the way you go about them
> (ἐπαινῶ σου τὴν προθυμίαν καὶ τὴν διέξοδον τῶν λόγων).[18] I really don't
> think I am a bad man, quite generally, and certainly the last man to harbour envy
> (φθονερός). Indeed, I have told many people that I admire (ἄγαμαι) you more
> than anyone I have met, definitely more than anyone in your generation. And I say
> that I would not be surprised if you became famous for wisdom (εἰ τῶν ἐλλογίμων
> γένοιο ἀνδρῶν ἐπὶ σοφίᾳ). We shall discuss these things later, whenever you
> wish. Now it is time to turn our attention to something else" (361d 7–361e 6).

Protagoras is speaking as someone whose membership in the circle of those
renowned for their wisdom is incontestable. If a much younger man, like
Socrates, has done so well in a discussion with him, it would not be surprising
if he too joined the circle. However we might appraise this exit strategy, Protagoras understands very well that his own wisdom was at stake in the proceedings he has just had with Socrates. He does not depict the situation as
one in which he himself has suffered any loss; none the less he grants that

---

[18] Alternatively: "I commend your eagerness and the way you went about the discussion". Since
   Protagoras echoes here the form of words Socrates had previously used—τὴν προθυμίαν at
   361d 8 recalls Socrates' πᾶσαν προθυμίαν ἔχω, "I am most eager," at 361c 3—he may well be
   referring to the specific discussion the two have just had. The reference to οἱ λόγοι, arguments
   or discussion, may thus be understood as referring to that discussion. However, Protagoras'
   words have generality: he may be praising not only the way Socrates handled their discussion,
   but also his habitual passion for argument.

Socrates has gained something, which puts him on his way toward achieving the sort of fame that Protagoras now enjoys. Protagoras presents himself as not begrudging this.

The erotic field as it appeared at the beginning of Socrates' narration has been put under considerable pressure by the conversations that have taken place meanwhile. In a brief response to the "encomium" with which Protagoras brings their debate to an end, Socrates brings up Callias as the reason why he had not left the house earlier:

> "That is what we should do [sc. end the conversation], if it seems right to you [if you please, εἴ σοι δοκεῖ]. It was in fact time a while back for me to go where I said I was going, but I stayed as a favour to Callias the Beautiful (ἀλλὰ Καλλίᾳ τῷ καλῷ χαριζόμενος παρέμεινα." (362a 1–3)

A reference to the host, especially such a generous one, might be appropriate when one is about to leave the house. However, Socrates is doing more with his words here. A remark that Socrates as narrator makes early in the dialogue should be recalled. He suspected that Protagoras was preening himself on the idea that Socrates and Hippocrates had come to Callias' house as his lovers, ἐρασταί (317c 6–d 3). Now as the conversation ends, Socrates makes it clear that he had not come to Callias' house as Protagoras' lover. He is a rival, and has been all along, whose aim it is to detach his companions, including the host Callias, from Protagoras.[19]

At this point Protagoras has granted to Socrates that he is likely to become famous for wisdom. Wisdom is what attracts young men like those present. When someone's presumed wisdom is challenged, as has just happened to Protagoras, the erotic attraction might easily also find itself in a precarious situation. In calling Callias beautiful in his own presence, while taking his leave of Protagoras, Socrates appears to be suggesting that Protagoras' claim to his host's attention was compromised in the course of the conversation.

---

[19] Callias is the first person mentioned by Socrates as he describes to the unnamed interlocutor those in Protagoras' retinue (314e 4–5). Many other highly desirable young men are also in the audience. Charmides, Plato's uncle, is among them (at *Chrm.* 155d 3–e 2 Socrates reports how he was nearly knocked out by the sudden glimpse of his naked body). Also present is a future tragic poet Agathon, described in the *Protagoras* as of fine character and very beautiful in appearance (τὴν . . . ἰδέαν . . . πάνυ καλός), who Socrates guesses is Pausanias' young love (παιδικά, 315d 7–e 3). Agathon and Pausanias also appear as a couple in the *Symposium*; Agathon is the host of the banquet. The overlap between the characters of the *Protagoras* and the *Symposium* is striking. It is as if Plato wants, when he comes to write the *Symposium*, to offer a retroactive commentary on what must be his earlier work. Like the *Symposium*, the *Protagoras* is an erotic dialogue. The philosophical eros Plato has been interested in all along gets an explicit elaboration in the later dialogue. The puzzlingly detached character of Socrates' dealings with Alcibiades in the *Protagoras* receive an elaboration in the *Symposium*, which offers a commentary on the unconventional eroticism of Socrates.

Socrates pays a compliment to Callias' beauty using the same form of words he had previously applied to his own presumed beloved, Alcibiades (316a 4: 'Alcibiades the Beautiful'). In this instance, however, he is not responding to a provocation; he is the one who is acting provocatively. There is irony in his words: he did not have to leave; it was not Callias' beauty that made him stay. The alleged need to go elsewhere was merely a pretext he used to express his dissatisfaction with the terms of the debate, which was on the point of breaking down. As a conventional come-on to Callias, the words are almost certainly ironic. But the provocation to Protagoras contained in his words to Callias, his challenge to Protagoras' mesmerizing appeal, is genuine.

Plato seals the erotic and dramatic reversal in the final words of the dialogue, where Socrates returns to his interlocutor to say, "Having said so much and heard so much, we left" (362a 4). 'Aπῆμεν, "we left," must refer to Hippocrates and Socrates. They left together. What Socrates is telling his friend is that Hippocrates did not stay on in Callias' house to become a student of Protagoras.

3. The Souls of the Dead

Socrates' description of the scene at Callias' house takes the anonymous interlocutor, and Plato's reader, into the next book of the *Odyssey*, Book 11, which tells how Odysseus, following Circe's instructions, goes to the outer edge of the underworld to speak with the souls of the dead. The relationship between the two situations is established by two brief quotations from the *Nekyia* which Socrates uses to introduce the two Sophists other than Protagoras who are present at the gathering, Hippias of Elis and Prodicus of Ceos.

Like Protagoras, Hippias and Prodicus are seen lecturing in Callias' house in front of an audience. Like Protagoras, they have attracted Athenians to their audience besides the foreigners who journeyed with them. To be sure, Callias, the rich host himself, and the two sons of Pericles are all in Protagoras' retinue, but there are prominent Athenians around Hippias and Prodicus as well.

At the end of Book 10 of the *Odyssey*, Circe informs Odysseus that he must meet with the souls of the dead, as the two are lying and sitting on her bed, in the pre-dawn darkness. Odysseus is unhappy that he must go to the abode of the dead, so unhappy he would rather be dead. What follows in Book 11 of the *Odyssey* is the memorable scene of his encounter with the souls from Hades.

Socrates' quotations link Hippias with the soul of Heracles (most probably), and Prodicus with that of Tantalus—two mighty chthonian heroes, whose shadows Odysseus encounters among other souls from the underworld.

The phrase with which Socrates introduces Hippias, τὸν δὲ μετ' εἰσενόησα, "and after him I spotted" (315b 9) is formulaic. It is used by Odysseus to introduce both Orion (10.572) and Heracles (10.601). The "him" in "after him I spotted" refers to Protagoras, whom Socrates had mentioned first, comparing him with Orpheus (314e–315b). The formula thus retroactively places Protagoras/Orpheus into Hades, where he is of course very much at home.[20] The formulaic phrase thus serves to transpose the whole scene in Callias' house to the realm of the dead.

The phrase when used as part of Socrates' narration is incongruously grand. The Homeric language is his way of mocking the trappings of the celebrity status the Sophists have assumed. It makes one think of the vanity of stars and the gullibility of the starstruck audience gasping for another sighting. Celebrity status is of necessity hierarchical. The standing of each of the three lecturers in Callias' house is matched not only by the social position of those in his audience but also by the quality of the space he occupies, the chair or bed on which he sits or reclines. Protagoras is in a grand and spacious colonnade; Prodicus in a converted storeroom.

It is much likelier that the reference of τὸν δὲ μετ᾽ εἰσενόησα is to Heracles than to Orion. Hippias' teaching of the many branches of knowledge nicely corresponds to Heracles' countless heroic labors. Heracles is a superhero, whose boundless, and sometimes outrageous, energy and enterprise seem to mock the ordinary hero. He is an apt ironical stand-in for Hippias' encyclopedic ambitions.[21]

The citing of Heracles builds on the symbolism Socrates introduces when he likens Protagoras to Orpheus. Orpheus was reputed to be a founder of mysteries; Heracles for his part was a prototypical mystery initiate. Heracles had additional links with the underworld. Among this hero's exploits was a κατάβασις, descent to the underworld.

In entering Callias' house, which Xenophon locates down in the Peiraeus (*Symp.* I. 2), Socrates and Hippocrates have entered no ordinary place. It is like that twilight place, the "house of Hades," as the poets are fond of calling the underworld.[22] As with the house of Hades, a fierce presence guards the door: Cerberus, the porter at *Prot.* 314ce.[23] Inside one encounters mighty heroes, but they are shadowy and not fully real. In the Homeric underworld, they are flitting about "smokelike" and "dreamlike."

By presenting them as heroes of the nether world, Socrates seems to be making an ironical comment on the image the three Sophists have of themselves. They like to think of themselves, and to come across, as extraordinary. Socrates attempts to deflate, with irony, what he regards as the Sophists' pompousness.

---

[20] Orpheus is himself a chthonic figure; vase painters often depict him in Hades.

[21] Contrast Adam and Adam *ad loc.*: "The reference is not to be pressed beyond the words quoted: for there is no special likeness between Homer's Heracles . . . and Plato's Hippias".

[22] E.g. *Od.* 10.491, 564; Sappho 55.

[23] The parallel with Cerberus is owed to Klär, "Die Schatten im Höhlengleichnis", 256.

Placed in the underworld, the three Sophists appear as shadowy figures, lacking in full-blooded life. Theirs is a different world—a world of εἴδωλα, images, or appearances. One thinks of Protagoras' endorsement of appearances—his claim that things *are* for each person as they *appear* to him—and of Socrates' own conviction that the Sophists are lost in the world of appearance, never getting hold of the truth.

Prodicus is the Sophist who receives the least sympathetic treatment, both here and in the rest of the dialogue. The portrayal of him later in the dialogue helps throw light on his casting as Tantalus. Prodicus is much concerned with the correct use of language.[24] He is at pains to distinguish between closely related expressions. But, like Tantalus' food and drink, the truth about words always seems to recede. Prodicus' linguistic analyses later on in the dialogue appear laborious, while invariably missing what matters. Socrates cannot hear what Prodicus is lecturing on, since his deep voice has set up reverberation in the room (*Prot.* 316a 1–2). The voice of the expert on language, who strives after an account that is exact and clear, appears to produce only something indistinct and blurred (ἀσαφῆ). Finally, Prodicus' mild illness, when put side by side with Tantalus' great torments, seems paltry.

Socrates' ironic representation of Hippias and Prodicus as the shadows of heroes is certainly not mere playfulness. Like Tantalus, Prodicus appears as a thwarted character. None the less, by placing them in the Homeric underworld and representing them as the souls of mighty heroes, Socrates draws an intriguing image. The Sophists emerge with pretensions to be larger-than-life, provocative figures.

4. The World of the *Protagoras*: Odysseus, Circe, and Hermes

Before Protagoras appears in the flesh in the dialogue, he appears as a force. It is his astonishing power to attract that makes its way to Socrates' house before dawn in the form of a fluttering Hippocrates. When Socrates and Hippocrates reach Callias' house, this power to attract, much amplified, is finally in full evidence.

Protagoras has drawn a large crowd in Callias' house. As he lectures, a number of people are walking with him up and down the portico, flanking him on both sides. The host himself, Callias, is next to him. Protagoras' star student Antimoiros of Mende is on the other side, close by. Many in the group are ξένοι, foreigners, which is to say, non-Athenians. Protagoras, says

---

[24] We have evidence that the historical Protagoras, and other Sophists, shared this preoccupation. Prodicus' distinctions were evidently regarded as especially subtle (witness the reaction of his audience to the distinctions he introduces at *Prot.* 337c 5–6).

Socrates, collects them from each city he goes through—enchanting them, κηλῶν, with his voice like Orpheus. Spellbound, κεκηλημένοι, they follow him around (315a 7–b 1).

However, it is not only foreigners who have followed Protagoras as if he were Orpheus. Some of Socrates' fellow Athenians are in the group flanking him, while others have come to hear Hippias and Prodicus. Some of the Athenians present are, moreover, Socrates' own companions, as we know from other dialogues of Plato. They have now, however, collected in Callias' house in order to hear not Socrates, but Protagoras or one of the other two Sophists present.

For his part, Socrates arrives at Callias' house alone, but for Hippocrates, his young charge. In this situation, the charm of Alcibiades, now at its peak, conjured up for us by the combined words of Homer and Socrates, has weight. Alcibiades is not at the gathering when Socrates arrives. He and Critias enter Callias' house shortly after Socrates and Hippocrates, as Socrates puts it, "from behind us" (κατόπιν δὲ ἡμῶν, 316a 3). Alcibiades and Critias will both back Socrates. They will come to his defense in his conversation with Protagoras, or rather in its breakdown—Alcibiades as ever flamboyantly, Critias more discreetly, and perhaps cunningly. However, Alcibiades alone is formally cast in the role of Socrates' beloved.

The acclaimed beauty of Alcibiades is a reminder and visible proof of Socrates' own power to attract. As Socrates reports on Alcibiades and Critias entering the house, he—for once—breaks the narration, and addresses the unnamed interlocutor directly.[25] "We had just arrived when from behind us entered Alcibiades the Beautiful—as *you* call him, and I am not arguing—and Critias son of Callaeschrus," 316a 3–5. This sudden leap out of the smooth flow of narration into direct address, as Alcibiades' beauty is mentioned, helps to underscore the special place of Alcibiades in the dramatic setup of the dialogue.

Alcibiades' beauty plays a formal, rather than a material, role in the dialogue. It represents Socrates as a locus of a certain kind of power. He, we are meant to understand, is hardly resourceless in the face of the Orpheus-like power of Protagoras. The younger man's beauty is a presentiment of what Socrates will accomplish by the end of the dialogue.

The Homeric parallel born of the quotation at *Protagoras* 309b 1, combined with the pair of quotations that follow, casts Socrates in the role of Odysseus. Like Odysseus, Socrates is ἀκηλητός (*Od.* 10.329)—singularly capable of resisting spell or enchantment. He is being ironical when he claims to have sat spellbound (κεκηλημένος) for a long time at the end of Protagoras' Great Speech, for really he was waiting to see if Protagoras had actually finished (328d 4–6). In fact, Socrates seems to be the only person in Callias'

---

[25] Socrates' narration runs otherwise uninterrupted to the very end of the dialogue. He returns to the unnamed interlocutor very briefly, in the last sentence, cited above.

house—with the possible but somewhat ambiguous exception of Alcibiades—
not under Protagoras' spell.

By the time Socrates meets the unnamed interlocutor, he appears to be an-
imated by the conversations he has just had and eager to relate them. But he
seems not to have had any intention to attend the gathering on his own, despite being very well informed about Protagoras' arrival in Athens (310b 8),
his whereabouts, and other guests present (314b 8–c 2). (Recall Odysseus,
who, unhappy about going to Circe's house, and mindful of danger, says that
he is impelled to go by a "powerful necessity": *Od.* 10.273.) Seemingly reluctant, Socrates none the less moves to go to Callias' house, having warned Hippocrates of the risk. He has in effect now taken charge of Hippocrates, and
undertakes the trip to Callias' house on his behalf.

In connection with the situation Socrates encounters at Callias' house we
must recall that when Odysseus arrives at Circe's, half his companions are
there, transformed into pigs. As Circe had intended (10.236), the noxious
drugs made them forget their native land. Their minds (*νοῦς*, 240) are otherwise unchanged. The transformation which the sorceress brings about is like
an expression of an ancient dread: forgetting who one is, where one has come
from, and how to return to what one is and to where one belongs. The conversation Socrates will have with Protagoras is undertaken by Socrates as a
way of coming to the aid of his friends, who have experienced a peculiar
transformation at the hands of Protagoras.[26]

In modeling Protagoras after Circe, and later explicitly likening him to
Orpheus, Plato represents the Sophist in the role of a *γόης*, a magician or sorcerer.[27] Magicians can communicate with the souls of the dead, and have the
power to cast and lift spells. We know from Herodotus that the ability to effect transformations was also associated with *γόητες*. Herodotus applies this
designation to the tribe of Neuri, on account of the reputation they have of
becoming wolves for several days every year.[28] Plato will later, in the *Sophist*,

---

[26] In Christa Wolf's rewriting of the role of Medea, Medea recalls her aunt Circe telling her: "Yes,
it *had* so happened that she'd chased a gang of men off the island as swine, thinking that perhaps this might help them attain a glimmering of self-knowledge" (C. Wolf, *Medea* [London,
1998], 81). The symbolism is exactly the reverse of that implied in Plato's association of Protagoras with Circe. Wolf's positive recasting of Circe gives the sorceress a Socratic role.

[27] The Orpheus comparison is made just a few lines before Socrates introduces Hippias by quoting
τὸν δὲ μετ' εἰσενόησα. *Pace* Klär, "Die Schatten im Höhlengleichnis", 256, R. B. Rutherford, *The
Art of Plato: Ten Essays in Platonic Interpretation* (London, 1995), 126, and Capra, 'Αγὼν λόγων,
67, this should override the inclination we might otherwise have to identify Protagoras with Sisyphus, to whom τόν refers in the original Homeric context. In effect, Plato has directed us to disre-
gard, for once, the original context. Sisyphus was a villainous trickster, but he did not command
the magical powers of Circe and Orpheus.

[28] Herodotus 4.105.

explicitly characterize the Sophist's art as γοητεία, magic or sorcery, and the Sophist as a γόης.[29]

The etymology of the word γόης (from γόος, lamentation) connects it with funerary rites.[30] A γόης, in Plato and elsewhere, is a practitioner of a certain kind of magic. Plato's conception of γοητεία seems to be broad; divination and purification are among the activities of a γόης. In the *Sophist*, the notion that a γόης makes things *appear*, things which in fact are *not*, seems to have become a salient characteristic of this figure in Plato's mind. Whereas effecting transformations is recorded by Herodotus, the ability to transform one's own appearance was not central to ancient magic. The use of γόης and γοητεία in the *Sophist*, however, shows that Plato strongly associates changing shape and appearance, including one's own, with the activity of a γόης.

In *Republic* 2 Socrates asks Adeimantus whether a god might be a γόης (380d 1). It turns out that the gods would be sorcerers if they changed their shape, or presented a φάντασμα, image or apparition, of themselves in a changed shape, or again if they made human beings believe falsehoods (such as that gods change shape). He argues that this is impossible (380d–383a), and concludes that the gods are not γόητες (383a 2–5). The passage presupposes that it is characteristic of γοητεία to transform appearances or present images of transformed appearances. The same conception of γοητεία is found in the *Sophist*, where at 241b it is used to motivate the dialogue's great metaphysical discussion of being and non-being.

We must note that magic at this time was not regarded as diabolical in the sense this term was later to acquire. Circe is a divine figure. Her drugs are harmful to those against whom she decides to apply them, but she lives by the rules of her own nature—her power inspires admiration as much as fear. She can heal and purify, as well as cast noxious spells. Olympic gods, the established and admired divinities, perform what can be seen as magic tricks in Homer, including transformations of themselves and others.[31] Once won over, Circe will be helpful not only to Odysseus, to whom she swore an oath, but also to his companions, with regard to whom she did not specifically commit herself.

---

[29] *Soph.* 234c 5, 235a 1, 235a 8, 241b 7. Γόης is peculiarly mistranslated by N. White as "a cheat," in the Hackett *Plato. Complete Works*, edd. J. M. Cooper and D. S. Hutchinson, and as "juggler" in N. Notomi, *The Unity of Plato's 'Sophist'* (Cambridge, 1999), pp. 17n.55, 77, 100n.12, 128, 145 and 279. They have been misled by LSJ *sv*.

[30] See the excellent account of γοητεία in S. I. Johnston, *Restless Dead* (Berkeley, Los Angeles, etc., 1999), 102–122, and a more general account of Greek magic in F. Graf, *Magic in the Ancient World* (Cambridge, Mass., and London, 1997).

[31] Athena uses her ῥάβδος, magic wand, to change the appearance of Odysseus: she turns him into a beggar (*Od.* 13.429–38), restores his appearance in front of Telemachus (16.172–6), and turns him into a beggar again (16.454–7).

As Homer portrays her, Circe behaves a lot like a very powerful human. It is not her business to think of how the people feel whom she turns to boars, wolves or lions. A freely roaming power like Circe's needs to be bound if a human dealing with her is not to come to grief. That is why it is crucial for Odysseus to make her swear a great oath.[32] An oath binds, and can serve as an antidote to magic powers. Such antidotes are magical as well.[33]

Socrates, however, is undoubtedly focusing on the dangerous and noxious side of Circe. When he warns Hippocrates of the risk he is running if he goes to Protagoras intending to become his student, we are left in no doubt as to what type of magic he is associating with Protagoras' influence on his students.[34]

In comparison with Circe, Odysseus is a thoroughly human character. He does not have, or claim to have, any higher powers. He makes do with what he is endowed with, his eloquence, shrewdness, and persuasiveness, and his otherwise human kind of intelligence. Even when he receives help from Hermes, or more often from Athena, that is not his to command.

Like Odysseus, Socrates has insight into people, and himself. His approach to his interlocutors is highly personal. He has the Odyssean cunning intelligence, $\mu\tilde{\eta}\tau\iota\varsigma$, which is an ability to devise schemes that get to their goal—often by indirect means. Using masks or screens and pretending are part and parcel of this sort of cunning.

One virtue that Odysseus strikingly possesses is courage. In this he seems to far outstrip Circe. Once the magic devices she attempted to deploy on him fail, she will be frightened by the sword he menacingly draws. Since she is divine, Odysseus could not take her life. Gods can be hurt by weapons, however, and Circe shrinks from pain.

To the extent that the *Protagoras* is about any single virtue, it is about courage. The dialogue starts by depicting what Socrates calls Hippocrates' $\dot{\alpha}\nu\delta\varrho\varepsilon\dot{\iota}\alpha$—his impulsiveness and readiness to act, which, however, is ultimately only a semblance of the true virtue of courage. Towards the end of the dialogue, Plato will have Socrates give an account of courage as he understands it. Although the issue of Protagoras' courage is not tackled directly, it is very likely that Socrates would see Protagoras' preoccupation with his own safety, and the emphasis he puts on forethought, as evidence of his lack of courage. Protagoras thanks Socrates for having forethought, $\pi\varrho o\mu\dot{\eta}\vartheta\varepsilon\iota\alpha$, on his behalf (316c 5). A foreigner going about cities and educating young men

---

[32] She swears the kind of oath that gods themselves swear. See Heubeck and Hoekstra, *ad* 10.299.

[33] Circe's potion is a magic agent, $\varphi\acute{\alpha}\varrho\mu\alpha\kappa o\nu$, and so is $\mu\tilde{\omega}\lambda\upsilon$ (according to Heubeck and Hoekstra, *ad* 10.302–6, $\mu\tilde{\omega}\lambda\upsilon$ may be an early technical term in the practice of magic).

[34] There is a report according to which Protagoras studied with Persian magicians ($\mu\acute{\alpha}\gamma o\iota$). See Diels-Kranz 80 A 2: Philostr. *V. Soph.* 1.10. This cannot be taken as reliable biography. Yet if Protagoras had such a reputation in Plato's lifetime, Plato could be playing on it.

is liable to incur envy and odium. Protagoras believes that Socrates had something of the sort in mind when he left it to Protagoras to decide whether the conversation between them should be public or not (316b3–6). Socrates, however, has no such thing in mind. He and Hippocrates, he says, are simply indifferent on the issue of privacy (316b 5). Protagoras' preoccupation with his own safety stands in stark contrast with Socrates' attitude to such matters, both here and in the *Apology*. Protagoras' inability to give a satisfactory account of courage in the dialectical debate also indicates—for Socrates at any rate—an absence of this virtue.

Hermes, invoked by Socrates at the outset, is the god who counteracts the forces that lead astray, and who points the way. He guides the souls of the dead to their final destination in the underworld, helping them as it were to find their way home. Although Socrates directly associates Alcibiades with Hermes—through his initial Homeric quotation—the spirit of Hermes is more at home with Socrates himself than with Alcibiades.

The power to resist Protagoras is Socrates' own. He will be, moreover, a Hermes to Hippocrates: he serves as the younger man's guide, descending with him to the "underworld" of Callias' house, enabling him in the end to resist Protagoras' misleading charm.

In the world of erotic forces Plato is describing, the power of a lover spreads through his erotic counterpart. They are symbolically a unit. When Hippocrates at dawn indicates to Socrates the need to go to Callias' house, this corresponds to Circe telling Odysseus in pre-dawn darkness of his need to descend to the underworld. But Protagoras is the force that drives Hippocrates, and the active bewitching force. He is the one more properly conjoined with Circe. Similarly, Socrates is the one properly aligned with Hermes. Alcibiades will, in the rest of the dialogue, throw himself into the task of standing by the side of Socrates. Yet he does not provide direction, and does not play the role of a guide.

Plato's employment of the Homeric material does not stop with the symbolic pairings of characters. There is a dynamic element to the material, which is reflected in the dynamic of the Platonic text. Odysseus is on a journey, trying to bring himself and his companions safely home, contending with powerful forces attempting to deflect him. He succeeds in compelling them to serve his purpose. Socrates is on a similar quest, aiming to release his companion from Protagoras' grip. Like Odysseus, he meets with success.

Or rather, from a dramatic point of view he meets with success. He forces Protagoras to acknowledge that he has not fully held his end in the argument. He succeeds in taking Hippocrates away with him. But the substantive outcome of their philosophical debate is more ambiguous, and requires separate analysis. The debate deals with the nature of παιδεία—seen by Socrates as a way of improving the soul—and its very possibility. The dramatic reversal which takes place at the end of the *Protagoras* is brought about almost exclusively by means of a philosophical argument; and its effectiveness directly depends on the force of that argument. This reveals that the link between the dramatic and the philosophical in the dialogue does not run in only one direction. The Homeric setup puts onto the map the very issues treated more discursively and argumentatively in the later part of the dialogue. Conversely, the philosophical force of Socrates' argument against Protagoras has a literary function. Only if the argument works, not merely dialectically but as a substantive rebuttal of Protagoras' position and his claim to wisdom, can the picture of Protagoras as Circe come convincingly alive.[35]

[35] On Protagoras' position itself, the content of his claim to wisdom, see my 'Protagoras' Political Art', chap. 1 above.

Three ~

No One Errs Willingly: The Meaning of Socratic Intellectualism

ἑκὼν ἑκὼν ἥμαρτον, οὐκ ἀρνήσομαι.
(Willingly, willingly I erred; I won't deny it.)
  —[Aeschylus], *Prometheus Bound*, 266

Video meliora proboque, deteriora sequor.
(I see what is better and approve of it, but pursue what is worse.)
  —Ovid, *Metamorphoses*, 7. 20

Concepts, just like individuals, have their history and are no more able than
they to resist the dominion of time, but in and through it all they nevertheless
harbour a kind of homesickness for the place of their birth.
  —Søren Kierkegaard, *The Concept of Irony*, 13. 106

I

The Western philosophical tradition is deeply indebted to the figure of
Socrates. The question 'How should one live?' has rightly been called 'the Socratic question'. Socrates' method of cross-examining his interlocutors has often been seen as a paradigmatic form of philosophical enquiry, and his own
life as an epitome of the philosophical life. What philosophers and non-philos-
ophers alike have often found disappointing in Socrates is his intellectualism.
A prominent complaint about Socratic intellectualism has been memorably
recorded by Alexander Nehamas: 'And George Grote both expressed the consensus of the ages and set the stage for modern attitudes toward Socrates when
he attributed to him "the error . . . of dwelling exclusively on the intellectual
conditions of human conduct, and omitting to give proper attention to the
emotional and volitional".'[1]

I am grateful to Myles Burnyeat, David Furley, John McDowell, and Julius Moravcsik for their
helpful comments on earlier versions of this paper. I also wish to thank the editor of *Oxford
Studies in Ancient Philosophy* for his generous criticisms and corrections.

[1] Alexander Nehamas, 'Socratic Intellectualism', in his *Virtues of Authenticity* (Princeton, 1999),
24–58 at 27; the reference is to George Grote, *Plato and the Other Companions of Sokrates*, I
(London, 1865), 399–400.

The complaints against Socratic intellectualism take two main forms. According to some, Socrates ignores or overlooks—or at least vastly underestimates the importance of—the emotional, desiderative, and volitional sides of human nature, being too preoccupied with the intellect. The error attributed to him by Grote belongs here. The second line of criticism does not charge Socrates with ignoring or marginalizing desires, emotions, and volitions, but rather with giving an inadequate, over-intellectualist, account of them. These two lines of criticism have sometimes been combined, and sometimes confused. What they have in common is the thought that the desiderative, the emotional, and the volitional are not given their due by Socrates.

I wish to challenge this understanding of Socrates. He holds that living a good life is a matter of living in accordance with a certain kind of knowledge. Since knowledge is an accomplishment of reason, his view is in some sense intellectualist or, perhaps more appropriately, rationalist. However, I argue that desiderative, emotional, and volitional propensities and attitudes are an integral part of the knowledge in which Socrates locates virtue. This is meant to undermine the more prevalent first line of criticism. Towards the end of the paper I address the second line of criticism and suggest a different overall understanding of Socratic intellectualism, one that centres on the view that every act of the human soul involves an act of reason. I work my way towards this understanding of Socratic intellectualism by looking into the role that volitions, emotions, and desires play in Socratic virtue.

A large part of this paper deals with two Socratic theses. The first, that no one errs willingly, has long been recognized as crucial to Socratic intellectualism; however, the precise meaning of this thesis has remained elusive. I argue that 'willingly' is used here in a highly specific sense. The text which in my view offers the clue to the proper understanding of the No One Errs Willingly thesis is a passage in the *Gorgias* that has been much slandered in the literature on Socrates. The argument has often been thought confused, and the whole passage has sometimes been treated as a deliberate exaggeration on Socrates' part. I claim that the passage makes perfect sense, that Socrates intends it seriously, and that it plays a central role in the overall philosophical structure of the dialogue. I then turn to the second thesis, that *akrasia*—weakness of the will, as the Greek term is usually rendered—does not exist. I offer an interpretation of the denial of *akrasia* based on my analysis of the No One Errs Willingly thesis. The joint reading of the two theses leads to a perhaps surprising result. Certain kinds of wantings and volitional propensities are constituents of moral knowledge. The same can be shown for desiderative and emotional attitudes and propensities. Far from disregarding the volitional, desiderative, and emotional, Socrates attempts to build them into his account of virtue as knowledge. Furthermore, his remarks on wanting or willing, sketchy and conversational though they are, point—I argue—to a distinct notion of the will. If Socrates does have a concept of the will, this is the first appearance of such a concept in the Western philosophical tradition.[2]

This interpretation shows that it is wrong to assume (as people have done since Aristotle) that Socrates ignores or marginalizes the desiderative and the emotional side of human nature, focusing solely on the intellectual.

II

Socrates claims that no one errs knowingly.[3] Why an intellectualist would make such a claim, we might think, is not so difficult to grasp. The intellectualist believes that when a person does what is morally wrong, that moral failure is due to an intellectual error. If only the person exercised his intellect well—if he knew better—he would not do what is wrong. Hence what we have to do in order to make people better, an intellectualist would have us think, is help them see how things really are; in particular, help them see what really is good or bad. I do not dispute that Socrates is a rationalist or intellectualist of some sort, or that a line of thought roughly corresponding to the one just sketched may be linked to his claim that no one errs knowingly. What I wish to emphasize is that in order to determine what *kind* of intellectualist he is, we must see how he conceives of the knowledge the absence of which he takes to be responsible for wrongdoing. I shall argue that Socrates' conception of moral knowledge makes many of the objections traditionally lodged against his intellectualism unwarranted.

In addition to claiming that no one errs knowingly, Socrates also claims that no one errs *willingly*. Why does he make this latter claim? An answer to this question does not leap to one's eye from the pages of Plato's dialogues. One would expect that, if anywhere, an answer is to be found in the

---

[2] We should not conclude from the fact that ancients discuss *akrasia*, which we label 'weakness of the will', that they have a concept of the will. The term *akrasia* indicates only some kind of weakness: the weakness of one who acts against his knowledge or better judgement of what is best. It is not uncommon to find the literature associating a notion of the will with this or that ancient figure, including Socrates. But it is not by dint of translation that we should come to think of the ancients as having a concept, or concepts, of the will, but by dint of interpretation and argument.

[3] See *Prot.* 352c 2–7: 'Now, do you [Protagoras] too think that that is how things stand with it [sc. knowledge], or do you think that knowledge is fine and such as to rule the person, and if someone recognizes what is good and bad, he would not be overpowered by anything else so as to act otherwise than knowledge dictates, but wisdom is sufficient to help the person?' Protagoras promptly grants that knowledge has this power. See also 358b 6–c 1.

Protagoras, where Socrates argues at length for the view that *akrasia* does not exist, and where he also briefly formulates, and appears to endorse, the claim that no one errs willingly (*Prot.* 345c 4–e 6; cf. 352a 1–358d 4). But the *Protagoras* is silent on what precisely the dictum 'No one errs willingly' amounts to and how it is related to Socrates' denial of *akrasia*. In view of this silence, it is tempting to think that Socrates himself was in error. He must have thought, mistakenly, that 'No one errs knowingly' implies 'No one errs willingly'. Those who recall Aristotle's discussion of voluntary and involuntary action in the *Nicomachean* and *Eudemian Ethics* may be especially inclined to think that Socrates simply made an error in passing from 'knowingly' to 'willingly'.

Aristotle was the first Greek philosopher, as far as we know, to undertake a systematic analysis of voluntary and involuntary action, and to connect the voluntariness and involuntariness of actions with the agent's knowledge or ignorance. He tried to specify as precisely as he could the kinds of ignorance concerning the circumstances of an action that make it involuntary (see especially *EN* III. 1 and III. 4). He stressed that not every kind has this effect: for some sorts of ignorance people are neither forgiven nor pitied—as might be appropriate if their action were due to ignorance. Instead, they are blamed (*EN* III. 1, 1110b 28–1111a 2). In Plato, however, we find no comparable attempt at a careful philosophical analysis of voluntariness and involuntariness. So it would be plausible to think that Socrates perceived that knowledge of some kind is connected with voluntariness, but never looked into the thorny issue of voluntariness with proper care. That allowed him to overlook the blunder involved in passing from 'No one errs knowingly' to 'No one errs willingly'.[4]

Tempting as this line of thought might be, we should resist it. We should not assume without examination that when Socrates describes someone as acting willingly, the action in question would be of the sort Aristotle classifies as 'voluntary'. (Likewise, we must not assume that those who on Socrates' diagnosis act unwillingly are not to be blamed for their actions.) The intended meaning of 'No one errs willingly' should be gleaned in the first place through careful reading of Plato's dialogues. The relevant passages seem to me to reveal that Socrates was not the least bit confused when he said that no one errs willingly.[5] Rather, I shall argue, he proposed a coherent and interesting, albeit unusual, view.

[4] John McDowell takes this view in his unpublished piece 'Irwin's Socrates and an Alternative Reading'. The culprit, however, is ultimately Aristotle. See next note.
[5] It is not just our knowledge of the philosophical analysis of voluntary action provided later by Aristotle that might mislead us into thinking that Socrates was confused. The picture of him as confused about voluntariness probably originated with Aristotle himself. Evidence suggests that

III

In Plato's *Protagoras* Socrates introduces the thesis that no one errs willingly
(at 345c 4–e 6) while presenting an analysis of a poem by Simonides. That no
human being errs willingly is something, Socrates contends, which Simonides,
as a wise and educated person, would surely have known. He proceeds to use
this thought to guide his interpretation of Simonides, but he offers no gloss on
the thesis itself. Although the *Protagoras* provides us with indispensable material for understanding Socrates' ethical outlook, and hence also for understanding the No One Errs Willingly thesis, a more direct clue to the meaning
of this thesis comes from the *Gorgias*.

Our starting-point should be *Gorgias* 466a 4–468e 2. In his exchange with
Polus Socrates declares that orators and tyrants do not do what they want to
do (467b 2, 466d 8–e 1), and that they have the least power of any in the city.
Startled by this, Polus asks if it is not the case that orators, just like tyrants,
kill anyone they want (ὃν ἂν βούλωνται), and subject anyone they please
(ὃν ἂν δοκῇ αὐτοῖς) to expropriation or exile (466b 11–c 2). Socrates retorts
that Polus has raised two questions rather than one (466c 7, 466d 5–6), and
proceeds to draw a distinction between doing what one pleases, on the one
hand, and doing what one wants, on the other (466d 5–e 2). Applying this
distinction, he now grants that orators and tyrants do 'what they please' (ἃ δοκεῖ
αὐτοῖς, at 467a 3 and 467b 8) or 'what they take to be best' (ἃ δοκεῖ αὐτοῖς
βέλτιστα εἶναι, at 467b 3–4),[6] but denies that they do what they want to do
(ἃ βούλονται, 467b 2, b 6, 467a 10; cf. 466d 8–e 1)—presumably when engaged in the actions mentioned: killing, expropriating, banishing. The passage makes it fairly clear why Socrates claims that orators and tyrants do not
do what they want to do: what they do is not good, and one can only want
those things that are good (see especially 468c 2–7). But why should he construe 'wanting' in such a peculiar way? To answer this question, we should take
a broader look at the matters discussed at 466–8.

Aristotle saw Socrates as mistaken on two issues: first, the role of knowledge and ignorance
in voluntary and involuntary action (see, in particular, *EN* III. 1 on τὸ ἑκούσιον and τὸ
ἀκούσιον), and second, the issue of the proper object of βούλησις—rational wish or wanting (*EN* III. 4).

[6] See also the variants: ὅτι ἂν αὐτοῖς δόξῃ βέλτιστον εἶναι (466 E 1–2) and ἃ ἂν δοκῇ αὐτῷ
βέλτιστα εἶναι (466 E 9–10). The two expressions 'what they please' (ἃ δοκεῖ αὐτοῖς) and 'what
they take to be best' (ἃ δοκεῖ αὐτοῖς βέλτιστα εἶναι) are treated by Socrates as equivalent
throughout the passage under consideration (466a 4–468e 2). A reader with no Greek will observe that the two expressions are rendered quite differently in English, but actually they look
very similar in Greek. To capture the similarity, one could translate respectively 'what seems to
them' (meaning roughly: as they see fit, or as they please) and 'what seems to them to be the best'.

Socrates' claim that neither orators nor tyrants do what they want to do is meant to be startling. What in common opinion distinguishes a tyrant from others is precisely the enormous power he has. As Polus had observed at 466b 11–c 2, the tyrant can put to death anyone he wants; he can dispossess or exile whomever he pleases. Thus he can visit what in common opinion are the worst of evils upon the head of anyone he wants. Another bit of common lore is that having power consists in being able to do what one wants. Power is so understood by Socrates' interlocutors in the *Gorgias*, and Socrates raises no objection. What Gorgias and Polus add to the common view is the claim that orators are at least as powerful as tyrants, and probably more so (see especially 452e 1–8). This, of course, is advertising on behalf of oratory by its practitioners or sympathizers. The advertisement none the less correctly identifies some of the aspirations, and some of the accomplishments, of oratory in the ancient world. Faced with Gorgias' and Polus' claims on behalf of oratory, Socrates does not take the obvious course, to reject as an exaggeration the claim that orators are so powerful. Rather, he takes the entirely non-obvious course of saying, first, that neither orators nor tyrants do what they want to do when they engage in the actions mentioned, and second, that they consequently have no great power in the cities. In making the transition from the first claim to the second, he relies on the above-mentioned assumption about power: to have power is to be able to do what one wants to do; to have a lot of power is to be able to do much of what one wants to do.

There can be no doubt that Socrates wants to shock his interlocutor by his apparently bizarre claim about orators and tyrants. Polus reacts as intended: he describes the claim as 'outrageous' and 'monstrous' (σχέτλια, ὑπερφυῆ, at 467b 10). It would be a serious error, however, for us to understand the claim as a piece of histrionics, or an exaggeration meant to bring into sharper relief some other views that Socrates seriously holds.[7] He means what he says: orators and tyrants do not do what they want to do. If Polus is shocked by this claim, the shock is meant to prepare him for a more general claim which Socrates wants to be taken quite as seriously.[8]

---

[7] *Pace* Roslyn Weiss, in 'Killing, Confiscating, and Banishing at *Gorgias* 466–468', *Ancient Philosophy*, 12 (1992), 299–315. Her contention that the argument of 466–8 'deliberately . . . exaggerates and distorts' views that the Socrates of Plato's early dialogues 'seriously holds' (p. 299) strikes me as a counsel of despair in the face of the fact that the argument has persistently resisted coherent and plausible interpretation.

[8] The way Socrates proceeds here is not unusual. Something similar goes on during his interpretation of Simonides' poem in the *Protagoras* (338e 6–347a 5). In the course of making a peculiar sort of display, he introduces views he seriously holds, including the No One Errs Willingly thesis. A further similarity between his exercise in literary criticism in the *Protagoras* and his handling of Polus in the section of the *Gorgias* we are discussing is that he seriously proposes his thesis while being mockingly playful. Later in the *Gorgias*, as I shall point out below, he subjects Callicles to similar treatment.

That doing what one pleases or what one sees fit ($\hat{a}$ $\delta οκε\hat{ι}$ $α\mathring{υ}τ\hat{ω}$) amounts to acting in accordance with one's opinion ($\delta όξα$) is suggested in Greek by the very form of the words ($\delta οκε\hat{ι}ν$ is a verbal counterpart to the noun $\delta όξα$). This suggestion is further supported by *Gorg.* 469c 4–7. There Polus explains to Socrates what, on his understanding, a tyrant is. A tyrant, he says, is someone who is 'in a position to do whatever he pleases [$\mathring{ο}$ $\mathring{α}ν$ $\delta οκ\hat{η}$ $α\mathring{υ}τ\hat{ω}$] in the city, whether it is killing a person or expelling him from the city, and doing everything [$πάντα$ $πράττοντι$] in accordance with his opinion [$κατ\grave{α}$ $τ\grave{η}ν$ $α\mathring{υ}το\hat{υ}$ $\delta όξαν$]'. Polus here treats doing 'whatever he pleases' and doing everything 'in accordance with his opinion' as equivalent. The phrase quoted, $πάντα$ $πράττοντι$ $κατ\grave{α}$ $τ\grave{η}ν$ $α\mathring{υ}το\hat{υ}$ $\delta όξαν$, which I have rendered 'doing everything in accordance with his opinion', could equally well have been rendered 'doing everything as he pleases'.[9]

If doing what one pleases amounts to acting in accordance with one's *doxa*, opinion or belief,[10] and there is, Socrates suggests, a sharp contrast between doing what one pleases and doing what one wants, it is not unreasonable to suppose that doing what one wants is linked with acting in accordance with one's *epistēmē*, knowledge. I shall defend the view that this is indeed so. In fact, I shall propose that wanting, as understood by Socrates in the present context, is even more intimately connected with knowledge than the phrase 'acting in accordance with knowledge' might suggest. Before I do so, let me make some remarks about the appropriateness of bringing knowledge into the picture.

The contrast between *doxa*, opinion, and *epistēmē*, knowledge, is at the heart of the *Gorgias* as a whole. Socrates recoils from oratory, which he considers dangerous to the human soul. Oratory is dangerous because it enshrines mere *doxa*, opinion, and aims to convert it into $πίστις$, conviction, without regard for the truth of the opinion, hence *a fortiori* without regard for knowledge. $πίστις$, conviction, is what persuasion ($πειθώ$), if successful, leads to, and producing persuasion is the business of the orator. Following Gorgias' descriptions, Socrates characterizes the orator as a $πειθο\hat{υ}ς$ $\delta ημιουργός$, 'a manufacturer of persuasion' (*Gorg.* 453a 2). Socrates sees himself, by contrast, as concerned with knowledge; hence he keeps denouncing practices that systematically bypass this concern. The orator and the tyrant, each in his own way, stand accused by Socrates of being mired in such practices.

---

[9] In Greek, the difference between acting $κατ\grave{α}$ $τ\grave{η}ν$ $α\mathring{υ}το\hat{υ}$ $\delta όξαν$ and doing $\hat{a}$ $\delta οκε\hat{ι}$ $α\mathring{υ}τ\hat{ω}$ lies merely in choosing between a noun-based idiom and a verb-based one. The difference can be illustrated in English by a choice between, say, acting 'as one wishes' and acting 'in accordance with one's wish'.

[10] I use 'opinion' and 'belief' interchangeably. 'Opinion'—a more common rendition of $\delta όξα$ in Plato—may be too narrow for the passages of the *Protagoras* and *Gorgias* under consideration here. Roughly, one has a $\delta όξα$ when one takes something to be the case, correctly or incorrectly. This corresponds to 'belief' fairly well, as well as to 'opinion' loosely understood.

To say that doing as one pleases is to be understood as acting in accordance with one's opinion or belief invites the question: an opinion or belief about what? Likewise for acting in accordance with one's knowledge. As far as opinion or belief is concerned, the very fact that Socrates treats ἃ δοκεῖ αὐτοῖς, what pleases them (467a 3, b 8), as interchangeable with ἃ δοκεῖ αὐτοῖς βέλτιστα εἶναι, what they think (believe, opine) is best (467b 3–4), suggests an answer. The opinion is about what is best, or perhaps more generally about what is good, better, or best. Although I think we can take our cue from the expressions Socrates uses, I do not mean to suggest that his understanding of these matters is determined by the peculiarities of certain Greek idioms. Socrates has philosophical reasons for seeing the matter this way—reasons which will emerge as we proceed. These reasons stand behind the form of words he uses.

My suggestion was that Socrates describes orators and tyrants as not doing what they want to do because in doing what they do they do not act in accordance with knowledge. But what does wanting have to do with knowledge? Why should only those who have knowledge, or perhaps those who have the relevant knowledge, be correctly described as doing what they *want* to do?

I propose the following, preliminary, characterization of the notion of wanting which Socrates relies on in the orators-and-tyrants passage: the agent wants to ϕ just in case he desires to ϕ taking ϕ-ing to be the good or right thing to do (in the circumstances in question), and his ϕ-ing (in those circumstances) is (or would be) good or right in the way he takes it to be. The point of glossing 'good' as 'right' is that wanting to do something, as wanting is understood here, does not merely involve a desire to ϕ because ϕ-ing is seen by the agent as having some goodness in it; the agent wants to ϕ only if he desires to ϕ seeing it as the right or correct thing to do.

Now this sort of wanting, which I shall call *Socratic wanting* or *willing*, is presumably still a desiderative state of some sort, in a broad sense of the word 'desiderative'. How can the ascription of a desiderative state to an agent possibly depend on the object of the desiderative state being in fact good? Whether an agent wants something, wishes for it, longs for it, and so on, depends on how he sees, or conceives of, the object of his wanting, wishing, or longing. Must we not leave open the possibility that the agent is wrong in his conception of the object desired, whatever the modality of his desire?

That, I take it, is how many people think of desiderative states; clearly, it is how Polus thinks of them. Socrates, however, is putting forward a different proposal. The issue here is not whether, generally speaking, one can be mistaken about the object of one's desire. Of course Socrates would agree that one can be. The issue is whether every end of desire or volition that can be ascribed to a person is independent of the correctness of the person's conception of the object desired or wanted. A parallel may be of help here.

In claiming that orators and tyrants do not do what they want to do, Socrates is inviting us to think of *wanting* as a volitional state that is in some ways like perceiving. I do not perceive an object if I have some images; I perceive it only if my sensory impressions derive from the object itself in the right kind of way. Socratic volition is likewise a receptivity of the soul to certain evaluative properties of the object of volition, the properties Socrates designates by the term 'good'. However, wanting is not sheer receptivity; it is mediated by a correct conception of the object of desire as the good or the right thing to do. Just as perception latches on to that aspect of reality that has an impact on our sensory apparatus, so Socratic volition latches on to a certain evaluative aspect of reality. Thus this kind of wanting can be correctly ascribed to the agent only if the object of his volition has the required evaluative properties and the agent recognizes, and responds to, these properties. We should call to mind again the relationship between belief and knowledge. Whereas having a belief consists in taking something to be true,[11] knowing on Socrates' view is the secure grasp of truth. Likewise, he seems to suggest, whereas desire involves believing that the object of desire is good,[12] wanting—the sort of wanting referred to in the *Gorgias* passage—implies knowing that the object of volition is good.

I can now offer a more precise characterization of Socratic wanting: I Socratically want to ϕ just in case I want[13] to ϕ, recognizing that my ϕ-ing (in the given circumstances) is the good or right thing to do.[14] Thus I (Socratically) want to ϕ only if my wanting to ϕ is linked to my recognition of the goodness of ϕ-ing; if it is a mere coincidence that I believe that ϕ-ing is the right thing to do and that ϕ-ing in fact is the right thing to do, my wanting to ϕ is not Socratic wanting.

This characterization is meant to bring Socrates' notion closer to us, while staying reasonably close to his own idiom. Its drawback is that it unravels a unitary notion: Socratic wanting is meant to be, I think, *both* a volitional *and* a cognitive state. On the best reading, the wanting would be a volitional state *in virtue of* being a certain kind of cognitive state. Socrates has philosophical reasons for offering us this notion of wanting. Before turning to them, let me make a few remarks in defence of my interpretation of the orators-and-tyrants passage.

---

[11] If we want to be fastidious, we can say that believing is taking something to be the case, which implies that something—some proposition or statement—is true.

[12] See *Meno* 76b 6–78b 2. I shall come to this passage below.

[13] In this occurrence, 'wanting' should be taken in its generic sense, not implying a correct conception of the goodness of the object of the want. I take bitter medicines because I want to be healthy; I try to preserve my health because I want to live well, and so on.

[14] Compare with this Socrates' formulation of what people take *akrasia* to be: the many [who believe that there is such a thing as *akrasia*] say that 'a lot of people, recognizing what is best [γιγνώσκοντας τὰ βέλτιστα], do not want to do it [οὐκ ἐθέλειν πράττειν], when it is possible for them to do so, but do something else instead' (*Prot.* 352d 6–7). The relevance of this comparison, which connects Socratic wanting to his denial of *akrasia*, will become clear below.

IV

I have already pointed to one line of thought that makes it difficult to understand why orators and tyrants do not do what they want to do. This is the idea that the claim is a deliberate exaggeration or a piece of histrionics. Another, more widely shared, line of thought is the following. To understand the orators-and-tyrants passage one first has to settle the question whether Socrates uses the verb 'to want' in a special sense. For, if he does not use it in a special sense, then it appears that his claim cannot possibly be true; but if he does use it in a special sense, then he and Polus are not speaking of the same thing; hence his disagreement with Polus, or with anyone who shares Polus' point of view, is not genuine.[15] The prevalent interpretation of the passage seems to be that Socrates does introduce a special sense of 'wanting' in the passage under consideration, but that for this

---

[15] Terry Penner's interpretation of the passage is driven by an attempt to avoid the second horn of the dilemma. He consequently aims to preserve the ordinary sense of 'wishing' (his rendition of βούλεσθαι). According to Penner, Socrates' position is this: orators and tyrants (like everyone else) do what they want to do only if they get what they want. Whatever they may think they want, it is their real happiness that they want in everything they do. The only action one ever wants to do (or desires to do: there is no difference, on this view, between desiring and wanting or wishing to do something) is the one that in fact leads to the ultimate end, one's own happiness, through the chains of means and ends that one has correctly envisaged (Terry Penner, 'Desire and Power in Socrates: The Argument of *Gorgias* 466a–468e that Orators and Tyrants Have No Power in the City', *Apeiron*, 24/3 (Sept. 1991), 147–202; see esp. pp. 170, 182–97). To use Penner's own example, if the tyrant's killing of his prime minister does not lead to the tyrant's happiness, in the way envisaged by him, we have to conclude that he did not want to kill his prime minister. I cannot offer here a detailed analysis of Penner's rather intricate interpretation. Anticipating the analysis I am about to provide, for Socrates there is indeed a legitimate sense in which we want to do things if the doing of them is good and otherwise we do not want them. This wanting is conditional not, as in Penner, upon what one *gets* from the action in the future, but upon the goodness of what is wanted through the action. The virtue of Penner's interpretation (as of his previous work on Socrates) is that he takes Socrates at his word, refusing to settle for 'charitable' readings of his claims. Thus I think that Penner is right in insisting that for Socrates the object of wanting (in one sense) is what really is good, rather than what one believes to be good. However, Penner in this article attributes to Socrates—and apparently himself subscribes to—an implausible general theory of desire (what we want or desire when we desire to do anything is, without exception, the whole chain of means leading to one's actual happiness, and if we don't obtain happiness by means of an action, then we did not want to do what we did), and an unattractive theory of action (no action is ever undertaken for its own sake). As I am about to argue, the dilemma which motivates Penner's interpretation is not, as he believes, inescapable. In the appendix below I offer an analysis of Socrates' argument at 467c 5–468e 5, and show that an instrumentalist account of action cannot be the correct interpretation of this passage.

very reason his overall argument is marred by equivocation, and hence flawed.[16]

As Socrates uses the verb 'to want' (βούλεσθαι) in the orators-and-tyrants passage, a sentence saying that someone wants something is false if what the person is said to want is not good. When βούλεσθαι is used in this way, the sentence in question has truth conditions that are different from those that the sentence would have if βούλεσθαι were used as Polus uses it, and as presumably most Greeks of this time would use it. So Socrates does use the verb 'to want' in a special way here. But from this it does not follow that he and Polus are speaking of different things, and hence cannot disagree. The notion of Socratic wanting is meant to express a truth about the underlying structure of human motivation. If we recognized this structure, Socrates appears to think, we would see that the notion is legitimate and useful. Not everyone would agree with his picture of human motivation, and he can disagree with those who reject it.

Socrates is aware that his construal of 'wanting' is not ordinary. When he introduces the distinction between doing what one wants, on the one hand, and

[16] For a statement of this view see Robin Waterfield's note on *Gorg.* 468d: 'The problem with the argument is that "want" is ambiguous, in a subtle way. To use the familiar philosophical example, Oedipus wants to marry Jocasta, but he does not want to marry his own mother; one can want and not want the same thing under different descriptions' (Plato's *Gorgias*, translated with explanatory notes by R. Waterfield (Oxford, 1994), 142). Further down, Waterfield accuses Socrates of trading on the ambiguity between 'good' and 'apparent good'. ('Just as importantly, Socrates' argument has not really dented Polus' position because of the ambiguity within "good"', ibid. 143; for this, compare Aristotle's discussion at *EN* III. 4 on whether the good or the apparent good is the proper object of βούλησις.) Terence Irwin similarly claims that Socrates' question, 'Does A do what he wants?', is misleading, since the answer may be Yes when the action is considered under one description the agent believes true of it, and No when it is considered under another description. Consequently, Irwin takes Socrates' conclusion, that the orator and the tyrant lack power, as 'unjustifiably strong' (Irwin's notes to his translation of the *Gorgias* (Oxford, 1979), 145–6). According to Kevin McTighe, Socrates confuses *de dicto* and *de re* analyses of the verb 'to want'—see McTighe, 'Socrates on the Desire for the Good and the Involuntariness of Wrongdoing', *Phronesis*, 29 (1984), 193–236; repr. in Hugh H. Benson (ed.), *Essays on the Philosophy of Socrates* (Oxford, 1992), 263–97. McTighe provides a useful survey of the received interpretations of the orators-and-tyrants passage, all of which he sees as flawed (see esp. pp. 264–7). The interpretation that seems to me closest to the truth is that of E. R. Dodds. I cannot agree with him when he says, in his classic commentary on the *Gorgias*, that the concept of wanting employed in the orators-and-tyrants passage—which he construes as the concept of what one really wants as opposed to what one thinks one wants—is 'perhaps only fully intelligible in the light of Plato's later distinction between the "inner man" who is an immortal rational being and the empirical self which is distorted by earthly experience' (Plato's *Gorgias*, edited with a commentary by Dodds (Oxford, 1959), 236). The passage appears to me to be fully intelligible without any such distinction. None the less, Dodds seems to me to be quite right in taking the notion of wanting here as special, and in recognizing that this does not vitiate Socrates' argument.

doing what one pleases, on the other (*Gorg.* 466c 9–467c 4), he deliberately goes against Polus' prior implicit identification of the two. He has quite a bit of explaining to do before it becomes clear what he means by his claim that Polus has raised two questions rather than one (466c 7–e 2). None the less, he speaks as if Polus is in some way committed to the distinction, whether he realizes this or not. The very fact that Socrates proceeds to produce an argument, at 467c 5–468e 5, for the thesis that orators and tyrants do not do what they want to do indicates that he does not take himself to be merely stipulating a new sense for the verb 'to want'. His argument starts from a more or less ordinary sense of 'wanting'. He begins by making claims about wanting that appear acceptable to Polus, as a person with commonsensical views about such matters, but somehow, at the end of the argument, Polus finds himself obliged to agree to the claim he had a little earlier labelled 'outrageous' and 'monstrous'.[17] So it seems that the not exactly ordinary construal of wanting which Socrates proposes to Polus is meant to be connected with what Polus and others normally understand by 'wanting'.

At 468b 1–4 Socrates formulates the following general claim about human motivation for action: 'Therefore it is because we pursue what is good that we walk whenever we walk—thinking that it is better to walk—and, conversely, whenever we stand still it is for the sake of the same thing that we stand still, [namely, for the sake of] what is good.' Although Socrates does not mention desire (other than wanting) in the *Gorgias* passage, he presumably would not deny that desires move us to act. However, looking at actions in terms of desire, the same principle holds—that we do whatever we do because we pursue what we take to be good—since Socrates believes that people always desire what they take to be good.

For this understanding of desire, we should look at *Meno* 77b 6–78b 2. The argument in this passage is meant to bring Meno round to the view that everyone desires good things. Socrates puts the following question to Meno: 'Do you assume that there are people who desire bad things [τῶν κακῶν ἐπιθυμοῦσιν], and others who desire good things [τῶν ἀγαθῶν]? Do you not think, my good man, that everyone desires good things?' (77b 7–c 2). Further below, the object of desire turns out to be what the person who desires takes to be good, not what as a matter of fact is good. As for those who at first appear to Meno to desire what is bad (77c 2–3), Socrates argues that they desire what they do thinking (οἰόμενοι) that it is good, and not recognizing (γιγνώσκοντες) that it is bad (77c 3–e 4). Those who appear to desire what is bad are also described by Socrates as being ignorant about the object of their desire (ἀγνοοῦντες αὐτά [sc. τὰ κακά], 77e 1 and e 2).

The object of desire according to the *Meno* passage is what people take to be good, whether or not their belief is correct. We should think of this as

---

[17] An analysis of Socrates' argument at 467c 5–468e 5 is provided in the appendix.

holding of all desiderative and volitional states: no one desires or wants a thing unless he takes it to be good. The sort of wanting Socrates invokes when he says that orators and tyrants do not do what they want to do is no exception; it fits entirely into the general theory of desire outlined in *Meno* 76–8. One does not Socratically want something without taking it to be good. But the notion of Socratic wanting is stronger, because the agent who Socratically wants to ϕ does not merely take ϕ-ing to be good; he recognizes ϕ-ing to be good. Thus Socrates does not waver between two different accounts of desiderative and volitional states, unclear whether it is the good or the 'apparent good' (that is to say, what people take to be good) that is the object of such states,[18] as some have suggested. He has a unified view of desire that covers all its modalities, plus a special notion of a volitional or desiderative state that is also a cognitive state. Socrates does think that this sort of wanting in some way underlies all other desiderative and volitional states. This, however, is part of a substantive philosophical position, not the result of an elementary confusion. I shall address this position in Section VII below. In the two sections that follow, I wish to bring out the larger significance of the orators-and-tyrants passage.

V

The ostensible conclusion of the discussion between Socrates and Polus at *Gorg.* 466a 9–468e 5 is simply that orators and tyrants—when engaged in killing, expropriating, and banishing—do not do what they want to do (468e 3–5; see also 468d 6–7). But Socrates' concern is clearly with anyone who does τὰ κακά, what is bad or wrong. Much later in the dialogue, at 509e 2–7, he expressly formulates the conclusion of the argument in these wider terms. Talking now to Callicles, he refers back to his discussion with Polus. He says:

> Why don't you answer at least this question, Callicles? Do you think that Polus and I were rightly forced to agree in our previous discussion [ἐν τοῖς ἔμπροσθεν λόγοις] that no one does what is unjust (or what is wrong)[19] wanting to [μηδένα βουλόμενον ἀδικεῖν], but that all who do what is unjust (wrong) do so unwillingly [ἄκοντας]? (*Gorg.* 509e 2–7)

The conclusion of the discussion with Polus is now formulated as follows: no one who does what is wrong does so βουλόμενος, wanting to. βουλόμενος is directly contrasted with ἄκων, unwillingly, suggesting that we should construe

---

[18] The term 'apparent good' is Aristotle's. It is, however, used by interpreters of Plato, especially to refer to the confusion Socrates is alleged to suffer from. See n. 16 above.

[19] The term ἀδικεῖν, 'to do what is unjust', can be used more broadly to include doing anything that is wrong.

βουλόμενος here as equivalent to ἑκών, willingly.[20] If so, the conclusion of
the orators-and-tyrants passage turns out to be the claim that no one errs willingly. For a more familiar wording of this claim, see *Prot.* 345e 1–2: *οὐδένα*
ἀνθρώπων ἑκόντα ἐξαμαρτάνειν, no human being errs willingly. The *Pro-*
tagoras passage reads in full:

> For [says Socrates] Simonides was not so uneducated [ἀπαίδευτος] as to say that he
> praised whoever did nothing bad willingly [ὃς ἂν ἑκὼν μηδὲν κακὸν ποιῇ], as if
> there were anyone who willingly did bad things [κακά]. I am pretty sure that none
> of the wise men thinks that any human being errs willingly [οὐδένα ἀνθρώπων
> ἑκόντα ἐξαμαρτάνειν], or willingly does anything shameful or bad [αἰσχρά τε καὶ
> κακὰ ἑχόντα ἐργάζεσθαι]. They know well that all who do what is shameful or
> bad [πάντες οἱ τὰ αἰσχρὰ καὶ τὰ κακὰ ποιοῦντες] do so unwillingly [ἄκοντες
> ποιοῦσιν]. (*Prot.* 345d 6–e 4)

The Greek verb translated as 'to err', *ἐξαμαρτάνειν* or *ἁμαρτάνειν*, ranges
over a wide territory. It covers both doing wrong, in a moral sense, and simply
going wrong, in the sense of making an error. This suits Socrates' purposes very
well. We might try to capture the way in which *ἁμαρτάνειν* is suitable for his
purposes by stating his position this way: no one commits injustice or does what
is wrong willingly, but everyone who does wrong goes wrong. When wrongdoing
is thought of as involving an error or mistake, it is easy to conclude that this is
something one would not want to do. But however felicitous *ἁμαρτάνειν* may
be for Socrates' purposes, he does not rely too heavily on the properties of this
particular word.[21] When he suggests that Simonides was not so uneducated as to
imply that a human being errs willingly, he may well be ironic, and in more than
one way. None the less, he associates a recognition that no one errs willingly
with education and wisdom, thus treating it as something that requires insight.

VI

At *Gorg.* 509e 2–7 Socrates gets Callicles to agree that no one does what is unjust or wrong wanting to, but that all those who do so do it unwillingly. The
larger immediately relevant passage starts at 509c 6. Socrates has been focusing
his and Callicles' attention on two evils—the evil of suffering injustice

---

[20] I am not suggesting that Socrates always uses *ἑκών* as equivalent to *βουλόμενος*, but only that
he does so in this specific context. For that matter, he does not always use *βουλόμενος* in the
sense of Socratic wanting either. He does not do so, for instance, later in the *Gorgias*, at 511b 4.

[21] A lot has been written about *ἁμαρτία*, especially in connection with Greek tragedy and Aristotle's *Poetics*. From the point of view of this paper, the most useful discussion is that of T.C.W.
Stinton, 'Hamartia in Aristotle and Greek Tragedy', *Classical Quarterly*, NS 25 (1975), 221–54;
repr. in Stinton, *Collected Papers on Greek Tragedy* (Oxford, 1990), 143–85.

(ἀδικεῖσθαι) and the evil of doing it (ἀδικεῖν). Now he raises the question of what it would take for us to save ourselves from falling into each of the two evils. In each case, he asks, is it δύναμις, power, or βούλησις, wish—as βούλησις is customarily translated—that enables us to avoid the evil in question?

To avoid being treated unjustly, Socrates and Callicles quickly agree, one needs power (509d 3–6). But what about doing what is unjust: is it δύναμις or βούλησις—power or wish—that saves us from this evil? Socrates permits Callicles to say that one needs power in this case as well (510a 3–5), even though just a moment ago he had secured Callicles' agreement to the conclusion of the previous discussion with Polus, that no one does what is unjust βουλόμενος, wanting to so do (509e 5–7). He intends Callicles to make the required connection between βούλησις and βουλόμενος. Like Polus before him, Callicles does not quite get Socrates' point. But Callicles is not entirely wrong in his answer, and this may be the reason why Socrates lets him off as he does. βούλησις—as construed by Socrates—is sufficient for a person not to do what is unjust. But this βούλησις, of course, is not merely a *wish*, but rather *wanting* or *willing* in the highly specific sense that Socrates had introduced in his discussion with Polus, and reintroduced here in his discussion with Callicles. This kind of wanting or willing is (in a certain sense) power. Socrates' point is the following. To avoid becoming a victim of an unjust action, one needs power in the straightforward sense; indeed, the power often needed is brute force. To avoid committing injustice, on the other hand, what a person needs is that his will be in a certain condition. When one's will is in this condition, one has all the power one needs, and all the power one can have, not to do what is unjust.

In speaking here of one's will being in a certain condition, I am of course relying on some more current notion of the will. There has been a long-standing dispute over the question whether the ancients had any notion of the will. Presumably, given the large number of widely different conceptions of the will that have emerged in Western philosophical thought since antiquity, the question is whether any of the ancient thinkers had a notion that is in some important way linked to one or more of these later notions. In his claim that orators and tyrants do not do what they want to do, as well as his claim that no one errs willingly, as I have interpreted these claims, Socrates introduces—apparently for the first time in Greek philosophical thought—a certain notion of the will, or something very much like such a concept. This notion of the will is in some ways peculiar. The βούλησις in question—the will, understood as I have suggested—prevents us from doing anything that is wrong. If so, this will—which is essentially the good will—cannot be weak. (This point is linked to Socrates' denial of *akrasia*, which I discuss below.)

We should not fail to notice the playfulness with which Socrates takes up the question whether it is δύναμις or βούλησις that can save us from the evils of suffering and of doing injustice (509d 2–510a 5). The playfulness in part depends on the usual meaning of βούλησις—that of a wish. Socrates asks about δύναμις and βούλησις in the course of renewing his argument for the view that the evil of suffering injustice is utterly trivial in comparison with the evil of doing injustice. To acquire things that are much prized by people, a great deal of power is usually needed. What makes the tyrant so enviable to many is the tremendous power he has—power so unrestricted that he can deprive people of what are considered to be their greatest goods: their life, their property, a place in their own city. It now turns out that the evil which it is incomparably more important to avoid—the evil of doing injustice—does not require the usual machinery of power. It would seem, in fact, that nothing could be easier than securing something by means of a wish. Neither the brute force the tyrant employs, nor the skilful manipulation of the soul by words that the orator relies on, is required here. What one needs, Socrates appears to suggest, is hardly anything at all: a mere wish, βούλησις. However, if one follows him to the end of his thought, it transpires that this thing—βούλησις in the sense of Socratic wanting or willing—is something that it is tremendously difficult to have.

Power was also the main ground on which earlier in the dialogue the great orator Gorgias had defended and praised oratory. In arguing that orators are at least as powerful as tyrants, Gorgias had relied on the enormous and nearly universal appeal of power. Polus inherited his argument from Gorgias. Thus in discussing the tyrant's actions of killing, expropriation, and banishing with Polus, Socrates is still addressing Gorgias' defence of oratory. Socrates now in response leaves his three interlocutors, Gorgias, Polus, and Callicles, with the following dilemma: either the power that enables a person to inflict what people consider to be the greatest evils on others is not good, and hence not something to be in the least admired, coveted, or envied; or else if power as such is good, orators and tyrants have none of it.

The notion that power as such is something good—clearly a notion that all three of his interlocutors are eager to push—undergoes a peculiar, deliberate transformation at Socrates' hands. He in effect offers his interlocutors an option of choosing between two concepts of power. In both cases power is the ability to do as one wants. On the first concept, a person is powerful if he can do what he wants or desires, as the words 'wants' or 'desires' are usually understood. On the second concept, a person is powerful if he can do what he wants in the more special sense—in the sense of what I have called Socratic wanting. Socrates is not blind to the fact that this notion is a novelty to his interlocutors. What he wants is to recast the debate in a novel way. Gorgias, Polus, and Callicles may insist as much as they please that power, as they understand it, is good. They are simply wrong about this. Relying now on the second concept of power—the one that Socrates himself is pushing—virtue is power. To express his thought in a different way: a certain kind of knowledge, and a certain kind of will, are power.

VII

Socrates seems to propose his special notion of wanting—that of Socratic wanting—not as a notion we already have at work in our language, but rather as a notion that we occasionally grope for, and a notion that we need. We need it because it enables us to express something that is of relevance to all the willing, wishing, and desiring that we ordinarily do and ordinarily speak of.

The notion of Socratic wanting announces a certain ideal. There is nothing arbitrary, however, about this ideal. Desires and wants of all varieties are, as we would put it, intentional phenomena. They are directed towards something. In Socrates' view, they embody a certain direction of the soul: a striving of the soul for what is good, and a striving of the soul for its own good, or perhaps for the good proper to a human being. The ideal of wanting that he introduces in the orators-and-tyrants passage, and in its follow-up later in the *Gorgias* (509c 6 ff.), is meant to embody the shape that this striving of the soul takes when the soul has got a grip on what the good that it is after in fact is.

The Socrates of Plato's early dialogues does not often invoke human nature. But here is what we find him saying about it in the *Protagoras*:

> Now, no one goes willingly towards things that are bad [ἐπί γε τὰ κακὰ οὐδεὶς ἑκὼν ἔρχεται] or towards those one thinks are bad [οὐδὲ ἐπὶ ἃ οἴεται κακὰ εἶναι], nor is it in human nature [ἐν ἀνθρώπου φύσει], so it seems, to want to go towards what one thinks is bad instead of to what is good [ἐπὶ ἃ οἴεται κακὰ εἶναι ἐθέλειν ἰέναι ἀντὶ τῶν ἀγαθῶν]. And when one is forced to choose between two bad things, no one chooses the greater if he is able to choose the lesser. (*Prot.* 358c 6–d 4)[22]

We, humans, are hardwired to seek our own good. What we want is, ultimately, to do well for ourselves. The striving for this condition of doing well, which Socrates calls 'the good', is something that every human soul comes equipped with. Striving after the good is as basic to the human soul as is its striving after the truth.

With regard to the considerations that impelled Socrates to introduce his special concept of wanting, it may be useful to quote a passage from outside what we consider Plato's Socratic writings, even if we do not, as we should not, treat it as evidence for the Socratic view:

> And isn't this also clear? In the case of just and beautiful things [δίκαια . . . καὶ καλά], many would accept things that are believed (reputed) to be so [τὰ δοκοῦντα], even if they are in fact not so, and they do such things, acquire them, and get a reputation for doing and acquiring them [ὅμως ταῦτα πράττειν καὶ κεκτῆσθαι καὶ

---

[22] I return to this passage in sect. x below.

δοκεῖν].[23] But when it comes to good things, no one is content to acquire things that are believed to be so [ἀγαθὰ δὲ οὐδενὶ ἔτι ἀρκεῖ τὰ δοκοῦντα κτᾶσθαι], but everyone seeks things that are in fact good [ἀλλὰ τὰ ὄντα ζητοῦσιν] and spurns mere belief [τὴν δὲ δόξαν ἐνταῦθα ἤδη πᾶς ἀτιμάζει] . . . This, then, [sc. the good] is what every soul pursues [διώκει] and for the sake of which it does everything it does . . . (Rep. 505d 5–e 1)

Whatever special interpretation Plato might be putting in the Republic on the distinction between τὰ δοκοῦντα and τὰ ὄντα—things that are reputed (opined, believed) to be good, on the one hand, and things that are good, on the other—there can be no doubt that the Socrates of the early dialogues is interested in a similar distinction: a distinction between what *appears* to be good, and what *is* good. Towards the end of the Protagoras, Socrates announces that it is the power of appearance (ἡ τοῦ φαινομένου δύναμις) that makes us wander all over the place and regret our actions and choices (356d 4–7). We mistakenly take for good things that in fact are not good, but merely appear to us to be so. If we had knowledge about what is good and bad, the appearing (τὸ φάντασμα) would lose its grip over us (become ἄκυρον, 356d 8); consequently, we would achieve peace of mind (ἡσυχία, 356e 1) and salvation in life (σωτηρία τοῦ βίου, 356d 3; see also 356e 2, e 6, e 8, and 357a 6–7).

Furthermore, both the Socrates of the Republic and the Socrates of the Protagoras take goodness to be an evaluative property of a special sort. No other question is of more importance to the business of living than the question 'Is this (what I am about to do, what I contemplate doing, what I am doing) really good?' We might believe that the action we are considering is admirable or useful; or that we shall be envied for it; or perhaps that it is in keeping with our outlook, although we shall be despised for it. But the nagging question

---

[23] Older English translations of this passage seem to me greatly preferable to the more recent ones. The first English translator, Spens (1763), is very much on the right track: 'But what, is it also not evident, that with reference to things just and beautiful, the multitude chuse the apparent, even though they be not really so, yet they act, and possess, *and are reputed of accordingly*; but the acquisition of goods . . .' (emphasis added). The best rendition, to my mind, is that of Davies and Vaughan (1852), who clearly take ταῦτα πράττειν καὶ κεκτῆσθαι as the antecedent of δοκεῖν: 'Once more: is it not evident, that though many persons would be ready to do *and seem to do*, or to possess *and seem to possess* what seems just and beautiful, without really being so; yet when you come to things good . . .' (quoted from the 4th edn. (1868); emphasis added). καὶ δοκεῖν is misconstrued by Lindsay (1935), Grube (1974), and Grube-Reeve (1992). Until they provide a parallel for their construal of δοκεῖν, the older translations must take precedence. The Grube-Reeve translation reads: 'In the case of just and beautiful things, many people are content with what are believed to be so, even if they aren't really so, and they act, acquire, *and form their own beliefs* on that basis' (emphasis added).

always remains whether the action under consideration is really good; whether in acting as we do, we do good for ourselves.[24] This concern is the driving force behind much ethical reflection. But it is a concern that is operative already at a pre-reflective level. What the nagging question brings out is that we aim—pre-reflectively no less than reflectively—not at what appears good, but at what is in fact good.

Thus the special, Socratic wanting is what wanting becomes when we have tracked down what we have been after all along. What we have been after all along—what our desiderative states are always tracking down—is where our well-being in the world lies.

VIII

In saying that no one errs willingly Socrates has in mind, roughly, that no one does what is wrong recognizing it as wrong and wanting it as one wants things one recognizes to be good. We might find it helpful to put the thought this way: no one does what is wrong knowingly and willingly. But Socrates has no need to add 'knowingly' to 'willingly', since his claim that no one does what is wrong willingly implies that no one does it knowingly. If 'willingly' is understood as I have suggested, the claim is clearly not that wrongdoing is involuntary in Aristotle's sense of the word (see EN III. 1). If one thinks that Socrates takes wrongdoing to be involuntary in Aristotle's sense of the word (or in something close enough to this sense), one will feel a need to explain how he came to embrace such a view. This, I think, is what gives rise to the mistaken belief that he infers that no one does what is wrong willingly from the idea that wrongdoing involves ignorance. He fails to realize—unlike Aristotle after him—that only certain kinds of ignorance concerning one's action make that action involuntary (cf. Section II above). On the reading I have proposed, Socrates' claim makes perfect sense; it does not reflect any such gross failure of judgement.

Special as the notion of Socratic wanting or willing is, it is part of a larger disagreement with many of us. Socrates believes, for instance, that all who do what is wrong do so simply because they go wrong. Wrongdoers do not aim at something they recognize as wrong or bad; rather, they are misguided and ignorant about the nature of their action and its goal. Further, the thesis that no one errs willingly, as will transpire shortly, implies that *akrasia* is not possible.

---

[24] We should set aside the complaint that Socrates wavers between two different questions—the question of what is good, and the question of what is good for the agent. The more basic question for him is: what is good? He does also think that everyone seeks his own good. However, since 'what is good for the agent' has little antecedent content, it is left open what the content of the ultimate good will turn out to be. The ultimate good need not be egoistic.

This is certainly not what many of us today think about weakness of the will, or what many people thought about *akrasia* in Socrates' own time.[25]

We ought to start, however, with the position that Socrates takes himself to be denying when he rejects *akrasia*. At *Prot.* 352d 4–7 Plato formulates with some care the position that Socrates rejects:

> You [says Socrates to Protagoras] know that the many [οἱ πολλοὶ τῶν ἀνθρώπων] are not going to be persuaded by us. They say that a lot of people [πολλούς], recognizing what is best [γιγνώσκοντας τὰ βέλτιστα], do not want to do it [οὐκ ἐθέλειν πράττειν], when it is possible for them to do so [ἐξὸν αὐτοῖς], but do something else instead [ἀλλὰ ἄλλα πράττειν] . . .[26]

The view that Socrates rejects—imputed to and indeed put into the mouth of 'the many'—is that a lot of people act against their recognition, that is to say, against their knowledge, of what is best. This I take to be Socrates' primary, or official, characterization of *akrasia*.

Nowadays weak-willed action is often characterized as action against one's better judgement—one's judgement of what, under the circumstances, is the better thing to do. When understood in this way, there is no reason why an akratic action could not in principle be a good thing to do, or at any rate better than the action which the agent (incorrectly) takes to be better. However, according to the characterization of *akrasia* which Socrates gives in the passage quoted, akratic action is by assumption wrong: the akratic agent does what is wrong knowing that it is wrong, considering or having considered a different course of action that is open to him,[27] which he knows to be better

---

[25] To be sure, we should be careful here. We are dealing with more than one party. We are not Socrates' interlocutors: when he discusses *akrasia*, his interlocutors are the 'the many' that he conjures up (see, in particular, *Prot.* 352b 2–3 and 352d 5). The notion of *akrasia* that Socrates rejects is somewhat different from the notion (or notions) that we nowadays have of weakness of the will. None the less, as I shall later argue, there is some reason to think that he would not only deny the existence of *akrasia* as (he thinks) his contemporaries conceive of it; he would also deny the existence of *akrasia* as many of us nowadays think of it.

[26] Having formulated what an akratic action is, Socrates goes on to state the cause, τὸ αἴτιον, that the many cite to explain such an action. I shall follow him in keeping the issue of the 'cause' separate.

[27] Davidson argues that Socrates—or, strictly speaking, G. Santas, whose interpretation of Socrates Davidson discusses—fails to realize that an alternative course of action need not in fact be open to the agent, because the agent's *belief* that the course of action is open to him is sufficient. (Donald Davidson, 'How is Weakness of the Will Possible', in *Essays on Actions and Events* (Oxford, 1980), 21–42 at 22 n. 1; the reference is to Santas's article 'Plato's *Protagoras* and Explanations of Weakness', *Philosophical Review*, 75 (1966), 3–33). Davidson's remark is appropriate given his perspective on weakness of the will. But Socrates is not in error here. His characterization reflects his approach to *akrasia*. Unlike us (and, to some extent, unlike Aristotle), Socrates approaches *akrasia* from outside in. He focuses on putative akratic actions that are

·or best. It is because Socrates construes *akrasia* in this way, and not merely as action against one's better judgement, that his denial of *akrasia* follows from his No One Errs Willingly thesis.

One important aspect of the official characterization of *akrasia* at *Prot.* 352d 4–7 has been generally overlooked. The many, Socrates says, claim that a lot of people, recognizing what is best, do not want to do it (οὐκ ἐθέλειν πράττειν), when it is possible for them to do it, but do something else instead. He invokes wanting here, and builds it into the characterization of *akrasia* offered by the many (see also ἐθέλει at 355b 2, ἐθέλειν at 358d 2, and ἐθελήσει at 358e 3). Thus the thesis he intends to deny is not just that one can fail to do what one recognizes is best, but more fully that an agent may recognize what is best and yet not want, or not be willing, to do it, and consequently, not do it. By contrast, we have to assume, Socrates contends that a person who knows what the right thing to do is, does want to do it and, other things being equal, will do it. (The more neutral word for wanting, ἐθέλειν, that he uses here is appropriate since the position he is denying is that of the many, who would not put their own point in terms of Socrates' special notion of wanting or willing. To express his own position, Socrates could use either the more neutral ἐθέλειν or the more specific βούλεσθαι.)

If Socrates uses 'willingly' in a special way when he claims that no one errs willingly, to designate a volitional act that is also cognitive, does this not make his claim problematic? His concept of willing is not ours. What can we do with such a peculiar concept? In response, I shall match these questions with another one. Socrates' rejection of *akrasia* amounts to the view that one cannot act against one's knowledge of what is best. Now the conception of knowledge that underlies this view should strike us as at least as peculiar as the concept of Socratic wanting. Here is what Socrates has to say about the relevant kind of knowledge:

> Now, do you [Protagoras] too think that that is how things stand with it [sc. knowledge], or do you think that knowledge [ἐπιστήμη] is fine and such as to rule the person, and if someone recognizes what is good and bad [ἐάνπερ γιγνώσκῃ

---

in fact cases of wrongdoing, where an alternative course of action is available to the agent and is *recognized* by the agent as available to him. Socrates is interested in (putative) *akrasia* as an ethical problem—primarily an ethical problem of wrongdoing of some kind. One could, of course, restate his views on *akrasia* by taking in an inside-out approach, focusing on the beliefs that the agent has about the action he takes and about the alternative course of action available to him. I shall go on to address this approach (which Socrates to some extent adopts later on in the *Protagoras*: see 358c 6–d 4), but only after I have looked into what I take to be the primary account of *akrasia*, given in a preliminary fashion at *Prot.* 352b 5–8, and then, more carefully, in the passage just quoted, 352 d 4–7.

τις τἀγαθὰ καὶ τὰ κακά], he would not be overpowered by anything else so as to act otherwise than knowledge dictates, and wisdom [τὴν φρόνησιν] is sufficient to help the person? (*Prot.* 352c 2–7)

We no more share with Socrates his conception of *knowledge* than we share with him his conception of wanting or *willing*. But if this is so, should we regard his claim that no one errs willingly as more suspect than his claim that no one errs knowingly? As I pointed out at the beginning of this paper, the wanting or willing that the expression 'willingly' refers to involves recognition of what is good or bad; it has now turned out that the knowledge of what is good and bad involves wanting that accords with the knowledge in question. Hence, one claim is as problematic or as unproblematic as the other; both claims stand or fall together. They should also be examined together.

IX

Socrates does not want to deny that we have episodes which we incorrectly describe as akratic or weak-willed. We should now take a look at his characterization of the 'cause' of *akrasia*, which is kept separate from the characterization of *akrasia* itself. We have heard what the many believe: that a lot of people, recognizing what is best, do not want to do it, but do something else instead (352d 4–7). When asked what they think the cause (αἴτιον) of this is (d 7–8), the many—according to Socrates—reply that 'those who act in this way do so being overcome [ἡττωμένους] by pleasure or pain, or being overpowered [κρατουμένους] by one of the things I [Socrates] referred to just now' (352d 8–e 2). Socrates has in mind the things he referred to at 352b 5–8, the passage in which he gives his first, informal characterization of *akrasia*. According to this characterization, the many believe that 'often, although knowledge is present in a person, what rules him is not knowledge but something else: sometimes anger [θυμόν], sometimes pleasure [ἡδονήν], sometimes pain [λύπην], at other times love [ἔρωτα], often fear [φόβον] . . .'. So, on the account given by the many, people act akratically—i.e. against their knowledge of what is best—because they are overcome by pleasure or pain, by desire, or by any of a number of passions.

At *Prot.* 352e 5–353a 2 Socrates says that he and Protagoras should now attempt to persuade and teach the many what the πάθος is which the many describe as being overcome with pleasure, and which in their view is why they don't do what is best when they recognize what it is. He refers to the same thing as a πάθημα a few lines below, at 353a 4–6: the many, he says, will demand an explanation from him and Protagoras as to what this πάθημα is, if it does not amount to being overcome by pleasure.[28] Thus Socrates grants that a certain πάθος or πάθημα—a particular way of being afflicted—is present. What is presumed to be missing is a correct characterization of this affliction. The two words, πάθος and πάθημα, which are here used interchangeably, refer, I believe, not to the experience associated with putative *akrasia* but to the affliction of the putative akratic—namely, what a person undergoes when he undergoes what the many think of as *akrasia*. The usual translation of πάθος or πάθημα as 'experience' does not seem to me to be accurate. When Socrates draws attention to what is happening with the presumed akratic agent, he may have in mind an experience that the agent has, but he need not. For instance, when he further down declares that the πάθημα in question is in fact ignorance (357c 7), he is not saying that the *experience* characteristic of putative *akrasia* is ignorance, but rather that the condition of the agent's soul that is wrongly attributed to *akrasia* is in fact ignorance.

Keeping in mind Socrates' preliminary formulation of *akrasia* at 352b 5–8, and bypassing the hedonistic assumptions from which the discussion of *akrasia* in the *Protagoras* proceeds,[29] the description 'being overcome by pleasure' should be taken as representative of a number of related descriptions that the many had offered to explain *akrasia*. The presumed akratic was described at 352b 5–8 as being overcome not only by pleasure, but also by pain, desire, fear, love, and so on. In speaking of the condition of being overcome by passion below, I use 'passion' broadly, to refer to any of these states.

It would be wrong to assume that Socrates has an easy task here. Once we strip the phenomenon commonly described as *akrasia* of all the descriptions Socrates would find incorrect, it is not quite clear what remains. This, I take it, sets him a task. We speak of our akratic episodes; we know what it feels like to be in the grip of one; we understand what others have in mind when they describe theirs. This presumably is not what Socrates wants to deny. But when the many say, for instance, that people are overcome (ἡττώμενοι or κρατούμενοι) by passion, they seem to have in mind a contest of two forces: one that wins and one that is defeated (being defeated is a usual meaning of ἡττώμενος). Socrates, as we shall see, rejects the picture of contest between two forces as a proper description of what happens in putative *akrasia*. The agent is not really acting against his knowledge; nor is he, as I am about to argue, acting against his better judgement. If this is so, Socrates should be able to tell us how to identify the putative phenomenon of *akrasia* in a way that is

---

[28] Socrates comes back to this πάθημα at 357c 7. He is now ready to provide his answer to the question pressed by the many. The πάθημα in question, he now claims, is ignorance (ἀμαθία). See 357e 2–4.

[29] Here and in what follows I am interested in Socrates' general position on *akrasia*. I thus aim to reconstruct the considerations on which he based his rejection of *akrasia* in a way that should be of interest to hedonists and non-hedonists alike.

independent of all the incorrect descriptions usually given of it. In the *Protagoras* he does not endeavour to do this.

X

Let me now turn briefly to a broader notion of *akrasia*, one that involves acting against one's judgement or belief[30]—not necessarily against one's knowledge—that some course of action is best. The characterization of *akrasia* in the *Protagoras* discussed so far has not included this kind of case. However, in the course of arguing against *akrasia* as officially characterized, Socrates makes observations that amount to grounds for rejecting *akrasia* in a broader sense, viz. *akrasia* thought of as action against one's judgement as to what is best.

The main thought behind this denial can be expressed in the following way. *Akrasia* presupposes an awareness on the part of the agent of alternative courses of action available to him. What supposedly happens here is this: the agent considers two courses of action; he believes that one of them is correct; none the less, he does what he believes to be wrong. The main reason why Socrates thinks this is not possible is that our actions embody our evaluative beliefs, and that they embody them in a very strong sense. By going for one of the considered alternative courses of action rather than the other, the agent shows that he takes the preferred course of action to be better. Recall again Socrates' statement about human nature:

> Now, no one goes willingly towards things that are bad [ἐπί γε τὰ κακὰ οὐδεὶς ἑκὼν ἔρχεται] or towards those one thinks are bad [οὐδὲ ἐπὶ ἃ οἴεται κακὰ εἶναι], nor is it in human nature [ἐν ἀνθρώπου φύσει], so it seems, to want to go towards what one thinks is bad [ἐπὶ ἃ οἴεται κακὰ εἶναι ἐθέλειν ἰέναι] instead of to what is good. And when one is forced to choose between two bad things, no one will choose the greater if he is able to choose the lesser. (*Prot.* 358c 6–d 4)[31]

In saying that no one goes willingly towards bad things (ἐπὶ . . . τὰ κακά), Socrates has in mind that no one goes willingly towards things that are bad, when it is transparent to the person's mind that they are bad. (Similarly for choosing between two bad things.) One reason why one cannot act against one's knowledge of what is better is that by acting so one would show one has a belief that contradicts the knowledge in question. But Socrates' practice of

---

[30] One might argue that making an evaluative judgement can fall short of holding an evaluative belief. However, I think that Socrates would not want to make a distinction between belief and judgement. To judge that something is good is to take it as good, and taking something to be such-and-such is on his view a δόξα, opinion or belief.

[31] Compare also 358e 2–6.

cross-examining his interlocutors implies that he thinks that a person who has a body of knowledge cannot have a belief that contradicts it.

The main intuition behind Socrates' denial of *akrasia* in the broader sense— the intuition that evaluative beliefs are both embodied and displayed in our actions—seems sound. This intuition is presumably something that would be understandable and in some form acceptable to the many. Socrates, however, pushes this thought much further than the many. He presumably believes that taking something to be good and going for it are connected far more tightly than people tend to think.

Now when I ϕ, where this ϕ-ing is a presumed akratic action, and I take myself to be acting against my belief that my ϕ-ing (here and now) is wrong, or worse than an alternative action open to me, is my belief that I have such a belief an illusion? Socrates' views on *doxa*, opinion or belief, seem to push him in two different directions. On the one hand, having a belief on his view implies having a commitment. Evaluative beliefs in particular involve practical commitments. So he might well argue that the presumed akratic is not committed to his professed evaluative belief to the degree that would be necessary for the ascription of the belief to him to be correct. If he took this line, what Socrates would be telling the presumed akratic is this: you claim to believe that your ϕ-ing (here and now) is wrong, but in fact you don't believe that. What you in fact believe, as your action shows, is that ϕ-ing (here and now) is good or right.

However, Socrates often uses *doxa* in a considerably more relaxed way. For instance, each of his interlocutors is said to have an opinion or belief whenever he sincerely agrees with the view that Socrates proposes for consideration. When we read in our translations of the *Protagoras* that this or that interlocutor 'concurred with' Socrates or 'agreed with' him, the word not infrequently used is συνδοκεῖν. The very word indicates that the interlocutor shares Socrates' *doxa*; that he believes (opines: δοκεῖν) that things are as Socrates says they are. The interlocutors often have a poor grasp of the content of what they agree to, and this (among other things) leads them to contradict themselves. Socrates takes such a contradiction as an indication that the interlocutor does not have knowledge, not that he does not have the relevant opinion or belief.[32]

---

[32] For συνδοκεῖν see 358b 6, c 3, c 6, and d 4. The four occurrences of συνεδόκει are part of an important global dialectical move Socrates makes at 358a 1–359a 1, at the end of his case against *akrasia*. He secures the agreement here not only of Protagoras, but also of Hippias and Prodicus, to the claim that pleasure is the good (358a 5–b 6); to his denial of *akrasia* and his diagnosis of what in fact happens in putative *akrasia* (b 6–c 3), along with his explanation of what ἀμαθία is (c 3–6), and to the claim that no one willingly goes towards what he thinks is bad (c 6–d 4). In each case, συνεδόκει punctuates the concurrence in belief among the four principal interlocutors. What is at issue at 358a 1–359a 1 is what Protagoras, Hippias, and Prodicus

When *doxa* is understood in this relaxed way, Socrates should say, as before, that the agent believes that his ϕ-ing (here and now) is right or good, since this belief is implied by his action. However, Socrates should now also grant that the presumed akratic agent believes that his ϕ-ing (here and now) is wrong. Now if Socrates takes this line, then on his view an agent can after all act against his belief that his ϕ-ing (here and now) is wrong. Would this amount to a recognition of *akrasia* on Socrates' part? I have in mind here a recognition of *akrasia* understood in the broader sense, i.e. *akrasia* thought of as action against one's belief about what is better or best. Although it is true that on this analysis the agent acts against his belief, I am inclined to think that this is not what those who hold that *akrasia* exists for the most part have in mind. Being akratic does not consist merely in acting against a belief, in a weak sense of this word, that something is good.[33] Although of course there are many conceptions of what *akrasia* consists in, the agent is usually thought to be acting against something a bit stronger than this sort of belief. I shall come back to this question in a moment.

Let me return to *akrasia* as originally defined—namely, as action against one's knowledge of what is better or best—and look at the diagnosis Socrates would give of the presumed akratic's predicament. It seems reasonable to assume that Socrates sees the putative akratic as himself believing that he acts against his knowledge of what is best. Admittedly, in his official characterization of *akrasia* at *Prot.* 352d 4–7 Socrates does not explicitly state that the many believe *of themselves* that they often know what is best and yet do something else; his claim is rather that the many (οἱ πολλοί) allege that akratic episodes happen to many (πολλοί). Although this invites us to think that the relevant ascriptions of knowledge involve self-ascriptions, the formulation itself does not settle the question whether such self-ascription of knowledge is constitutive of (what passes for) *akrasia*.

There is some reason to think that it is. What makes it so difficult to deny *akrasia* is precisely the repeatedly insistent first-person claim: 'but—whatever your theory—I knew full well that what I was going to do was bad; yet I did it.' When we find it difficult to go along with philosophical worries concerning the existence of *akrasia*, we do so not because we are confident about third-person ascriptions of knowledge to agents who happen to act against their knowledge. What makes it difficult to deny *akrasia* is rather the first-person

---

believe, or rather have come to believe, having been persuaded by Socrates (see the instances of δοκεῖν at 358a 3 and a 4, d 7, and e 6). Socrates then moves on to secure the agreement of all three to his definition of fear (358d 5–359 a 1). Having secured these admissions, Socrates immediately (starting at 359a 2) moves to show that Protagoras' position on the unity of virtue is incompatible with the admissions he has just made.

[33] This, I presume, is why Aristotle comes to think of *akrasia* as action against the agent's προαίρεσις, choice. As he understands it, προαίρεσις involves a firm practical commitment.

experience of going against one's own firm conviction that something is bad, often because of some powerful desire or impulse. Is the firmly held conviction taken by the akratic himself to be a case of knowledge? In everyday life people often describe their weak-willed episodes this way; they do it when they say, for instance: 'But I *saw* clearly that this was bad; yet I did it.' This conception of *akrasia* is vividly conveyed by Ovid's memorable 'video meliora proboque, deteriora sequor', cited at the head of this paper. Except for being couched as a first-person statement, Ovid's formulation is strikingly close to Socrates' own (at *Prot.* 352d 4–7): the akratic acts against what he *sees* is better—the Greek γιγνώσκειν to recognize, has become the even more emphatic Latin *videre*, to see.[34]

If the akratic agent believes, Ovid-style, that he acts against his knowledge of what is better or best, Socrates' case against *akrasia* implies that this belief is false. Socrates would diagnose the Ovid-style akratic as suffering from the affliction he believed it was his task to unmask, and if possible, eradicate (see the *Apology*): ignorance of one's own ignorance. The akratic agent not only lacks knowledge of what is better or best; he also wrongly believes that he possesses this knowledge. When Socrates declares that the πάθος or πάθημα of being overcome by pleasure (or, in general, passion) is in fact ἀμαθία, ignorance[35]—indeed, ἀμαθία ἡ μεγίστη, the greatest ignorance—he might have in mind the ignorance of what is good or bad. However, every wrongdoer is on Socrates' view ignorant of what is good or bad. What is specific to the central type of wrongdoing that the many incorrectly describe as akratic is the specific ignorance of one's own ignorance that this type of wrongdoing involves.

Now what would be Socrates' diagnosis of the putative akratic condition if *akrasia* is construed more broadly, as action against one's better judgement? Here the diagnosis would have to await a more precise description of what *akrasia* is. There is a view according to which we can go for something without taking it in any way as good. Values are here seen as being at some remove from the desires or impulses on which we act. So on this view an akratic may, for instance, do something in spite of his judgement that what he is about to

---

[34] One interesting difference is that Socrates does not find it necessary to make separate mention of the approbative attitude that goes along with the recognition of what is better or best. The relevant knowledge or recognition, on his view, implies an approbative attitude.

[35] See *Prot.* 357e 2–4: 'So this is what being overpowered by pleasure [τὸ ἡδονῆς ἥττω εἶναι] is, the greatest ignorance [ἀμαθία ἡ μεγίστη], which is what Protagoras here and Prodicus and Hippias claim to cure.' What Protagoras professed to teach earlier in the dialogue was (civic) virtue (318e 5–319a 2). It is because he claims to teach this (among other reasons) that Socrates, ironically, counts him as being on his side in the argument against the many. Protagoras had better know what putative *akrasia* is, since this issue is at the heart of his professed expertise.

do is bad; he does so simply because he 'feels like it', not because he values it in some way. If this is what it means to act against one's better judgement, Socrates would deny that such *akrasia* exists. He would do so because he would reject the view that the agent can act without taking anything to be good or bad. As the *Meno* passage referred to above indicates (as well as the statement in the *Protagoras* about human nature quoted above, 358c 6–d 4), when an agent acts on a desire, he acts in accordance with the value judgement involved in the desire. This judgement is the one that motivates his action.

But suppose the opponent grants a part of Socrates' point, admitting that our actions are shot through with value judgements, and that value judgements are not motivationally inert; suppose he also agrees that it is not possible to go for something without considering it good in some way. The opponent might none the less think that it is possible to act against one's reflectively considered scheme of values, and he might propose that the 'better judgement' against which the akratic acts be identified with such a reflectively considered judgement. Would Socrates deny this?

Socrates would not be the one to deny that reflective thought can generate values. He could also hardly deny that one's impulses might go against reflectively generated values. However, *akrasia*, as usually understood, is not an affliction that consists merely in holding contradictory evaluative beliefs, and acting sometimes on one such belief and sometimes on another. *Akrasia* is more than confusion about values. A proponent of *akrasia* usually regards the so-called 'better judgement' as something more than a mere judgement that some course of action is better. The 'better judgement' is 'better' because it is reflectively endorsed; or because it has higher epistemic credentials; or because it is the judgement with which the person more fully and directly identifies.

For instance, having considered the evaluative point of view that pushes me into this action, I may form a judgement that the evaluative viewpoint in question is not one that I can ultimately embrace; a more carefully considered judgement, or a judgement that rests on a wider point of view, or a judgement that expresses more directly my will—these are the candidates for that 'better judgement' against which I act when I act akratically. But the more weight we thus put on the notion of better judgement, the less likely it is that Socrates would agree with us. It is likely that he would stick to his basic intuition that our actions reveal more about us and our values than any product of detached reflection might. As he would see it, the mere fact that a desire is a second-order one, or that it is endorsed by some second-order thinking on our part, is neither here nor there. The reflection he is interested in is practical reflection: one that changes preferences, and goes all the way down, to influence the very valuations on which we act. The more we add to the notion of better judgement in terms of one's identification with it, the closer we get to the grounds on which Socrates refused to admit that one can ever act against one's knowledge of what is better.

On his understanding of what knowledge is, in order to know that a course of action is good, it is not sufficient to believe that it is good, and to hold this belief for the right reasons. If one knows something, then on Socrates' view, one cannot have a belief that contradicts that knowledge. Knowledge of what is good precludes false appearances of goodness. This suggests that knowledge—the sort of evaluative and practical knowledge that he has in mind when he speaks of the knowledge of good and bad—cannot be had in bits and pieces. To have the relevant sort of knowledge is to be in possession of a certain regulative and organizing principle that is in control of the overall condition of the soul. Socrates seems to think of knowledge as a condition in which none of one's doxastic commitments ever goes unheeded. One does not concur with a certain opinion, and then proceed to concur with a contradictory opinion a little later; one does not say 'Yes', and fail to recognize what this 'Yes' implies. Hence knowledge could be ascribed only to someone who has thoroughly thought things out. Only someone who grasps what his beliefs imply and how his various beliefs hang together possesses knowledge.

Although the considerations that I have suggested might impel Socrates to reject *akrasia* in the broader sense (thought of as action against one's better judgement) must remain speculative, the considerations he relies on in denying *akrasia* as action against one's knowledge give the impression that he might not be easily persuaded into accepting the existence of *akrasia* by its latter-day proponents. I do not mean to suggest here that he would be likely to reject the possibility of a weak-willed action on most, or even many, present-day conceptions of weakness of the will. For instance, there is no reason why he should reject the notion that a person may act in a way that stands in conflict with some of his second-order desires. In denying *akrasia*, Socrates is denying a certain picture of how human motivation operates. Thus he would be likely to deny weakness of the will as thought of by those who subscribe to the wrong picture of human motivation. In my next section I turn to the issue of what conception of the human soul and its workings he intends to reject when he rejects *akrasia*.

XI

Socrates can deny *akrasia* without ever mentioning desire.[36] Citing the link between actions, on the one hand, and motivating beliefs or opinions, on the other, suffices to bring out the most general grounds on which he denies *akrasia*. However, his view of desires—and also more broadly of passions or feelings ($\pi\acute{a}\theta\eta$)—is central to his rejection of what he presents as the cause,

---

[36] Indeed, that is what he does. In the *Protagoras* Socrates does not mention desire until his argument against *akrasia* is completed.

αἴτιον, of *akrasia*: the account the many give of how it comes about that one acts against one's knowledge (or belief) of what is better. Socrates' understanding of desires and passions is also central to his own full account of what actually goes on in putative cases of *akrasia*.

The common explanation of *akrasia* that he wants to reject has it that one acts akratically (weakly, as the Greek term indicates) because one is overcome by desire or passion. Recall again the view of the many: 'often, although knowledge is present in the human being, what rules him is not knowledge but something else: sometimes anger, sometimes pleasure, sometimes pain, at other times love, often fear; they [the many] think that his knowledge is dragged around by all of these just like a slave' (*Prot.* 352b 5–c 1).

At *Prot.* 358d 5–7 Socrates characterizes fear as προσδοκία τις κακοῦ, some kind of expectation of something bad. The word προσδοκία, translated usually as 'expectation', means something like 'anticipatory belief'—the component - δοκια is closely related to δόξα, belief or opinion.[37] By adding τίς to προσ- δοκία (in Greek, *x* τις means, roughly, some *x*; a sort (kind) of *x*; *x* of a sort). Socrates apparently wants to indicate that not every sort of expectation of, or anticipatory belief about, something bad qualifies as fear. What sort of expectation of something bad in fact qualifies as fear is at least in part connected with the sort of bad or evil (κακόν) that is the proper object of fear. Socrates intends this as a genuine (even if not fully spelt out) definition of fear. However he would want to spell it out, he appears to take fear as a certain, highly specific, case of taking something to be bad. Other passions would presumably be characterized too in terms of their specific way of taking something to be good or bad. I have already argued that Socrates thinks of desires as involving beliefs that something is good. If we can think of desires as passions of some kind, it would follow that desires too are ways of taking something to be good.

Socrates is sometimes said to reduce desires or feelings to mere beliefs. The assumption seems to be that, in doing so, he is leaving something out. Being in the grip of a passion can be a harrowing, wrenching, or delightful experience. How can having such an experience, people tend to ask, be a matter of holding a mere belief? I suggest that Socrates' characterization of fear need not be thought of as reductive. His view might well be the following: the very motion of the soul that constitutes the passion of fear is what it takes for us to believe that this or that thing is frightful. If this is his view, it need lose nothing from the phenomenological richness of our experiences of fear. What holding a belief amounts to depends on the sort of belief that is being held. Many evaluative beliefs have motivating force; some evaluative beliefs— those that on this view constitute desires and passions—are of such a sort that having them amounts to having experiences of a particular sort.

---

[37] The definition of fear as προσδοκία τις κακοῦ is sandwiched between συνεδόκει at d 4 and ἐδόκει at d 7, in a way that puts emphasis on the -δοκια part of the definition. See n. 32 above.

The belief that being *afraid* cannot consist in *taking* something to be of some sort can perhaps be traced to the view that *taking* or *considering* something is, as such, an act of intellect, and that intellect, again, is something from which the stormy movements of the soul are removed. Contrary to that line of thought, I would suggest that Socrates need not be seen as reducing desires and feelings to something else, with the richness of experience being lost in the process. He can be seen as offering an alternative analysis of what it is to desire something, or what it is to have a certain feeling.

Similarly, in denying that a host of pleasures and pains, desires and emotions, can drag knowledge around 'like a slave', he need not be seen as denying the heterogeneity of states of the soul (mental states, as we might want to put it) that move us to act. That he does so is a fairly frequent misconception. What he rejects is a picture according to which passions or feelings are psychic states independent of reason. Against this, he believes that in every passion reason is in some way exercised. There is nothing in this view that would commit him to denying that the ways in which reason takes things to be good or bad are many, or even that some of these ways of taking things to be good or bad are irreducibly distinct from others.

What on Socrates' view accounts for wrongdoing—akratic and otherwise— is not the condition of being vanquished by the forces of desire and passion. Rather, wrongdoing is in each case due to an improper functioning of reason. When passion leads us astray, what leads us astray is the incorrect valuation that our reason has adopted. It is perhaps easy to jump from this view to the position that passions as such are nothing but states in which reason has gone off track, and hence to the conclusion that we should get rid of them. (Likewise, it is easy to suppose that Socrates' memorable rejection of the image of knowledge as a slave dragged about by a myriad of passions implies hostility to passions.) But according to the discussion of courage that follows upon Socrates' definition of fear, in the last pages of the *Protagoras*, courage is not a state in which fear is extinguished. Far from it. Courage is a state of the soul which makes one fear those things that ought to be feared, that is to say, things that are genuinely bad. The courageous, as he puts it, do not 'fear disgraceful fears' (*Prot.* 360a 8–b 2). But they do fear. The courageous person's fear—which is some kind of abhorrence of vice—would admittedly be very different from the sort of fear an ordinary soldier might feel in a battle; none the less, one should not be too quick and on account of this difference deny it the status of fear. Socrates does think that the knowledge that is virtue involves a certain peace of mind—ἡσυχία (*Prot.* 356e 1). We are given no ground, however, to take this kind of tranquillity to be freedom from passions—ἀπάθεια. On the contrary, Socrates' discussion of courage in the *Protagoras* provides us with a picture of the virtuous person as prone to the right kind of fear.

Virtue is a condition in which one's takings-to-be-good and takings-to-be-bad are not only correct, but are instances of knowledge. Those takings-to-be-good or takings-to-be-bad that constitute the passions of a virtuous person are also not just correct takings, but states of knowledge. The view here is not the more common one, that a virtuous person's passions are fully appropriate responses to the situations he encounters; rather the view is that virtue itself (in part) consists in such passions as are correct takings-to-be-good and takings-to-be-bad.

To put the same point differently: Socrates no doubt believes that someone who is not sensitive to the aspects of a situation that a virtuous person would be sensitive to does not know what there is to know about what is good and bad. However, he goes beyond this belief. He takes it that such sensitivities are themselves bits of the knowledge that is virtue. A comparison with Aristotle might make the point clearer. Socrates is often thought to differ from Aristotle in not including desiderative and emotional propensities—what Aristotle calls states of character—in virtue, making virtue instead into a mere excellence of the inert intellect that judges things correctly. On the interpretation I have offered, Socrates is precisely insisting that such propensities constitute virtue. I would locate the main difference between Socrates and Aristotle in the fact that excellent states of character for Socrates are at no remove from moral knowledge. The excellent states of character simply are states of knowledge. However close the two might lie for Aristotle (and this might be closer than some of his formulations suggest), he did want to make at the very least a notional distinction between the emotional and desiderative propensities that constitute virtue of character, on the one hand, and moral knowledge, on the other.

After Socrates gets Polus to agree to the conclusion that orators and tyrants do not do what they want to do, Polus in effect exclaims: 'As if you, Socrates, do not envy the tyrant!' (468e 6–9). Olympiodorus, who in his commentary on the *Gorgias* judges Polus' intervention to be vulgar (ἰδιωτικόν), entirely misses the point.[38] Polus' reaction is relevant, and revealing. Envying the tyrant is not a minor lapse that can be overlooked if the person in question professes the correct beliefs. Someone who forcefully argues that doing injustice is one of the greatest evils, yet envies the tyrant, displays a soul that lacks knowledge and is very much in need of repair. One reason why so many of Socrates' interlocutors contradict themselves on the issue of virtue is that they so glaringly lack it. They think, for instance, that what the tyrant does is disgraceful (αἰσχρόν), but also envy him.

Often, one of the first things Socrates wants his interlocutor to agree to is that virtue is something beautiful or fine (καλόν), and vice something ugly or disgraceful (αἰσχρόν). By concurring with this, the interlocutors commit

---

[38] See Olymp. *In Plat. Gorg.* 95. 22 ff. Westerink, and Dodds ad loc.

themselves to more than they had perhaps imagined. They commit themselves, for instance, to not envying the tyrant, and to abhorring the things the tyrant does.

The virtuous person's actions express his evaluative knowledge. The evaluative judgements embodied in one's emotions and actions—the values one lives by—are of paramount importance to Socrates. A part of what in his view accounts for putative *akrasia* is precisely the fact that people are mistaken about what values they live by. If putative *akrasia* is so frequent, this is so in part because people are often mistaken about this. In addition to inconsistencies among a person's evaluative beliefs, which testify to a lack of knowledge of what is good and bad, the condition people describe as *akrasia* also involves a certain lack of self-understanding.

XII

The many take it that sometimes, driven by a desire or emotion, we act entirely against what our reason tells us is good, better, or best. Against this, Socrates holds that our actions themselves embody judgements of value. Our reason speaks in the very passion that drives us, even if reason does not speak in a way that is consonant with our remaining opinions or judgements. We take ourselves to be fragmented where we are not. Socrates sees the human soul as one and undivided. In taking the human soul to be unitary and undivided, he is ruling out the possibility that there is an irrational or non-rational part of our souls that is capable of motivating us to act entirely on its own. But the unity of the soul he envisages has a further significance: it ties inextricably together the practical side of our nature—the desiderative, the emotional, and the volitional—with the supposedly non-practical side of us, namely the side that forms judgements and possesses knowledge.

On Socrates' view, it is an inadequate conception of reason that lies at the bottom of the belief that *akrasia* exists. An inadequate and impoverished conception of reason might also lie behind certain misunderstandings of his position. Socratic intellectualism is often criticized as one-sided, on the ground that it does not to do justice to the richness and complexity of our mental life. But on the account given here, the complexity and richness of our mental life, and of our nature, can remain untouched. Rather, Socrates' view might be that more of us goes into every state of our soul than we suspected; in some sense the whole power of the soul goes into every state of the soul. If our reason is at work in more places and in more ways than we might have thought, it should not be too surprising if it turned out to malfunction more often than expected. Specific malfunctionings of reason are also at the bottom of what people call *akrasia*.

One would expect that an intellectualist would propose an intellectual cure for an intellectual ailment. So, for instance, if virtue is knowledge, as

Socrates appears to think, it might seem that all we need to do in order to in-stil virtue in those who lack it is instruct them about what virtue requires. But he never recommends such simple instruction; on the contrary, he insists that becoming virtuous involves much care and therapy of the soul. Reason is quite vulnerable. Susceptible to more maladies than we might have expected, it also requires more extensive and complicated care than expected. If we do not stick to the characterization of *akrasia* given in the *Protagoras*, we could concede that on Socrates' view humans are prone to a condition that might deserve to be labelled *akrasia*. The Greek word simply indicates weakness, and Socrates does take it that weakness of reason is displayed in the episodes usu-ally considered akratic. What he presents as powerful—as not dragged about 'like a slave'—is not reason as such, but knowledge, which is a stable overall condition of a well-functioning reason.

When Socrates describes virtue as knowledge, it is not just any kind of knowledge that he has in mind. Certain desires and feelings are part of the knowledge that is virtue. In addition, Socratic volition as discussed above is part of moral knowledge. This volition is an aspiration; it is part of an ideal of the good life. The virtuous person alone on Socrates' view does entirely what he wants to do. The virtuous person can do what he wants to do because the taking-to-be-good that his willing amounts to is itself a state of knowledge: it is an accurate grasp of what is in fact good. Being instructed on what one ought to want typically does not produce the desired wanting; this holds good for Socratic volition as much as it holds for volition as usually understood. Socrates would certainly agree with those who think that becoming good re-quires that one's whole soul be turned around. What he might disagree with is what happens in the process of turning the soul around. On his view, any change in the desiderative, volitional, or emotional condition of the soul is it-self a change in the condition of reason.

APPENDIX

Gorgias 467c 5–468e 5

Through his argument at *Gorg.* 467c 5–468e 5, Socrates gets Polus to agree, even if reluctantly, that orators and tyrants do not do what they want to do. I have argued above that Socrates' position is coherent and does not involve confusions of the sort interpreters have attributed to him. I wish now to show that the argument he uses at 467c 5–468e 5 to support his claim that orators and tyrants do not do what they want to do is likewise not flawed. In addition, the argument is worth looking into in its own right for at least two reasons. First, Socrates introduces here important concepts concerning human action, and second, his treatment of Polus is a paradigm of a kind of irony that he often displays in Plato's Socratic dialogues. In fact, one cannot properly assess the philosophical content of the argument at 467c 5–468e 5 without paying attention to the way Socrates treats Polus.

Socrates asks Polus if people who take medicines prescribed by their doctors want what they are doing (βούλεσθαι ὅπερ ποιοῦσιν), namely, taking the medicine and being in pain, or that for the sake of which they do this, namely, being healthy (467c 7–10). Polus agrees that they want to be healthy. Similarly, seafarers do not want sea voyages with all the danger and trouble that these involve; what they want is wealth (467d 1–5). Socrates then secures Polus' agreement to the claim that this is so in all cases (περὶ πάντων)—when a person does something for the sake of something, he does not want what he is doing (οὐ τοῦτο βούλεται ὃ πράττει), but the thing for the sake of which (ἐκεῖνο οὗ ἕνεκα) he is doing it (467d 6–e 1).

The troubling clause is 'he does not want what he is doing'. The form of words chosen here might suggest that Socrates intends to assimilate all action to merely instrumental activities like taking bitter medicines. On the strict instrumentalist view ostensibly proposed here, no one ever wants what he does; the agent merely wants the beneficial result which he expects his action to have. Hence, like everyone else, orators and tyrants do not want what they are doing in killing, expropriating, and banishing. Now we know that the conclusion Socrates wants to reach is that orators and tyrants do not do what they want to do. How is the transition made from orators' and tyrants' not wanting what they do to their not doing what they want? The instrumentalist account of action seemingly embraced at the beginning of the argument does not provide means for this transition. But in that case, why did Socrates start by drawing our attention to actions such as the taking of bitter medicine? I suggest that he is not in fact proposing to assimilate all action to merely instrumental activities like this. To see what he is up to, we have to look a bit ahead in the argument. Let me quote an important claim he makes further on:

P1   Therefore it is because we pursue what is good [τὸ ἀγαθὸν ἄρα διώκοντες] that we walk whenever we walk,—thinking that it is better to walk [οἰόμενοι βέλτιον εἶναι],—and, conversely, whenever we stand still it is for the sake of the same thing [τοῦ αὐτοῦ ἕνεκα] that we stand still, what is good [τοῦ ἀγαθοῦ] . . . And don't we also kill a person, if we do, expel him from the city, or confiscate his property thinking that doing so is better for us than not doing it [οἰόμενοι ἄμεινον εἶναι ἡμῖν ταῦτα ποιεῖν]? . . . Hence it is for the sake of the good [ἕνεκα . . . τοῦ ἀγαθοῦ] that those who do all these things do them. (Gorg. 468b 1–8)

I propose to view everything that precedes the quoted passage, starting from 467c 5, not as endorsing an instrumental account of action, but as an attempt to bring Polus to acknowledge the general picture of motivation offered in the lines just quoted. Socrates attempts to do this in two stages.

The first stage is the opening passage at 467c 5–e 1, where the drinking of bitter medicines and navigation are discussed. Socrates introduces here the notion of an end or goal of an action—that for the sake of which (ἐκεῖνο οὗ ἕνεκα) an action is performed—and connects this notion with the notion of wanting (βούλεσθαι). What we want in whatever we do is that for the sake of which we do it. This point holds regardless of how the goal is related to the activity in question—whether it is separate from it, includes it, or is identical with it. The claim is simply that the proper object of wanting is the goal, whatever this goal might happen to be.

The second stage of his attempt to get Polus to subscribe to the picture of motivation painted in the lines quoted above is found at 467e 1–468b 1, the passage immediately following the section on bitter medicines (and immediately preceding the lines quoted). In this passage, Socrates links the goal of an action with something that is good. He gets Polus to accept a division of things into good, bad, and those that are neither good nor bad; he also gets Polus to agree that we do indifferent things for the sake of good things. That we do bad things for the sake of good things is not explicitly stated, but Polus is meant to have in mind examples like the taking of bitter medicines—something that in itself is bad—which he had already agreed we do for the sake of something good, namely health.

Having thus provided the basic concepts of the theory of action he is trying to get Polus to subscribe to, Socrates is now ready to state a central principle of that theory. This is expressed in P1 above. What we are after—or what we pursue (διώκειν)—in everything we do is the goal (that-for-the-sake-of-which), and this in each case is something we take to be good. Our 'pursuing what is good' (at 468b 1) is specifically glossed as thinking (note οἰόμενοι at b 2 and b 6) that doing what we do is 'better' (note βέλτιον at b 2 and ἄμεινον at b 6).

It is at this point (at 468b 8) that Socrates invokes what he takes was agreed upon at the very outset. He says: 'Now didn't we agree that we want not those things that we do for the sake of something, but that for the sake of which we do them?' (468b 8–c 1; the reference back is to 467c 5–e 1, especially to 467c 5–7 and 467d 6–e 1). I have interpreted the passage which he refers to here as establishing a conceptual connection between wanting and the goal: the goal is the proper object of wanting. If this is the point of 467c 5–e 1, isn't it distinctly misleading for him to insist that people do *not* want, say, to make troublesome and dangerous journeys at sea? According to my reading of the opening passage, the point Socrates makes there is in a sense trivial: *provided* that making troublesome and dangerous journeys at sea is not the goal, it is not wanted. That making such journeys is not the goal is simply built into his example. (This fits well the statement with which he ends the opening passage: '*If* someone does something for the sake of something, he does not want that which he is doing, but that for the sake of which he is

doing it', 467d 6–e 1.) What he has in mind is clear from what he says immediately after he has reminded Polus of their previous point of agreement. Having received a positive answer (at 468c 1) to the question 'Now didn't we
agree that we want not those things that we do for the sake for something, but
that for the sake of which we do them?' (468b 8–c 1), he goes on to say:

> P2 Hence [ἄρα], we do not simply [ἁπλῶς] want [βουλόμεθα] to slaughter peo-
> ple, expel them from the cities, or confiscate their property, just like that
> [οὕτως]; we want to do these things if they are beneficial [ἀλλ' ἐὰν μὲν
> ὠφέλιμα ᾖ ταῦτα, βουλόμεθα πράττειν αὐτά], but if they are harmful, we
> don't [βλαβερὰ δὲ ὄντα οὐ βουλόμεθα]. (468c 2–5)

The lines just quoted contain the second central principle of the theory of action Socrates advocates here. The claim now is that we want to do such things
as killing, banishing, and confiscating, if they are beneficial; but if they are
harmful, then not. So, on the view now expressed, we precisely *do* want to
make dangerous journeys at sea—provided, that is, that we shall gain wealth
by them. But Socrates cannot have forgotten here the point he had made
when bringing up such examples as taking bitter medicines and making dangerous journeys at sea, since at 468b 8–c 1 he invokes what he takes to be the
conclusion of that discussion, and does so precisely in order to establish the
point he is now making (in P2). His current point is that we want to do those
things the doing of which is beneficial, and we do not want to do those things
the doing of which is harmful. This is a new point, quite different from what
we find in P1, and made expressly for the first time here in the lengthy argument he is presenting to Polus in support of the conclusion that orators and
tyrants do not do what they want to do. And it is this new claim that he needs
if he is to reach that conclusion.

So what was Socrates up to when he reminded Polus (just before stating
P2) of the opening part of the argument, namely, their agreement concerning
actions such as the taking of bitter medicines and the making of troublesome
sea voyages? I suggest that he uses these examples to lead up to P2. Even the
things that people generally would not want to do–drink a bitter potion, say,
or risk one's life at sea—they will want to do, and will do, if the doing of them
is beneficial. The attraction some find in adventures at sea is not a counter-
example to the point he is trying to make, just as someone's liking of bitter po-
tions is not such a counter-example. The instances he cites are simply of
things that are commonly regarded as highly undesirable. One generally does
not want to do them. If this is so, the instrumental reading of the opening
passage, 467c 5–e 1, turns out to be beside the point.

Does Socrates manage to establish his claim that orators and tyrants do not
do what they want to do by the argument we find at 467c 5–468e 5? The considerations adduced in support of his claim amount to a certain theory of
action. Does the argument make it clear what this theory is and how it might

be defended? Socrates, I contend, at the very least makes a move in the right direction. Admittedly, he does not say enough within the scope of his exchange with Polus fully to support P2. In claiming that we want to do things if they are beneficial and otherwise not, he has moved from speaking of things that are merely *taken to be* good (recall οἰόμενοι at 468 в 2 and в 6; see also οἰόμενος at 468d 3, quoted immediately below) as proper objects of wanting to speaking of things that (as a matter of fact) *are* good as proper objects of wanting. Is his transition from P1 to P2 surreptitious? The answer to this depends on whether we should take 'surreptitious' to mean attained by fraud or attained by stealth. Some stealth perhaps, but certainly no fraud, is involved.

Let me observe first that he makes the transition deliberately. He is not himself in a muddle. That the two passages quoted above impose different conditions on wanting is noted clearly, even if implicitly, by Socrates himself at the very end of the argument. He says:

> Since we are in agreement about that, then, if someone, whether tyrant or orator, kills someone or expels him from the city or confiscates his property because he thinks that [doing] this is better for himself [οἰόμενος ἄμεινον εἶναι αὐτῷ] when as a matter of fact it is worse [τυγχάνειν δὲ ὂν κάκιον], this person presumably does what pleases him [οὗτος δήπου ποιεῖ ἃ δοκεῖ αὐτῷ], doesn't he? . . . And is he also doing what he wants [ἃ βούλεται] if these things are in fact bad [εἴπερ τυγχάνει ταῦτα κακὰ ὄντα]? Why don't you answer? [POLUS:] All right, I think that he isn't doing what he wants. (468d 1–7).

Socrates here deliberately reserves the term 'wanting' for an attitude that hits upon what is in fact good, knowing of course that most people do not use the term in this way. Is he warranted in thus construing the term? I would like to argue that, dialectically speaking, he is. At 467e 1–468b 1 he got Polus to adopt the objective point of view: there Polus accepted the division of things into those that are good, those that are bad, and those that are neither good nor bad. The talk there was of things that actually are good, bad, or neutral, not merely of things that are considered to be so. Polus further agreed to the claim that people act for the sake of (actually) good things. It is this agreement that Socrates exploits further down, at 468c 5–7, while moving towards P2. He says: 'For we want things that are good [τὰ γὰρ ἀγαθὰ βου-λόμεθα]—as you say [ὡς φῆς σύ]—whereas we don't want those that are neither good nor bad, nor those that are bad.'

Polus is free to object here; he could interject that he had previously only meant to say that we go for—and want—things we take to be good, not things that are in fact good. But he does not object. Not only is he free to protest; Socrates repeatedly nudges and prods him to do so. When Socrates says 'For we want the things that are good, *as you say* . . .', he is clearly warning Polus that the conclusion has been reached using something Polus himself had previously said or agreed to. This is undoubtedly an invitation to Polus to reflect on what he had previously agreed to and why. What is especially intended to serve as a prod is the palpable irony in that 'as you say'.[39] When Socrates then pointedly asks whether Polus believes that what Socrates is saying is true, Polus, again, does not stir. Since he makes no objection, his prior agreements now commit him to saying that we want things that as a matter of fact are good.

Is Socrates deliberately confusing Polus? Given that Polus does not quite grasp what he is up to, should he move so nonchalantly from P1 to P2? It seems to me that by examining Polus as he does, he precisely intends to bring Polus' confusion into the open. He is suggesting to Polus that he has to re-think the whole issue since he does not understand what he is saying. In thus underscoring the need to think more carefully about the transition from P1 to P2, Socrates can hardly be muddling the issue. We must also bear in mind, as we wonder whether he might be confusing Polus, that he really believes what he describes Polus as saying. He decidedly believes that we 'want good things', namely, that we want things that are [as a matter of fact] good. It is therefore reasonable to think that when he says so, he is making a bona fide suggestion to Polus as to what he, Polus, ought to be saying. Finally, the shocking nature of the conclusion, that orators and tyrants do not do what they want to do— the conclusion which, as I have argued, Socrates embraces in all seriousness— is in itself a deterrent against muddles.

Socrates has philosophical reasons for maintaining that we want—in some legitimate sense of this word—what as a matter of fact is good, even if he has not fully set these reasons out in his exchange with Polus at 467c 5–468e 5. If in this argument he slips into the guise of the orator and tyrant, forcing what he takes to be true upon the unwilling Polus, we should perhaps be led to sus-pect that Polus lacks the sort of grasp of the matters discussed that would en-able him to follow Socrates willingly.

---

[39] Polus has not expressly said this. Since he has gone along with Socrates, Socrates can count him as having said so, but in that case Polus must be saying something he does not mean. He clearly does not understand the full force of the view he assents to; otherwise he would not be granting what in a moment will force him to embrace what he had not too long ago described as 'outrageous' and 'monstrous'. There is a hint of irony in the question Socrates will ask imme-diately after making the assertion (at 468c 5–7) that we want things that are good: 'Do you [Po-lus] think that what I am saying is true [$\dot{\alpha}\lambda\eta\theta\tilde{\eta}\ \sigma o\iota\ \delta o\kappa\tilde{\omega}\ \lambda\acute{\epsilon}\gamma\epsilon\iota\nu$])?' (468c 8). Since 'what I am saying' refers to Socrates' allegation about what Polus is 'saying' ('For we want the things that are good, as you [Polus] say, $\dot{\omega}\varsigma\ \phi\tilde{\eta}\varsigma\ \sigma\acute{v}\ \ldots$', 468 c 5–6), Socrates is in effect confronting Polus. He is questioning whether Polus has any idea not only what Socrates is saying and believing, but also what he, Polus, is saying and believing.

Part Two

Four ~

Aristotle on the Varieties of Goodness

*I*n the course of arguing against Plato's account of the good in the *Nicomachean Ethics*, Aristotle observes that honour, wisdom (*phronēsis*) and pleasure have different and dissimilar accounts (*heteroi kai diapherontes . . . logoi*) precisely insofar as they are goods (*tautē(i) hē(i) agatha*), which shows that the good is not some common element answering to a single Form (*EN* I. 6 1096b 23–6).

This remark is of considerable significance for understanding Aristotle's ethical theory. He has just said that having intelligence or wisdom (*to phronein*), seeing, and certain pleasures and honours are uncontroversially *kath' hauto* goods, things that are good in themselves (1096b 17–19). What he now adds is that Platonic Forms cannot account for the irreducible specificity of such intrinsic goods. Their accounts are different precisely insofar as they are goods. And Plato is not his only target, for Aristotle, as I shall argue later, directs the same line of criticism against the theory of something he calls the 'common good', and against the hedonism of Eudoxus.

Aristotle takes over from his predecessors—from Plato, and in a different way, from Eudoxus—the very discourse of *the good*, while wanting to reject the presuppositions on which this discourse was based.[1] His task is to show that his own ethical project, as an inquiry about the good, makes sense.

Aristotle starts from the striking variety of particular goods and kinds of good that people pursue in their actions. Equally striking is the variety of considerations people rely on in their everyday evaluative practices, when they judge this or that to be good. However, when one looks at ethical theories, one encounters an apparently overriding concern to find some single thing, or kind of thing, from which to derive the goodness of everything that is good. This project, Aristotle thinks, cannot succeed. The goodness of each of the many goods—pleasure, honour and intelligence, among others—is distinct and cannot be explained by reference to a good of some different kind.

The list of three goods-in-themselves that Aristotle cites against Plato at I. 6, 1096b 23–6 is not an arbitrary collection. Each of the three goods has

---

[1] Aristotle was influenced by other ethical theories as well. Protagoras, I believe, exerted a decisive, and largely unrecognized, influence. Yet direct textual evidence gives pride of place to Plato and Eudoxus. As I shall try to show, Aristotle worked out his own understanding of the good by attending closely to the Platonic and Eudoxan arguments. Most of his discussion of the two is highly critical. However, as I shall stress in the last section of this paper, he also owes a great deal to both.

figured as the centrepiece of an alternative view of what the human good is. Aristotle brings up these views in the preceding chapter, I. 5. You can tell, he says there, what people take to be the good from the most prominent types of life they go in for: the life of pleasure, the life devoted to honour, and the life of the intellect. In effect, pleasure, honour and wisdom have already been proposed as candidates for the human good. Admittedly, in I. 5 pleasure is proposed in the debased form it is pursued by the masses. But one has only to look at EN X. 4, or Aristotle's lyricism about the pleasures of philosophy at EN X. 7 1177a 22–7 (cf. Metaph XII. 7 1072b 14–26), to see that he accepts that pleasure, no less than honour and wisdom, is indeed a major good. Yet if their accounts are different precisely insofar as they are goods, no one of the three can explain the goodness of the other two. None can be the good.

In EN I. 5, Aristotle discusses the implicit identification of the good with some one special good as evidenced by the sort of life people lead. As he writes the Ethics, he undoubtedly also has in mind ethical reflection and theory which identifies the human good with pleasure, pursuit of honour, or the life of the intellect. He will later, at X.2, explicitly discuss and reject the view that pleasure is the good, which he identifies as the position of Eudoxus. The idea that the good lies in honour or reputation was deeply embedded in a more traditional and popular kind of moral reflection. The Sophists took the pursuit of honour especially seriously, providing theoretical underpinning for the traditional view. Finally, according to our sources, Socrates thought that knowledge must play a central role in any account of the human good. He does not seem to have identified the good with wisdom,[2] but he did identify virtue with wisdom or knowledge of a certain kind, and held that the good human life is a virtuous life.

Plato's ethical theory is quite different in style from these accounts of the good, moving at a much more abstract level. But in Aristotle's eyes it is ultimately driven by the same concern. The peculiarity of Plato's theory, as Aristotle understands it, is that it locates the good in something altogether different in kind from any good or kind of good by which people are motivated to act, or which they have in mind when in everyday life they praise what people go for in action, admire it, or otherwise evaluate it positively. The Form of goodness is something over and above particular goods and ordinary kinds of good; none the less, it is supposed to be the cause (aition) of the goodness of whatever is good. At EN I. 4 1095a 26–8, Aristotle sums up

---

[2] Possibly the identification is to be found in Socrates' associate Eucleides of Megara, although uncertainty remains; see Gabriele Giannantoni, Socratis et Socraticorum Reliquiae, 4 vols. (Rome 1990), IIA 30–32 and Nota 5. Plato has Socrates reject the identification at Rep 505bc, by way of preparation for introducing the specifically Platonic Form of the good in the simile of the Sun. Whether this amounts to rejecting a view implicit in Plato's early dialogues, or a view of the historical Socrates, is a matter for debate.

his understanding of the Platonic good: 'Some have held that over and above these many goods [sc. pleasure, wealth, honour, health, etc., cited just before to illustrate the sorts of thing people ordinarily identify eudaimonia with], there is some other good, in-itself, which is also the cause for all these goods of their being good.'[3]

I do not think that Aristotle is wrong to target together theories of the good that are clearly different in kind. He seems to be well aware that, when Plato describes the good itself as the cause which makes good things good, he intends this in a sense different from that in which a hedonist would claim that pleasure makes good things good. Similarly for wisdom and pleasure. Although one might think that these lie closer to one another than the Platonic good does to anything one ordinarily speaks of as a good, the way in which wisdom—probably conceived as identical with virtue in general—might be *the* good is not so close to the way in which pleasure, according to Aristotle's Eudoxus, is the good. Wisdom is most likely to be thought of as the controlling cause of action, pleasure as its accompanying reward. But what Aristotle is concerned to combat is the very idea of the good being subsumable under a single explanatory scheme.

Aristotle's point in rejecting such a scheme is not to affirm that there are a lot of different kinds of good out there, but to insist that ethical theory—theory concerned with how one should live—should give this variety its due weight. The plurality and variety of goodness is a datum too robust to be explained by any single-factor account. When he rejects the notion that pleasure is the good, he rejects both a certain ideal of life, a life devoted to the pursuit of pleasure, and the notion that the goodness or the rightness of conduct is to be judged by a single type of consideration. His concern is not to ban a single type of consideration, by letting in a few more say, but rather to preserve to a fair degree the richness of the types of consideration employed in everyday evaluative practices and followed in everyday ways of acting. For all the substantial differences between hedonist, Platonic, or the 'common good' theories, they share a common pattern, which justifies grouping them together—and rejecting the lot.

---

[3] Ἔνιοι δ' ᾤοντο παρὰ τὰ πολλὰ ταῦτα ἀγαθὰ ἄλλο τι καθ' αὑτὸ εἶναι ὃ καὶ τούτοις πᾶσιν αἴτιόν ἐστι τοῦ εἶναι ἀγαθά. Compare the nearly identical formulation concerning the Form of the good as the cause of goodness at *EE* i. 8 1217b 4–6, where Aristotle says of the Platonic good itself (αὐτὸ τὸ ἀγαθόν) that it is that ᾧ ὑπάρχει [. . .] τὸ αἰτίῳ τῇ παρουσίᾳ τοῖς ἄλλοις τοῦ ἀγαθοῖς εἶναι—'that to which it belongs [. . .] to be the cause, by its presence, for other goods, of their being goods.' The Platonic language Aristotle uses in *EE* i. 8 to characterize his own position is almost startling (especially at 1218b 11–12, where he calls what he is after, αὐτὸ τὸ ἀγαθόν, the good itself). However, the criticism of Plato in *EE* i. 8 seems to me to be entirely consistent with the criticism found in *EN* I. 6. For a different view, see Hellmut Flashar, 'Die Kritik der Platonischen Ideenlehre in der Ethik des Aristoteles', *Schriften zur aristotelischen Ethik* (1988), 201–24.

I wish to pursue further the claim that the objection to Plato I quoted at the beginning of this paper is indeed intended to be directed at other ethical theorists as well. But first let me look more closely into Aristotle's criticism of Plato's Form of the good.

1 The Human Good as a Practical Good

Aristotle argues that the sort of good Plato sets up in postulating the Form of the good could not, even if it did exist, be practical, *prakton*, or possessed, *ktē-ton*, by a human being (*EN* I. 6 1096b 31–5).

The claim that the Platonic good is not *prakton* is often understood as the claim that this good is not 'realizable' or attainable in human action. But understanding, or indeed translating,[4] the term this way misses the basic sense it carries when predicated of a good in Aristotle.

A passage in the *Eudemian Ethics* provides the clue for the correct understanding of *prakton*: 'But the good is so called in many ways [. . .] one good is *prakton*, another not. What is *prakton* is the sort of good which is that-for-the-sake-of-which (*to hou heneka*); but the good among unchanging things [*en tois akinētois*] is not that [sc. *prakton*]' (i. 8 1218b 4–7).[5]

Aristotle here connects the *prakton* character of good, its practicality as I shall call it, with the notion of a telos, or goal of action. He says that the practical kind of good is *to hou heneka*, 'that-for-the-sake-of-which', a phrase that he standardly uses to designate a telos. A good, then, is practical if it is, or can be, a genuine end of human action. A telos is primarily something that is aimed at in action. It moves a human being to action by being aimed at.[6]

If one aims at something in one's action and the action is successful in its purpose, one attains or realizes that end. Hence a good that is *prakton* is typically something that is realizable or realized in human action. Realizability of some sort is a condition for successful aiming. One cannot, for instance, aim

---

[4] So, for instance, Michael Woods, *Aristotle: Eudemian Ethics Books I, II, and VIII*, translated with a commentary (2nd ed., Oxford 1992). In the commentary, Woods calls the *prakton* requirement the 'requirement of realizability'. This, he says, is the requirement that the good be 'something that human action can bring into existence' (80). Ross renders πρακτόν as 'achievable' or 'achieved'. Irwin's translation of πρακτόν as 'pursued in action' is somewhat closer to what I argue is the primary sense of πρακτόν.

[5] Alternative construals of the same text are: '[. . .], but there is no such good [sc. a good that is *prakton*] among unchanging things', or: 'The sort of good that is *prakton* is that-for-the-sake-of-which, but the good among the unchanging things is not [sc. that-for-the-sake-of-which]'. On every reading, a good being *prakton* is connected with its being a telos.

[6] For a fuller account of the notion of telos in Aristotle, see my article 'Aristotle's Metaphysics of Action', chap. 5 below.

at having sacked Troy, or aim at one's favourite athlete winning a competition. Through derangement (laying aside the possibility of a corrupt action), a person might attempt to bring about something of the sort. However, under normal circumstances what the agent aims at in his action is the sort of thing that can be realized in the world through human action, and more specifically, through the agent's own action. Although realizability is thus connected with the practical character of the good, the requirement that the good sought by ethical theory be *prakton* is not in the first place a requirement of realizability. Realizability is a derivative feature.

Aristotle does not confine himself to complaining that the Form of the good is not practical. The problem, he thinks, is not just that we cannot desire the Form of goodness, or be moved to act by desiring it,[7] or that we cannot realize it in action. Having made the claim that the Platonic good is not *prakton*, Aristotle goes on at *EN* I. 6 1096b 35–7a 3 to consider a further suggestion, that it might none the less be better to get to know this Platonic, 'unpractical', good with a view to those goods which are *kteta* and *prakta*—which are practical and which we can possess. Perhaps, he says, it might be good to get to know this good, and 'having it as a pattern (*paradeigma*), we shall also come to know better the things that are goods for us, and knowing them we shall hit upon them' (1097a 2–3). Aristotle rejects this suggestion on empirical grounds: experience, he says, shows that the idea of the good, or rather the knowledge of it (*gnōsis*), is practically irrelevant, providing no guidance to craftsmen in their practice (1097a 4–13). Crafts do not proceed in this way; they leave out the Form of the good altogether.

Aristotle's move here may seem odd, since it is equally true that the ultimate good as he thinks of it himself does not make one better at, say, medicine or generalship. The *Eudemian Ethics* appears to be more to the point; the Forms, including the Form of the good, are described there as being of 'no help for the good life or for actions' (*oude chrēsimos pros zōēn agathēn oude pros tas praxeis*) (*EE* i. 8 1217b 23–5). This is just what one would expect Aristotle to say. However, I do not think that his objection to the Form of the good as useless for the practice of crafts in the *Nicomachean Ethics* is confused. What he probably has in mind is that, since the Form of the good is supposed to be the cause of the goodness of *everything* that is good, it should be the cause of goodness in the domain of technical production (*poiēsis*) as well as in the domain of practice proper (*praxis*); hence an adequate conception of it should in fact provide guidance in both. Aristotle does not give the same broad role to the ultimate good as he himself understands it. So his objection is not out of place.

[7] Given Plato's views on *erōs*, e.g. in the *Symposium*, it is not so clear that the Form of the good is not meant to be an object of desire. Furthermore, eudaimonia is the goal of human conduct for Plato as much as it is for Aristotle.

Yet his objection as it stands is not effective in dismissing the suggestion that Plato's good, while being 'unpractical' in the sense of not being itself a goal of action, might be practical in some sense if it—or rather, adequate knowledge of it (cf. *gnōsis* at 1097a 6)—could in some indirect way guide action. Aristotle concedes that the suggestion has some plausibility (*pithanotēs*, 1097a 3–4), and is prepared to take it seriously. None the less, he never looks into the theory in sufficient detail to provide an adequate rejection of the idea. The precise sense in which Forms are separate would have to be investigated before they can be labelled practically useless. However, it is true that Plato does have some trouble providing his reader with a picture of how knowledge of the Forms helps point the way in life. Aristotle exploits this weakness.

Aristotle does not explain what he means by his complaint that the Platonic good is not *ktēton*. I suspect this is connected with his *prakton* requirement. The agent's actions, and their results, in an important sense belong to him. Since it is neither the goal aimed at, nor the goal attained, in action, the Form of the good (unlike honour and pleasure) cannot be a part of human enterprise and achievement. Furthermore, as a good that is *chōriston*, separable or separated from sensible things, it stands inaccessibly apart from the human way of living.

The good, Aristotle believes, has to be something that is attained by specifically human powers, and linked to a human form of life. This thought is crystallized in the *ergon* argument of *EN* I. 7, which grounds the human good on some basic facts about the sort of creatures human beings are. The *prakton* requirement connects the good with *praxis*, which is a specifically human mode of life. The notion that the good 'we are after'—that is to say, the good which ethics is all about—is something *prakton* (*EN* I. 6 1096b 34–5) is part of what makes it a *human* good. Aristotle believes that his account of the ultimate good, unlike Plato's, is based on his insight into the specifically human capacities and the specifically human way of life.

Aristotle's criticism of the Platonic good as non-practical is a part of a more general disagreement with Plato over the question how one should proceed in ethics and politics:

> Since our purpose is to consider what form of political community is best of all for those who are most able to realize their ideal of life, we should examine the other constitutions, both such as actually exist in some of the states said to be well-governed, and any others propounded by certain thinkers and held to be of merit, in order that we may discern what there is in them that is right and expedient. (*Pol* II. 1, 1260b 27–33)

There follows a lengthy critique of Plato's political philosophy.[8]

The only proper and fruitful procedure, from Aristotle's point of view, is one which works its way up to a practical ideal from a reflective analysis of

---

[8] Compare the critique of mathematical derivations of what is good at *EE* i. 8 1218a 15–24.

concrete social forms of human existence, including an analysis of the existing types of political arrangement and existing evaluative practices. This reflective analysis, if it is to be fruitful, has to involve an exercise of practical reason. For Aristotle, such an exercise always presupposes an evaluative commitment (thus the existence of certain desires), even if the deliberative virtues also demand readiness to revise such commitments. Aristotle thinks that Plato's approach to ethics and politics—which starts from a clean slate in building the ideal city, and constructs a political and ethical ideal of life in an abstract and speculative fashion—is wrong-headed. In politics, one has to start with concrete forms of social life. This criticism, disregarding the question whether it is fair to Plato, tells us something about Aristotle's own approach to ethics and politics.[9]

2 Against the 'Common Good'

In the *Eudemian Ethics*, and apparently also in the *Nicomachean*, Aristotle criticizes and rejects the notion that there is such a thing as *to koinon agathon*, 'the common good' (see *EE* i. 8 1218a 38–b 4 and 1218b 7–10; cp. *EN* I. 6 1096b 32–5). The common good would be a single unique character common to all things that are good. One could call this 'goodness as such'. In both *Ethics* it transpires, importantly, that the common good is not to be thought of as a Form or any kind of transcendent entity. At *EE* i. 8 1218a 14–15, Aristotle says: '[. . .] nor is the common good identical with the Form; for it is common to all goods.' And at 1218a38–b2: 'Similarly, the common good is neither the good itself (for it would belong even to a small good), nor is it *prakton*.' Again at 1218b 7–10 Aristotle distinguishes between the Form of the good and the common good: 'It is clear that neither the Form of the good nor the common [good] is the good itself we are searching for, since the first is unchanging and not *prakton*, the second changing, yet still not *prakton*.' The so-called common good is unlike the Form of the good in that it is the inherent shared character of the changeable goods themselves, rather than something over and above them, to which the changeable things owe their goodness.

---

[9] Aristotle's criticism of Plato here resembles Hegel's criticism of Kant's ethics. Hegel's main charge is that by disregarding concrete forms of social existence (*Sittlichkeit*), Kant provides an ethics that is entirely formal and empty. This means, among other things, that Kantian ethics cannot provide the practical guidance that an adequate ethical system should give. See, in particular, Hegel's *Grundlinien der Philosophie des Rechts*, in *Werke*, Suhrkamp 1970, vol. 7, §§ 127–142 (section 'Das Gute und das Wissen'), and *Phänomenologie des Geistes, Werke*, vol. 3, p. 343ff. and p. 533. A modern relative of this type of view is David Wiggins, 'Neo-Aristotelian Reflections on Justice', *Mind* 113 (2004), 477–512.

The *Nicomachean Ethics* speaks not of the 'common good', but of 'some single good that is predicated in common'. At I. 6 1096b 32–5 we read: 'For if there is some single good which is predicated in common (*koinē(i) katēgoroumenon agathon*), or which is separated (*chōriston*), itself by itself, clearly it would not be *prakton* or *ktēton* by a human being; but that is just the sort of thing we are here searching for.'[10] It seems likely that 'the single good predicated in common' here refers to the same thing the *Eudemian Ethics* designates as the 'common good'. The point made is essentially the same: The good that is predicated in common is not separated; none the less, just like the separate Form of the good, it is not *prakton* for a human being.

Having made the claim that the common good is the *prakton*, at EE i. 8 1218a 38–b 2, Aristotle goes on to explain why: '[Similarly, the common good is not *prakton*], since (*gar*) medicine does not make it its business to see that something that may belong to *anything* shall exist (*hopōs hyparxei to hotōioun hyparchon*), but that health shall. The same holds of every other craft as well' (1218b 2–4). Every craft, as Aristotle had put it at 1218a 35–6 (just above the lines quoted), deals with *idion ti agathon*, some specific good.

Michael Woods runs into difficulties here.[11] Taking *prakton* to mean 'realizable', he observes:

---

[10] I translate according to the text of K^b, reading καί rather than τό at line 32: εἰ γὰρ ἔστιν ἕν τι καὶ κοινῇ κατηγορούμενον ἀγαθὸν ἢ χωριστόν αὐτό τι καθ' αὑτό, δῆλον ὡς οὐκ ἂν εἴη πρακτὸν οὐδὲ κτητὸν ἀνθρώπῳ· νῦν δὲ τοιοῦτόν τι ζητεῖται. Aristotle uses here his own technical term 'predicated' (κατηγορούμενον), and, on his view, things that are predicated cannot be separated in the way he takes Plato's Forms to be. One of Aristotle's arguments against the Form of goodness is precisely that this Form, being separated (χωριστόν), could not be predicated in common. An extended argument at EE i. 8 1218a1–15 to this effect ends by saying: 'nor is the common good identical with the Form; for it is common to all goods.' The clear implication is that the Form is not common to all goods. An alternative text of 1096b32 has καί earlier and τό later: εἰ γὰρ καὶ ἔστιν ἕν τι τὸ κοινῇ κατηγορούμενον ἀγαθὸν ἢ χωριστὸν αὐτό τι καθ' αὑτό, etc. as above—'For even if the good predicated in common is some single thing, or something separated, itself by itself, clearly it could not be *prakton* or *ktēton* [. . .].' This text, printed by Bywater, has good manuscript authority (L^b), and is adopted by most commentators (e.g. Burnet, Gauthier and Jolif, Ramsauer; also Irwin, Ross). However, the text I prefer here comes from the best manuscript, K^b, and makes best sense philosophically. As printed in the Bywater text, the sentence makes the following point: whether you take this good-predicated-in-common to be χωριστόν or not—i.e., whether you take it to be just some single thing, or else a single thing that is also separated—the problem you run into is the same: you get something that is not *prakton*. There are yet other ways of understanding the Bywater text, but under every reading, the *EN* passage refers to two distinct views, one Platonic, and one non-Platonic, the non-Platonic one being that the good is something common, but not separated. The non-separated common good is what I am discussing in this section.

[11] *Eudemian Ethics*, 78–82 ad 1218a 38–b 6.

At [1218] b 2–4, [Aristotle] says that no practitioner of a science or skill (*technē*) aims to secure the possession of "what belongs to anything", but always some specific good (e.g. health). This may be taken as adding further support to the claim that the common character is not realizable; if so, it seems fallacious, since the fact that it is impossible to seek to produce some good except by aiming at producing some specific form of good does not show that that good cannot be produced.

Woods points out that independently of the argument from crafts it is 'doubtful if it is *true* that the common good is not realizable. For if it is construed as the character shared by human goods, and is held to depend for its existence on their being possessors of that character, its existence *will* be dependent on human action' (emphasis his).

This criticism seems to me to misunderstand the primary meaning of *prakton*. Aristotle, as we saw in the previous section, explains what he means by this term at 1218b 4–7, a passage whose relevance Woods finds unclear.[12] That is where the *prakton* is said to be the sort of good which is *to hou heneka*, that-for-the-sake-of-which, namely, telos.

Woods is also puzzled about why Aristotle should discuss the common good at all, except as a 'consequence of the Platonic ideal theory'. The *EN* appears to him to be 'clearer and more coherent' on the topic of the common good, since there Aristotle 'recognizes the equivalence of saying that goodness is a single thing [. . .] and that it is common [. . .] and that it is universal [. . .].'

The common good may or may not be part of Plato's theory of the good. There is some indication that in addition to the Form of the large, Plato envisaged the large in us, which is presumably a common character belonging to the changeable things themselves (*Phaedo* 102d–e; cp. *Timaeus* 37a). It is possible that Plato also envisaged the existence of a character common to changeable *good* things. However, when speaking of the 'common good' Aristotle might have had other views in mind. He might well have thought that the Socratic quest for definitions of virtue was meant to capture the common immanent character of virtuous actions. Aristotle insists that Socrates did not separate forms (*Metaph* XIII. 4, 1078b 30–1); if he thinks that Socrates was after a common form in his definitions, he would assume this would not be the Platonic separate Form. Alternatively, Aristotle might have had in mind a theory of the good of some later Academic, who disagreed with Plato about the separateness of Forms. He does not identify for us the view he is criticizing. What is clear from his discussion is that the common good is for him a separate dialectical target. An ethical theory which thinks its business is to capture the character that all goods supposedly have in common is for Aristotle a paradigmatic instance of ontologically misguided theory of value. Such a theory also does not deal with the kind of good that is capable of exerting a

---

[12] *Ibid.*, 81.

motivational pull on us. The remark in the *Eudemian Ethics* about the goal of medicine, mentioned above, helps throw light on both points.

The common good, Aristotle maintains there, is not *prakton*, since medicine does not make it its business to see that something which may belong to *anything* shall exist, but that health shall. The same holds of other crafts. Every craft deals with *idion ti agathon*, some specific good (1218a 35–b 2).

A craft aims at something because its practitioners aim at that thing. The analogy with the medical art is meant to bring out a larger point. Every human goal-oriented action is directed at *idion ti agathon*, a good of some specific sort. Now in Aristotle's view whenever one aims at any particular intrinsic good, one aims at it *as* a good of a specific sort. Goodness as such, by itself, is not something one can aim at. A 'practical' good precisely is a telos, namely, something aimed at in action. This is the reason why, or perhaps one of the reasons why, the common good is not something *prakton*.

Aristotle says of the Platonic Form of the good that it is supposed to be something of which the good is truly predicated, other things being good through sharing in it, so that 'if the object in which things share were taken away, with it would go all the things that share in the Form and are called [what they are called] through sharing in the Form' (*EE* i. 8 1217b 9–13). This seems to explicate the sense in which the Platonic good is meant to be a cause, *aition*, for other goods of their being good. Aristotle wants to deny that any such grand 'cause' of goodness exists; there is no thing, which, if taken away, would rob all other things of their goodness.

He would undoubtedly make a similar claim about the common good. The character which all goods had in common, and which made them good, would, if taken away, rob the goods of their goodness. Yet no such universally shared character exists. The goodness of a given intrinsic good is *idion* in a strong sense; it is bound up with the ontological category to which the good in question belongs. The categories do not cross over, or reduce to, one another. This is why the common good theory is ontologically misguided. *Good*, like *being*, is spoken of in many ways. (See *EE* i. 8 1218b 4; *EN* I. 6 1096a 23–19; cp. *Metaph* IV. 2 1003a 33–b 10, VII. 1 1028a 10–13.)

What Aristotle thinks especially matters for ethics is that an abstract feature all goods had in common, even if it existed, would not be of the sort to motivate people to act. People go for things they find attractive in far more concrete ways. A sensual pleasure will engage our attention and move us to act in a way that is specific to the sort of sensual pleasure it is—a way that is entirely different in kind from the way in which, say, the prospect of some honour to be received will engage our attention and move us to action. That particular intrinsic goods, or kinds of intrinsic good, have their own specific motivational *modus operandi*, their own distinctive ways of affecting us and moving us to act, is as much a fact about us as it is a fact about the things we pursue for their own sake. This is not surprising. After all, what moves human beings to act are *aisthēta* and *noēta*, things perceived or conceived of in a certain way by the human beings they move. Goods of a practical sort fall into different kinds to some extent depending on how they tend to influence us. A proper ontological treatment of practical goods has to regard them as practical, namely, as specific objects of human aiming.

It will be observed that Aristotle is assuming here that there are some significant similarities in the ways we, humans, are moved to act. Without denying important motivational differences between one human being and another, he thinks that these ways are similar enough for the general claims he makes about human motivation to make sense. It would be the task of a more detailed psychological theory than we find in the *De Anima* to chart these significant similarities.

3 Aristotle against Eudoxus

Apart from Aristotle's criticism of the Platonic Form of the good and the common good, there are further passages that bear on his rejection of a monolithic ethical theory. One is his discussion of Eudoxus in *EN* X .2. Eudoxus, according to Aristotle, offers the following argument to support his view that pleasure is the good: 'when pleasure is added to any other good, for instance, to just or temperate action, it makes that good more choiceworthy; but the good is increased by [the addition of] itself' (X. 2 1172b 23–5). Aristotle replies that the argument shows pleasure to be just one among other goods, no more a good than any other, since 'every good when together with another good is more choiceworthy than all by itself' (1172b 26–8).

At first, it looks as if Aristotle must have missed the point of Eudoxus' argument. He speaks as if the argument Eudoxus had in mind could be used to show that any good one cared to name was the good. Add just action to pleasure: the addition makes pleasure more choiceworthy; hence—one would have to conclude—just action is the ultimate good.

However, Eudoxus' position presumably was that anything good is good only to the extent that it contains pleasure, or leads to it. When pleasure is added to just action, assumed itself to be a good, what it is added to is some pleasure already assumed to be there (or in the offing), as that which made just or temperate action good in the first place. A greater good emerges because extra pleasure has been added to the pleasure that just or temperate action already contains or leads to. That this is what Eudoxus must have had in mind is clear from his final remark: 'The good,' he says, 'is increased by the addition of itself' (1172b 25). One pleasure has been added to another.[13]

[13] If Eudoxus took pleasure to be a homogeneous quality, he probably thought that all pleasures are commensurable. However, he is not committed to such a view by the line of thought expressed in this argument. The additivity of goods does not require that they be commensurable.

Eudoxus probably did not intend this argument as a knock-down proof that hedonism is the true theory of the good. That just or temperate action, when conjoined with pleasure, yields a greater good is something he probably assumed was generally agreed; he saw himself as giving a particularly elegant explanation of this fact. In Aristotle's discussion of Eudoxus at *EN* X. 2, the argument appears as just one among several considerations Eudoxus adduced to show that hedonism is a plausible theory of the good.

Aristotle counters Eudoxus' argument with another. This is Plato's argument that pleasure cannot be the good, since the pleasant life is more choiceworthy when combined with wisdom (*phronēsis*) than without it, but nothing can be added to *the* good to make it more choiceworthy (1172b 28–32; cp. *Philebus* 60e–1a). Plato's argument turns on its head the Eudoxan argument, which attempts to use the additivity of goods in support of the thesis that pleasure is the good.

But Eudoxus need not be at a loss for a reply. He might grant that a pleasant life is better when combined with wisdom. If he did so, he would be taking 'a pleasant life' to mean a life that is pleasant to some degree. If the addition of wisdom makes an already pleasant life better, this is because it provides additional pleasure to the life initially described as pleasant. If, on the other hand, 'a pleasant life' is understood as a life that is as pleasant as a life can be, then Eudoxus simply would not grant that anything can be added to make it better.

Aristotle's reaction to Plato's argument is instructive. It is not clear whether he is happy with it; the argument as it stands is too imprecise and formulaic to be easily assessable, and Aristotle does not bother to expand it. What he unambiguously, and strongly, endorses is the more general moral of the argument, which he sums up in the following way: nothing that can be made more choiceworthy by an addition of *any* of the *kath' hauto* goods can be *the good* (1172b 32–4). In fact, he appears to turn this thesis into a programme governing his ethics. It is precisely, he goes on to say, a good of this sort—a good, namely, that cannot be made more choiceworthy by the addition of an intrinsic good—that is being sought after (*epizeteitai*, sc. in the ethical inquiry), provided that it is a good we human beings can share in (*hou kai hēmeis koinōnoumen*) (1172b 34–5).

This last clause clearly harks back to Aristotle's discussion of Plato's theory of the good in I. 6. There Aristotle argued that the Form of the good, being non-practical and separate, is not something we can share in. Yet Aristotle is in agreement with Plato about one thing: the good which ethics is all about is different in kind from any special good. The endorsement of this thought does not occur for the first time in X. 2. It is already expressed in I. 7,[14] Aristotle's programmatic discussion of the good. The good, he says there, is something

---

[14] Compare X. 2, 1172b 28–36 with I. 7, 1097b 16–20.

that is the most choiceworthy of all goods while not being *synarithmoumenon*, 'counted along'. For if it were counted along, he explains, it would be made more choiceworthy by the addition of the smallest of goods; for among goods the greater is always more choiceworthy (1097b 14–20).

Eudoxus grants that just and temperate actions have value. His additivity argument implies, when interpreted in the way I have proposed, that their value resides entirely in the pleasure they contain or lead to. But to assume this is to deny that acting justly or moderately has a value entirely its own, and that acting so can be worthwhile independently of the pleasure that attends a just or moderate action.

Aristotle firmly contradicts this: 'There are many things we would take trouble about even if they brought no pleasure, for instance, seeing, remembering, knowing, possessing the virtues. If pleasures necessarily accompany these, that makes no difference; we would choose them even if no pleasure resulted' (*EN* X. 3 1174a 4–8; cf. *Metaph* I. 1 980a 21–6).

Aristotle implies that we would be right to do so. Seeing, remembering, knowing and possessing the virtues are states and activities that in his view make for the good life. In the light of this, he might endorse an even stronger claim: the substance of a good life might to a large extent be preserved even if no pleasure was ever sought, or ever accrued, from such activities. Undoubtedly, life without the 'bloom' of pleasure is not one Aristotle advocates, or would welcome. It is, I believe, his own view that he refers to when he mentions the possibility that pleasures accompany some activities *ex anankēs*, necessarily.[15] What the remark quoted is meant to underscore is his view that goods other than pleasure have a considerable degree of independence from pleasure. They are not primarily engaged in as ways of attaining pleasure, and they are choiceworthy independently of the pleasure that is normally, and perhaps necessarily, entangled with them.

To think that when pleasure is added to just action, the value of the whole is just the sum of pleasures, is to deny the independent choiceworthiness of ends other than pleasure. They are abolished as separate worthwhile ends. Aristotle's diagnosis therefore is that the Eudoxan good is ultimately a good masquerading as the good. He could have put a part of his point against Eudoxus in the same terms he used when discussing Plato: different types of *kath' hauto* goods have different and dissimilar accounts precisely insofar as they are goods, so that they cannot all be reduced to one *kath' hauto* good, pleasure. The Eudoxan good does not give a true picture either of what ordinarily motivates us to act, or of where the value in our lives resides.

---

[15] A just action, done as a just man would do it, is in his view necessarily pleasurable (*EN* II. 3). More generally, complete or perfect activities, which are exercises of the subject in the best condition directed at the best sort of object relative to the capacity exercised (*EN* X. 4 1174b 18–19), are necessarily pleasurable.

Aristotle took hedonism far more seriously than some of his criticism of Eudoxus might suggest. Much of the discussion in *EN X*. 2 and 3 defends the Eudoxan position against Platonic and other criticism. Aristotle's own conception of the good owes a good deal to Eudoxus. His sympathy for Eudoxus comes in part from sympathy with pleasure. Pleasure is intimately involved in the activities that make up the good life, as the discussion in the subsequent chapters, X. 4 and 5, shows. Pleasures are so closely intertwined with activities, 'yoked together', that it is difficult to say whether they are something apart from the activities. At X. 4, 1175a 18–21, the question whether we choose life because of pleasure, or pleasure because of life, is put aside: 'Let us set this aside for now. For the two [life or activity, and pleasure] appear to be yoked together (*synezeuchthai*), and to allow no separation (*chōrismos*), since pleasure never arises without activity, and it also completes every activity.' As something most congenial to our nature (*EN X*. 1 1172a 20), and inextricably linked with all the activities in which living well resides, pleasure is a necessary and indispensable element in happiness.

Aristotle adamantly rejects the view that pleasure is homogeneous at *EN X*. 5; this discussion could be a continuation of his criticism of Eudoxus.[16] Yet Eudoxus would come under Aristotle's criticism even if he held that pleasures are immensely different in kind and value, even to the point of being incommensurable. While making room for some diversity in the structure of goodness, such a view would still regard pleasure as a universal motivational spring of action, and deny independent value to other goods.

At 1175b 32–3, Aristotle observes that pleasures—as opposed to desires—are close to activities and so little distinguished from them (*adioristoi*) that disputes arise whether the activity is the same as the pleasure. One can easily imagine that a hedonist might have claimed something of the sort. A hedonist could acknowledge the full range of differences among activities Aristotle speaks of in *EN X*. 5, and yet maintain that in each case it is pleasure that makes a good activity good. Pleasure, in all its variety, remains the sought-after goal of life.

A view of this sort would go some way toward appreciating the variety of goodness, yet still not close enough for Aristotle. He would repudiate any view that does not acknowledge the autonomous standing of goods other than pleasure. Not to acknowledge the specificity of goodness is to promote an impoverished vision of human motivation, and to fail to do justice to the plurality of value in human life.

---

[16] Aristotle does not explicitly attribute to Eudoxus a conception of pleasure as a single homogeneous thing. His discussion does not point to Eudoxus' acknowledgment of a variety of pleasures either.

4 Happiness as the Cause of Goods: Appearance and Practical Reason

Aristotle's emphasis on the diversity of values is unusual for antiquity. The only ethical theory that did full justice to this diversity might be called an anti-theory of the good. This is the position of Protagoras, or the Protagoreans. Protagoras was famous for saying that the human being is the measure of all things. In the ethical context, his view seems to have been that that which *appears* good to each person *is* good for that person.

Aristotle does not go for the view that that which appears good *to each person* is good for that person. When in *EN* III. 4 he discusses the aporia whether the object of rational wish, *to boulēton*, is the good or the apparent good, he rejects the view that what is wished for is the apparent good on the ground that 'different things, indeed opposite things, if it so happens, appear good to different people' (1113a 21–2). Soon afterwards, at III. 5, 1114a 31–b 3, he rejects the view that we have no responsibility for what appears good to us. Aristotle evidently wants to preserve objective truth in ethics; things may appear good to a person, and yet not be good for him. At least one of the pair of contradictory views on what is good for him must be mistaken. Just as sweet things might appear bitter to a sick person, an individual's appearance of goodness—the way things strike him as good or bad—may be distorted.

In Aristotle's view, Protagoras preserves appearances well enough, but at the cost of rejecting anything but appearance. He rejects any such thing as the objective ethical good. This gives us some clue as to why, on Aristotle's view at any rate, other ethical theorists of the period might have gone for the single-factor type of explanation. What they were after, in proposing their various theories of the good, was to secure the objectivity of ethical value. However, restricting the range of considerations on the basis of which the goodness or rightness of conduct is to be judged is not in Aristotle's view necessary for securing ethical objectivity.

Yet although Aristotle is not tempted by the view that the individual human being is the measure of value, he seems to have been inspired by Protagoras in some of his ethical concerns. His preoccupation with the role of *appearance* in ethics seems to me to be such a concern, one that is in evidence all over his ethical theory. I am interested here in the role it plays in his understanding of the human good.

At *EN* I. 7 1097b 2–5, Aristotle says:

[. . .] we choose honour, pleasure, understanding (*nous*), and every virtue on their own account (*di' auta*)—for we would choose each of them even if nothing resulted from them—and also for the sake of happiness (*tēs eudaimonias charin*), assuming (*hypolambanontes*) that through them (*dia toutōn*) we shall be happy (*eudaimonēsein*).

Happiness is a distinct goal of human life. We aim at it in action; in a sense, it is our most important goal. Yet happiness or the good life is not separable from the specific goals we pursue in concrete situations. We aim at happiness *through* the pursuit of honour or pleasure or virtue, as these present themselves to us in particular circumstances. Yet Aristotle maintains that we would choose the goods mentioned even if happiness did not result from them. They are choiceworthy on their own, and they move us to act on their own, each in their own way.

The claim that honour, pleasure, understanding and virtue are each irreducible intrinsic goods is, in a way, a vindication of the very theories we have witnessed Aristotle criticizing. Most ethical theorists of the time dismissed goods other than their favourite candidate for the good. A number of philosophers were especially dismissive of honour and pleasure, treating them as something it is just wrong to consider good at all.

Aristotle wishes to preserve appearances. This is evident in his desire to give its due to what ordinarily strikes us as good and motivates us to act. But his desire to preserve appearances is also a desire to preserve whatever truth there may be in competing theories of the good. The Sophists with their defence of honour saw something Socrates did not see. Eudoxus clearly understood how congenial pleasure is to our mode of life. Plato and others grasped the very special place understanding has in a human life. All of them, however, suffered from a peculiar one-sidedness which worked to obliterate the insights of their rivals.

The notion that an adequate ethical theory has to preserve the truth contained in theories of the good says something about the kind of objectivity that pertains to ethical inquiry. All practical goods are dependent on a human perspective. Their being good for us depends in part on our finding them, or thinking them, good. Happiness is equally dependent on a perspective. Where human happiness lies is in part constituted by what human beings consider a happy life to be.

In X. 2, Aristotle reports Eudoxus as saying that each [animal] kind finds its own good just as it finds its food. This appears as part of Eudoxus' argument that what all beings actually strive after is the good. For him, of course, this is pleasure. He takes hedonism as both a psychological and a normative theory. The notion that animal kinds, hence human beings, tend to find their own good left an impression on Aristotle. This is clear from his strong criticism further down in the same chapter of those who claim that that at which all aim is not good (1172b 35–6). These people, he declares, are talking nonsense. 'For we say that what everyone takes to be the case is so; and the man who attacks this belief will hardly have anything more plausible to maintain instead.'

To say that what everyone *takes* to be the case *is* so has a whiff of Protagore-anism about it. Yet his point is not Protagorean. Consensus about goodness does not by itself guarantee truth. Nor does Aristotle fully endorse Eudoxus' point. He will not admit that all, or most, people find their own good in the sense of living a fully choiceworthy human life. However, if most people con-sistently place a great value on certain pursuits, a philosophical theory of the good has to acknowledge this. Most people not only consider pleasure to be good, but find it so in their lives. This implicit belief in the goodness of plea-sure must be respected, not overturned. The reason for this is that our finding and considering things good is in part what makes them good. Theorists who are attentive to what people pursue and value in their lives, like Eudoxus, can nonetheless propound a one-sided theory of the good. They tend to obliterate those facts about human motivation and value which do not neatly fit their theory.

Aristotle goes so far as to call happiness *to aition tōn agathōn*, the cause of goods (*EN* I. 12 1102a 2–4). This may be puzzling. We have seen that he re-jects the notion that ethics should busy itself with anything that may be the cause of goodness in the sense in which he takes the Platonic Form to be the cause of goodness. In his view, the locus of value in human life lies in sub-stantive, irreducibly specific, goods. It would not be wrong to sum up this view by saying that specific goods are the cause of goodness: if *their* goodness were to be taken away, the goodness of a human life would go as well. Yet Aristotle retains the Platonic idiom with a purpose. The notion that the good, happi-ness, is in a certain sense fundamental, and prior to, other goods strikes him as correct. It is worth pursuing the question how he—or we—might understand this idea.

Practical reason gives unity to our various pursuits by introducing the standpoint of a life as a whole. Specific goods do not lose their independence when seen from this standpoint. Their full value is, however, determined by the place they occupy in this larger context, and how they interact with other goods. The unity that practical reason brings to deliberation about goals of ac-tion is not that of an aggregate. The value of a specific pursuit contemplated by a person is not computable. At each point it is subject to the agent's inter-pretation, and re-interpretation, of its meaning given his understanding of how it links with the other goals aimed at, his plans for the future, his assess-ment of past accomplishments. Honour has a value that is all its own. Yet whether seeking honour here and now has any value whatsoever depends on the agent's assessment both of the circumstances and of what matters in his life. The value of any particular goal is dependent on the place it assumes in this larger context.

The unity in question is akin to organic unity insofar as the whole is not a simple sum of its parts. The goals are dependent on each other, and dependent on the context of the life as a whole. Yet there is nothing organic about the unity of a good human life. The human good is not a naturally functioning entity, but—in a certain sense—a product of practical reason, a life lived under its guidance.

The fact that particular goods in the agent's life are assessed with reference to his life as a whole, and that their valuation is thus dependent on the larger framework, is what makes Aristotle speak of the good, happiness, as 'the cause of goods'. A conception of happiness is a general framework within which the good of any given goal is evaluated, and fixed. An agent's goals, he thinks, are context-dependent; they have full value only within a perspective that puts them in relationship with other goals. In this sense the good, happiness, invests them with value. Yet happiness is no part of the account of what makes honour, pleasure, or understanding good. Each is good in its own right, even if it is not the good I should pursue here and now.

Aristotle takes over from Plato (and possibly Eudoxus) another way of designating the good, while giving it a new interpretation. In *EN* I. 12, he points out that the good, which he had identified with happiness in I. 4, is something the attainment of which receives congratulation rather than praise. Things are praised, he claims, always in relation to something (*pros ti*—1101b 13); praise always implies such a reference (*anaphora*—1101b 20–1). Happiness, however, is not referred to anything else, and hence is not an appropriate object of praise. Aristotle says: 'By not praising pleasure although it is a good we indicate, he [Eudoxus] thought, that pleasure is better than the things which are praised; and god and the good are of this [better] sort, since the other things are referred to them (*pros tauta* [. . .] *kai talla anapheresthai*)' (1101b 28–31). (Cp. also the usage of *anapheresthai* in the *Eudemian Ethics*, at ii. 1 1219b 11–13 again in the context of a discussion of why happiness is not praised.) Although Aristotle disagrees with Eudoxus' identification of the good with pleasure, he takes Eudoxus to have shown by his remark that he has the correct notion of the good as something different from all other goods, something to which other goods are 'referred'. The good is thus a reference point of some sort.

Plato speaks of referring particular things to the relevant Form.[17] Again, while sticking to the language he inherits from others, Aristotle interprets it differently. The reference point for him is the general framework within which particular goals acquire their meaning. It is not a single thing that explains the goodness of the variety of things that are good. The *sui generis* status of happiness is, he thinks, evidenced in the different sort of evaluative attitude we take towards it.

When Aristotle says that we pursue honour, pleasure, understanding, and virtue assuming (*hypolambanontes*) that through them we shall be happy, he does not seem to have in mind an explicitly worked out scheme of values.

---

[17] *Phaedo* 76d, *Republic* 484c.

The verb *hypolambanein* is often used for an implicit conception of some sort. When we aim at happiness in our action we bring to bear an often implicit understanding of happiness to the particular circumstances of the action. Aristotle never speaks of this conception as an explicitly formulated blueprint for the whole of life. Rather, one's conception of the good life is a product of repeated deliberations in particular circumstances. When Aristotle demands that the good be practical, this in part means that the agent's conception of the good should be capable of effectively guiding his deliberations and actions.

In *EN* I. 7 Aristotle provides the first outline of his own theory of the good, and introduces certain general conditions on the concept of the good. Although he at no point mentions practical reason, which comes up for discussion in Book VI, the concept of the good outlined here depends on his understanding of the workings of practical reason, and especially of deliberative virtue.

Among the requirements on the concept of the good introduced in *EN* I. 7 are finality and self-sufficiency. As described by Aristotle, the concept of *finality* is formal, and comparative. A good pursued for its own sake is 'more final' than a good pursued for the sake of something else, and a good which is never pursued for the sake of anything else is 'more final' than a good pursued both for its own sake and for the sake of something else (*EN* I. 7 1097a 30–2). The ultimate good is 'most final'. Greatest finality includes in fact three elements. A good is 'most final' if it is pursued for its own sake, not for the sake of anything else, and everything else is pursued for the sake of it. Although the last condition is not formulated explicitly at 1097a 30–b 6 (it is implied at 1097b 4–5), it is central to Aristotle's understanding of the ultimate good.[18] A good could be pursued for its own sake and not for the sake of anything else, and yet not be most final. Some trivial amusements are often pursued in this way while not being most choiceworthy, or even choiceworthy at all.[19] What makes a good most final or end-like is above all the fact that it organizes the whole structure of aiming.

Aristotle defines the second condition, that of *self-sufficiency*, in the following way: 'That is self-sufficient which, all by itself, makes life choiceworthy and lacking in nothing' (*EN* I. 7 1097b 14–15). The claim that the ultimate good

---

[18] At *Rhet* I. 6 1362b 11–12, this condition is explicitly included among the conditions on the concept of the good; it is also mentioned at *EN* I. 7 1097a 22–4; *EN* I. 12 1102a 2–3, and *EE* i. 1 1219a 10–11.

[19] See *EN* X. 6 1176b 9–7a 11. The fact that Aristotle speaks of choosing for its own sake sometimes in the psychological and sometimes in the normative sense might make the discussion here confusing from our point of view. His main point, however, is clear. Some people, most strikingly tyrants, pursue trivial amusements as ends-in-themselves. Yet most people pursue relaxation for the sake of activity; and indeed relaxation should be pursued for the sake of activity.

makes life 'lacking in nothing' is in part a claim about desire. The good, as Aristotle puts it in the *Eudemian Ethics*, fills one's desire to the full (*EE* i. 5 1215b 17–18). Although self-sufficiency involves having one's desire fully satisfied, it is not as Aristotle presents it a purely subjective condition. A life that is self-sufficient leaves nothing to be desired. It is satisfactory as well as satisfying, and it is so all by itself, without any need for further additions.

Although choiceworthiness is implied in self-sufficiency, it will suit my purposes better to have choiceworthiness on hand as a separate condition. I shall assume, then, that Aristotle sets up the following three conditions on the ultimate good: finality in the purely formal sense, self-sufficiency, and choiceworthiness.[20] A list very close to this is found in the *Rhetoric* (I 6, 1362b 11–12). Eudaimonia, Aristotle says there, is something 'choiceworthy in itself (*kath' hauta haireton*), and self-sufficient (*autarkēs*), and such that we choose many things for the sake of it'.

These conditions, I believe, are best regarded as saying something about the way in which happiness emerges as a result of the proper exercise of practical reason. In order to attain the good, or live the good life, we should strive to adjust the way we go about pursuing goals in life—the 'how', or the mode of pursuit—to the value these goals, to our best judgment, have in our lives. Those ends which we consider to be more choiceworthy than others we should pursue as more final than others.

Akrasia is not the only obstacle that might stand in the way of conducting one's life in accordance with this precept. One can also fail to give the right level of priority to the projects in life which one judges to be important through, for instance, lack of foresight. Yet another obstacle is frivolity. One is frivolous—on a first understanding of frivolity—if one has a tendency to go for what one recognizes as trivial ends, and pursues them in a way that would only be appropriate for the ends which one does consider important. On a second

---

[20] Although he is indebted to his predecessors for these conditions, the way in which he employs them seems to me to be new. Eudoxus' influence is evident from the following paraphrase or quotation: '[. . .] most choiceworthy (μάλιστα [. . .] αἱρετόν) is what we choose not on account of, or for the sake of, anything else; and it is agreed that pleasure is of this sort, for we ask no one what it is for the sake of which he is pleased, on the assumption that (ὡς) pleasure is choiceworthy in itself (καθ' αὑτήν)' (*EN* X. 2 1172b 20–3). For the condition of finality, compare the statement made by Socrates in Plato's *Republic*: 'That then which every soul pursues and for the sake of which it does everything it does (τούτου ἕνεκα πάντα πράττει), the soul divines is something, but is puzzled and cannot adequately grasp what it is [. . .]' (*R* VI. 505d 11ff). The requirement that the good be 'sufficient' (αὐτάρκης) for happiness in the sense of lacking in nothing appears in Plato's *Philebus* under the title ἱκανόν (20d 1–1a2; 60c 2–1a 26). Although Aristotle never mentions the *Philebus* by name, there is every reason to think he was familiar with it. Compare especially *EN* X. 2 1172b 28–32, which discusses an argument advanced by Plato against hedonism, with *Philebus* 20e 4ff. For the good as 'lacking in nothing', compare μηδενὸς ἐνδεᾶ at *EN* I .7 1097b 15 with μηδενὸς ἔτι προσδεῖσθαι at *Philebus* 20e 6.

conception of frivolity, one is frivolous if one considers important, and pursues as important, ends which as a matter of fact are trivial. Each of these examples involves a failure in practical reason which undermines the appropriate fitting of finality and choiceworthiness.

The goal of adjusting the way in which one desires things, and aims at goals, to their rationally assessed value is something that requires a high degree of deliberative virtue. This virtue governs the ability to adjust one's desires and aimings to one's reasoned understanding of the relationship between the goals one is pursuing and what matters in life. It is this reasoned understanding that serves as a reference point in well-conducted deliberations.

Deliberation is a reasoned process whereby the agent's desiderative attitudes are shaped. If successful, it leads to a choice regarding what to do in the specific circumstances of one's life. Ethical deliberation is guided by a conception the agent has of the good life. As such, it directly guides life, and bears on the satisfaction attained in life. Whereas choice is a direct result of a successful deliberation, one's conception of the good life is changed in the process.

If one's life is to be not only satisfying but also satisfactory, one's reasoned understanding of the goals one pursues in life and their relation to happiness has to be a correct understanding. Aristotle allows room for error in one's conception of the good, and one's assessment of one's own life. Like Plato, he goes for ethical truth, not Protagorean appearance. Yet this truth for him does not lie on the other side of what appears to people to be good. A path to a correct self-understanding and a correct conception of the good life is a painstaking struggle with appearances of goodness.

The primary exercise of practical reason, through which a conception of the good life is formed and corrected, is not reflection but deliberation. Yet Aristotle believes that ethics—the kind of ethics he is writing—is importantly relevant to practice (see EN I. 3 1095a 2–6). Engaging in ethical reflection and theorizing is meant to help us live a good life. I suggest that part of the reason why this is so is that different ethical theories (which Aristotle discusses in his own ethical works) provide a variety of perspectives on the good, from which we can learn. To do so, we have to approach them dialectically, seeking out the truth in the appearances. We can, however, learn the right lesson only if, along with their insights, we recognize their one-sidedness.

Aristotle's emphasis on appearance is not strictly individualistic. There is nothing in his way of thinking that precludes the possibility that the good for different individual human beings can amount to strikingly different things. But the point of his emphasis on the variety of appearance is neither individualistic nor anti-individualistic. When looking at the situation of an individual with regard to the rest of the society, Aristotle is not motivated by alarm at the possibility that the individual might be constrained against his will to pursue things the society wrongly believes are good for him. He is alarmed primarily by the limited character of many people's ethical perspectives. This may be due to their own limitations, or to the one-sided influence of the society. Aristotle views exposure to different ways of thinking about the good as an opportunity to make one's life more choiceworthy than it otherwise might have been. If one's aim is to live as rich a life as one can, to close oneself off to another's way of seeing matters, and declare sacrosanct the way things appear to oneself, is a serious mistake.

Ethical deliberation has a distinctive point of view. The distinctive perspective of ethical deliberation becomes apparent when one focuses on the question of what it is to conduct such an inquiry well. Deliberation begins and ends with desires;[21] thus, to be a good deliberator, one has to have insights into one's own desires and the ability to direct them. A good deliberator has to be able to recognize which sorts of things would give substance to his life and bring him satisfaction, or—as Aristotle puts it—fill his desire to the full (*EE* i. 5 1215b 17–18). He has to be able to judge the particular circumstances of action with a view to his life as a whole, and able to arrange his life in such a way as to obtain satisfaction. Yet he also has to be able to form a correct conception of which courses of action will amount to a good life. His deliberations in particular circumstances ought to build up to an adequate understanding of his life as a good human life.

The agent's conception of the good life is embedded in the considerations that guide his choices. The subject matter of a well-conducted ethical deliberation, the goodness of one's life as a whole, seen as the framework for a choice as to what to do in particular situations, is what Aristotle designates the ultimate good. It is his choice for the role of 'cause of goods'.

---

[21]Aristotle treats choice, *prohairesis*, which is the end result of a successful deliberation, as a special kind of desiderative attitude.

Five ~

Aristotle's Metaphysics of Action

> [. . .] a human being is the origin and begetter of actions, as he is of children.
> —Aristotle, *Nicomachean Ethics* III. 5 1113b 17–19

*H*uman action has a point. It is the agent who supplies the point, by intervening in the world to realize a purpose of his own. Aristotle calls the agent's purpose "that for the sake of which," or more simply, *telos*. By relying on the concept of telos in his analysis of action, Aristotle, it is agreed, found a good tool with which to approach agency. In this paper I try to bring out what is distinctive in his approach. At several points I defend it against objections. I do this especially when it goes against assumptions common in current philosophy of action. I do not wish to subscribe to Aristotle's theory as it stands, or to offer a full defence of it. I am, however, interested in whatever insight into action it might give us today. Thus my concern is as much with the nature of human action as it is with Aristotle.

The agent who has a goal faces the world equipped with a conception of what he can get from making an effort in this or that direction. He has a view of the initial situation as something his action can modify, and some notion of the modification he is interested in bringing about. Not every action aimed at a goal is premeditated, but every such action is in a certain sense "preconceived," since it involves a conception[1] of some sort, namely, some way in which the circumstances of the action and his own goal *appear* to the agent. This appearance, which Aristotle calls *phantasia*, is firmly embedded in the telos structure of action.

For their help with earlier versions of this paper I am grateful to Myles Burnyeat, John M. Cooper, Michael Frede, David Furley, John McDowell, and Julius Moravcsik. My thanks also go to Charles Brittain, Nicholas Denyer, Eyjolfur Emilsson, Øyvind Rabbas, Malcolm Schofield, and two audiences that heard an early version of the paper: members of the Society for Ancient and Medieval Philosophy at the University of Oslo, and those present at my B Club talk at Cambridge. I worked on this paper while visiting Clare Hall, Cambridge.

[1] Broadly speaking. I use "conception" here in the sense of Aristotelian "appearance," not as a translation of *hypolêpsis* in the restricted sense of an intellectual conception. The scope of "appearance" is discussed below.

Whatever else may be involved in the agent's conception of his goal, Aristotle thinks that in each case the goal strikes the agent as good. Telos for him is not only a *phainomenon*, something that appears to the agent in some way, but a *phainomenon agathon*, something that appears good. I explicate this view, and defend it against certain objections that are likely to be raised against it. In invoking seemings of goodness, Aristotle does not abandon the project of explaining actions by citing desires that motivate it. Rather, he sees himself as carrying that project a step further. Seeing something as good, he thinks, is part of what it is for human beings to desire something. The upshot is that every goal-oriented action is seen as embodying an evaluative stand of some kind.

The notion of an apparent good should, I suggest, be placed within the context of Aristotle's dialectical approach to ethics. Apparent goods are among those "appearances" with which, he insists, the dialectical inquiry should start. I argue that this insistence is part of his deliberate attempt to incorporate into his own ethics the insights he found in Protagorean relativism, while reaffirming—against Protagoras—the standpoint of ethical objectivity.

The appearances that should serve as ethical starting points are not, I urge, only things *said* and *believed* about value, be it by those who have a reputation for ethical insight, or by the common folk. The appearances in question include the ways goodness and badness get represented to us in our desires, both non-rational and rational, and in passions of various kinds. My argument here relies on Aristotle's discussion of pleasure, which is a paradigmatic instance of an apparent good.

The seemings of goodness embedded in non-rational desires and passions often do not amount to full-blown value judgements. Many such seemings are predoxastic. Our lives, Aristotle believes, are shot through with evaluative appearances that do not amount to positions taken by reason. They ground our full-fledged value judgements, and sometimes—as in akrasia, weakness of the will—undermine the effectiveness even of the most carefully considered judgements. The notion that dialectical procedure in ethics should start from non-doxastic appearances of goodness as well as from views of experts and non-experts about values reflects Aristotle's belief that reason can bring such appearances to light, and subject them to scrutiny. If reason can, by proceeding dialectically, subject to scrutiny a whole range of appearances—from predoxastic ones to highly reflective and carefully calibrated ones—a hope opens up that some comparison and adjudication can be made between seemings that conflict with one another. Aristotle is committed to the belief that we can guide our lives by reason; he thinks that we can do so because reason is capable of bringing order and resolution to conflicting seemings of goodness, predoxastic and doxastic alike. Since *phantasia* that is embedded in action is the material upon which practical reason works, much of what Aristotle has to say about the structure of appearance in action is directly relevant to the account he will go on to give of practical reason.

As readers of Aristotle will know, he regards actions not only as goal-directed, but also as actualizations of various human capacities and dispositions. I attempt to bring into the open the link between goals of action, on the one hand, and dispositional states and their actualizations, on the other. In this, concluding, part of the paper, I make explicit a concept he made use of but did not articulate. My aim here is to sketch out how the notion of telos and that of actualization combine to form a distinctively new perspective on action.[2] This new perspective enabled Aristotle to make room in his ethics for the sort of success in life, spurned by other Greek philosophers, which ordinary Greeks of his time so much admired.

Aristotle's new account of action was a result of his determination to strike a balance between the Socratic and the Protagorean position on truth and appearance, and to avoid what he took to be the pitfalls of both these positions. Whereas Socrates' influence on Aristotle has long been recognized, the influence of Protagoras has not. The impact of Protagorean relativism on Aristotle's thinking about action and value goes, however, quite deep.

I. Aristotelian Telos

1.   A telos is in the first instance what the agent aims at in his action. If the agent hits upon what he aims at, this result is also called a *telos*. To count as a telos in this sense, the outcome of an action must be aimed at in the action and be a direct causal product of the aiming involved in the action. Let me call this kind of outcome an *Aristotelian outcome*. An Aristotelian outcome is a goal achieved. As such, it cannot be identified independently of what the agent who brought it about aimed at in action, nor independently of the way in which he saw the circumstances of his action and its point under those circumstances.[3]

To bring into focus the telos of an action in the sense of an Aristotelian outcome is not to bring into focus the outcome of the action as such, as the

---

[2] The notion of telos is found in Plato (see, for instance, *Prot.* 354b 7, *Gorg.* 499e 8, *Tim.* 90d 5). The terminology of *hexis* and *energeia* is Aristotle's own, but the concepts involved have Platonic antecedents. See *Euthyd.* 277e–278b, *Phil.* 11d, and especially *Theaet.* 196d–199c. What Aristotle did with these concepts is new.

[3] On the distinctive ways in which different moral characters see the world and the circumstances of their action, see John McDowell, "Virtue and Reason," *The Monist*, July 1979; "The Role of *Eudaimonia* in Aristotle's Ethics," in *Essays on Aristotle's Ethics*, ed. A. O. Rorty, Berkeley/Los Angeles 1980, his "Comments on 'Some Rational Aspects of Incontinence' by T. H. Irwin," *The Southern Journal of Philosophy*, vol. XXVII, 1989, Supplement, and "Some Issues in Aristotle's Moral Psychology," in *Ethics* (*Companions to ancient thought*, vol. 4), ed. S. Everson, Cambridge 1998. (These articles, except for the comment on Irwin, are collected in McDowell's *Mind, Value, and Reality*, Cambridge, Mass. 1998.)

notion of outcome is most often understood today, where outcomes are without history and without subjectivity. On this more recent understanding, outcomes are identified independently of the actions that bring them about, and independently of the conceptions under which the agents bring them about.[4] For some purposes, the agent's conception of the outcome may be of interest in this framework as well. Nonetheless, the agent's conception of the goal need not be the conception in virtue of which the outcome of his action is identified. By contrast, the specific conception of a goal that is involved in the agent's aiming at that goal is the very one in terms of which an Aristotelian outcome is identified.

By contrasting Aristotle's concept of telos, in one of its two guises, with that of an outcome as this is most often understood nowadays, I do not mean to suggest that current theories of action cannot handle the aspects of action that his concepts bring into particularly sharp relief. My intention here is simply to point out which aspects of actions he focuses upon when he adopts the two-sided concept of telos as his main theoretical tool for analyzing actions.

2.   What is the point of stressing that whenever the agent aims at some end, he does so under some conception of the end? Of course, one might say, if an agent aims at some state of affairs, he does not have that state of affairs in his head. He thinks of it, and necessarily thinks of it in some way or other. To initiate an action is to bring something to pass in the world; it would seem that our concern should be above all with how the world has changed as a result of an action, not so much with how the agent happened to think of his goal while aiming to bring it about.

The way in which the outcome is conceived when it is aimed at in action can of course be seen simply as a part of the apparatus that will, if all goes well, bring the outcome about. What should or should not matter here depends on what one is up to. It is thus necessary to look at the uses to which Aristotle intends to put his notion of telos.

One job that the concept of telos is meant to do is help us understand and explain actions. Getting a grip on how the agent sees the situation, and his own action within that situation, helps us throw light on why he acts as he does. Another use to which the telos model is put is ethical. Here Aristotle holds that the goodness or badness of an action depends as much on what the agent is minded to do as it depends on the goodness or badness of what comes to pass in the world as the result of the action. Since spelling out the conception under which the agent aims at his goal amounts to spelling out what motivates him to act as he does, specifying the conception in question is a step that has to be taken if the action is to be evaluated properly from an ethical point of view.

---

[4] One can, of course, narrow down one's focus by looking into certain kinds of outcomes. I am here focusing on the very concept of an outcome.

Although Aristotle's approach to action is teleological in some sense—namely, centered on the concept of telos—he does not embrace what is nowadays called a teleological ethical theory. If on his view the *effecting* of one's purposes in the world were the most significant aspect of action, we would be led to believe—or, more modestly, given the theoretical leap we are making here, to suspect—that the ultimate end to be sought from ethical conduct would be to bring about the most desirable, or best possible, state of affairs. Aristotle's ethical theory is not a theory of this type.

A good Aristotelian outcome is a successful realization of an ethically good purpose. But an ethically good purpose is not merely a sincere, or pure, purpose. To be fully ethically successful, an action must embody a correct evaluative appraisal of its object, and yield the result that it strives for. So although Aristotle's ethics is not teleological in the current sense of the word, for him the goodness of the actual states of affairs brought about by action does matter ethically.

The dual nature of Aristotelian telos makes it a good tool with which to capture the joint ethical significance of the motivation for an action, on the one hand, and of the actual state of affairs that the action brings about, on the other. A firm commitment to both of these aspects of action as ethically significant is a striking characteristic of Aristotelian ethics, setting it apart not only from many modern moral theories, but also from most ethical theories proffered in antiquity.

3. The telos model of action presupposes that it is possible to act in such a way as to attain one's conceived purpose, or, to use Aristotle's metaphor, to hit one's target. The metaphor of aiming at a target, *skopos*,[5] and of hitting or missing it, stands at the core of his approach to action. However, things other than simply hitting or missing one's target can surely happen. An action may disintegrate under the burden of the agent's disparate or conflicting purposes; the agent's purpose can shift, so that he does not end up carrying out what he took himself to be carrying out in action; he can achieve what he had not set out to achieve—as, for instance, when one aims at proving a certain result but ends up with a much more important result of a kind one did not envisage. (The agent's goal-directed action has to be appropriately related to the result attained, if that result is to count as the agent's own achievement.)

Why are these possibilities of interest? Some worries can be raised concerning the telos model of action. The concept of telos does double duty in explaining actions: it is both that which is aimed at, and that which is achieved if the action is successful. But the assumed overlap between one's

[5] For *skopos*, see especially *EN* I. 2 1094a 23–24 and VI. 1 1138b 21–25. Also relevant are *EN* VI. 12 1144a 23–27, VII. 11 1152a 2–3 and 1153b 24–25; *EE* i. 2 1214b 6–10; ii. 10 1226b 29–30 and 1227a 5–8, ii. 11 1227b 19–25, viii. 3 (=vii. 15) 1249b 23–25, and *Rhet.* I. 5 1360b 4–7.

goal and the aimed-for outcome may be seen as suspect. Agents, one might claim, in fact seldom attain precisely what they aim at. This point is empirical. Second—and this is a conceptual point—one's goal is not the same sort of entity as the outcome brought about by one's action. The Aristotelian model of action either assumes that they are, or leaves us in the dark how the two are related. Finally, this picture of action does not seem to be able to accommodate a variety of instances where the goal and the outcome appear to be out of alignment.

An Aristotelian reply to these worries might run along the following lines. The telos approach to action does not presuppose that everything of interest that goes on in action consists in hitting or missing the targets one has set up. Rather, it invites us to describe more complex and interesting situations in which there is some disparity between the goal and the outcome by taking the simple target model as the canonical case.

The second complaint mentioned raises some larger issues; I shall address only the basic worry I take it to express. The notion of telos has two sides, but so do actions themselves. Beside being events in the world, bringing about other events, there is an intensional side to actions, which has to do with the fact that they are directed at something perceived, or thought of, in a certain way. The possibility of our hitting or missing the mark in action presupposes that there is a point of contact between the object as it appears in the oblique context of our perception and thought, and the object which is a part of what there is in the world. That the telos model presupposes this should not be cause for complaint. The possibility of making the required contact is something without which neither meaningful thought and speech, nor effective action, would be possible.

What is left at the periphery when telos is what one focuses on is a way of acting, or rather a way of doing things, which one might describe by saying: she didn't know *what* she was doing. So, what lies at the limits of the goal-directed action is aimlessness, or too many fleeting, disparate or shifting purposes, which may well undermine the very activity of aiming. The telos model of action does not deny that human beings sometimes do things in a desultory sort of way. Rather, it assigns such doings a place on the margin of well-defined instances of action.

II. Desire and Apparent Goods

4.   To specify the goal of an action is to interpret the action by answering the question of what the person does in acting thus and so. To recognize that the goal in question is something seen by the agent as good is to answer the question why the person acts as he does. However, for Aristotle, the two answers do not stand far apart. He envisages a tight link between the notion of telos

and that of an apparent good.[6] To have a purpose in action is to be minded in a certain way about what one sets out to do. Going for a goal need not involve a full-fledged value judgement, but in Aristotle's view it does involve an evaluative endorsement of some sort.

Anything that appears to an agent in a favourable light is a *phainomenon agathon*, an apparent good, in the most relaxed sense Aristotle gives to this term. Seemings of goodness come in two varieties: an apparent good can be something that merely seems good to the agent, or strikes him as good, where a judgement of value is not present, or it can be something that the agent considers or judges to be good.

That a full specification of what the person does will indicate why he does it is not too surprising. When the agent perceives or considers something as good, one can see how the action aimed at securing it makes sense from his point of view. But the thought that whenever an agent aims at a goal that goal appears good to him is far more problematic. I address what I take to be the central problem with this view in Section III below. In the rest of this section, I consider some questions regarding the explanatory role of Aristotelian seemings of goodness.

5.   One question that comes promptly to mind is the following: in order to explain why the agent did what he did, could one not simply cite the operative desire, bypassing the alleged perception of the goodness of the object desired?

Aristotle frequently explains actions by referring to desires that motivate them. However, by invoking the perceived goodness of the end, one gives what he takes to be, in a certain sense, the preferred explanation. I can point to two lines of thought that led him to think so.

First, on his view, desires go along with certain ways of perceiving the world. By focusing on how the world is seen, or conceived of, by the agent, one may be able to shed light both on the agent's desiderative states, and on his actions. Second, Aristotle thinks that certain ways of going about things in life are not only seen as good, or taken to be good, by this or that person, but are genuinely good or bad (in a given context, I take it, and for the given

[6] As well as between telos and that which not only appears good, but is so. This is evident in the opening of the *Nicomachean Ethics*: "Every craft (*technê*) and every systematic inquiry (*methodos*), and similarly every action (*praxis*) and choice (*prohairesis*), are thought to go for (*ephiesthai*) some good, and for this reason the good has rightly been declared to be that for which everything goes (*ephietai*). But there appears to be a difference among ends (*tôn telôn*): for some of them are activities, others products over and above the activities" (1094a 1–5). Other relevant passages are *EN* I. 2 1094a 18–22, 1094b 6–7, I. 7 1097a 15–24 (esp. 18–22) and a 25–28 (cp. *EN* I. 4 1095a 14–17 and I. 6 1096b 35–1097a 3); *EE* i. 8 1218b 10–12, ii. 1 1219a 10–11; *Pol.* I. 2 1252b 34–1253a 1; *Rhet.* I. 6 1363a 5; *Top.* 146b 10, and *Met.* V. 2 1013b 25–28. I am addressing here the role apparent goods play in explaining actions. The question whether the object of aiming and wishing is an apparent good or a good is addressed in Section IV below.

agents). His thought here seems to be that starting from the notion of an apparent good he can work his way up to the concept of something that is objectively good, showing how by imposing restrictions on the original notion of an apparent good we construct the objective good through some kind of dialectical procedure. If something of the sort can be done, however exactly it may be done, it would seem more profitable to take the concept of a good as the more basic one, and treat desires as attitudes directed at goods, including the objective goods thus constructed.

Aristotle divides human desire into rational and non-rational. What ultimately sets a rational desire apart from a non-rational one is the causal role that an exercise of reason plays in the acquisition of the desire. The valuations that the two kinds of desire involve also tend to be different. Seemings of goodness, he thinks, may be present even where a reasoned evaluative stance is not.

If Aristotle takes a different view on the role desire plays in the explanation of action from the view that is often taken today, he does so because he has a different understanding of what is involved in desiring something. However, given his belief that everything is desired as being something good, in relying on desires to explain actions he does not take himself to be giving an explanation different in type from an explanation that invokes apparent goods.

We all cite desires in order to explain actions; the interesting question is what it is about desire that is relevant for explaining action. Aristotle thinks of desire as involving a movement of the soul toward an object one is attracted to, or, if "desire" is understood more broadly, also a movement away from something one is repelled from. He links desire to pursuit and avoidance at *EN* VI. 2 1139a 21–22: "Just as assertion and denial are to thought (*dianoia*), so pursuit (*diôxis*) and avoidance (*phygê*) are to desire (*orexis*)." The term used here, *orexis*, is his general term for a desire. It applies to all three types of desire that he distinguishes: *boulêsis*, a rational wish, and two non-rational types of desire, *epithymia*, an appetite, and *thymos*, a spirited desire (see *EN* III. 2 1111b 10ff).[7] If one wants to understand more about a desire—and consequently about the action which is motivated by the desire—than that it involves a movement toward, or away from, a given object, one has to specify what it is about the object that is found attractive or repellent by the agent. Aristotle takes it that in specifying such attractive or repellent aspects of the object, one is specifying those features of the object that are seen by the agent as being, respectively, good or bad.

---

[7] For different types of desire in Aristotle, see John M. Cooper's "Some Remarks on Aristotle's Moral Psychology," *The Southern Journal of Philosophy*, vol. XXVII, 1989, Supplement (Spindel Conference 1988), pp. 25–42 (reprinted in his *Reason and Emotion, Essays on Ancient Moral Psychology and Ethical Theory*, Princeton 1999, pp. 237–252).

The view that everything desired is desired as being something good does not by itself imply that there is a state of the soul—a mental state, as we might prefer to put it—that is both a state of desiring something and a state of perceiving something as good. The view is rather that in ascribing a desiderative state to a person we are committed to ascribing to him a perception of the object of desire as something good.

6.   If every goal-oriented action is directed at something that appears good to the agent, valuation is built into the very nature of action. This has the consequence that in order fully to determine whether an action is good or bad, one has to re-evaluate the subjective valuation that is built into the very tissue of action. Many accounts nowadays locate valuing at the level of second-order desires.[8] In the theories I have in mind here, valuation shows up at the level of a more or less reflective judgement. Aristotle, however, finds it suitable to talk of valuation at an unreflective as well as reflective, unreasoned as much as reasoned, level. (More on this in Sections III and IV.) The consequence that in evaluating an action as good or bad one is re-evaluating the agent's own valuation, is not at all unwelcome from his point of view. When we evaluate an action, what we in part do is judge whether we share the agent's evaluative standpoint, and to what extent and in what way we do so.

III. Is Everything Pursued as Being Something Good?

7.   Philosophers today tend to draw a sharper line between desiring or wanting, on the one hand, and valuing, on the other, than Aristotle (and other ancients) did. That I want or desire something, Bernard Williams points out, can be a brute fact. I can simply desire something without valuing it at all. It is on this ground that he rejects the view that everything pursued (or desired) is pursued (or desired) as being something good.

   The thought of something's being good, Williams claims, "imports an idea, however minimal or hazy, of a perspective in which it can be acknowledged by more than one agent as good." The most a person commits himself to by having a purpose, is that it "would be good for him if he succeeded." But even this modest claim is thought by Williams to "[imply] a perspective that goes somewhere beyond the agent's immediate desires, to his long-term

---

[8] For instance, Harry Frankfurt, "Freedom of the Will and the Concept of a Person," *Journal of Philosophy*, vol. 68, No. 1, January 1971, pp. 5–20; David Lewis, "Dispositional Theories of Value," *Proceedings of the Aristotelian Society*, Suppl. vol. 63, 1989, pp. 113–138. Cp. Gilbert Harman, "Desired Desires" in *Value, Welfare and Morality*, eds. R. G. Fray and W. Morris, Cambridge 1993, pp. 117–136.

interests or well-being".[9] When a desire is attributed to a person, however, no hint of intersubjectivity need be present.

By contrast, Aristotle holds that all desire is directed at something that appears good to the desiring subject, and that everything pursued as a goal in action is pursued as something good. This view, I think, ought not to be dismissed so easily. It has its merits, which deserve to be looked into.

8.   Basic though it is, Williams' claim that the very thought of something being *good* goes beyond a subjective perspective can be questioned. That I now find this thing here good seems to me to carry no implication whatever as to what others might find good or what I might find good at some later time, let alone as to what might be in my interest either now or later. Those who envisage a very sharp divide between valuing and desiring might think Williams' claim appealing. That he himself should take this position is somewhat puzzling, given some other views he holds.

Any reasonable view of desires and values should envisage some connection between desiring, on the one hand, and perceiving or thinking of things as good, on the other. Williams, I think, does envisage such a connection. In his "External and Internal Reasons,"[10] he claims that all (genuine) reasons we have for acting are internal. This means roughly that a judgement to the effect that I *have a reason* to do something is false (or does not make sense: cp. p. 111), unless that judgement is appropriately related to some *desire* of mine—or, more generally, to some more complex orectic item in my "subjective motivational set" (pp. 102 and 105)—that would be satisfied by my action. The simplest model for the internal interpretation of reasons, which is the model Williams starts from, is this: A has a reason to φ just in case A has some desire the satisfaction of which will be served by his φ-ing.

Now it is reasonable to assume that what is *good* for me to do is on Williams' view connected with what I *have a reason* to do, and what is *best* for me to do with what I *have most reason* to do. If this is so, then a parallel to his view that all genuine reasons for acting are internal should strongly recommend itself to him: a judgement to the effect that it is good for me to do something would be false or would not make sense unless that judgement could be appropriately related to my desires—or to some other item in my subjective motivational set—that would be satisfied by my action. On such a view, something being good for me "in the longer run" would presumably also have to be connected with some desire—perhaps with my present desire for my future well-being, or with what I would desire for myself in the future if some conditions obtained. Likewise for something being good in a way other people can recognize as good. If the parallel I have been developing here holds, the claim

[9] *Ethics and the Limits of Philosophy*, Cambridge, Mass. 1985, pp. 58–59.
[10] *Moral Luck*, Cambridge 1981, pp. 101–113.

that some things are good for me would be groundless unless an appropriate link can be found with what I desire, or would desire under some circumstances. Williams' view that any claim about what is good for me necessarily transcends a subjective point of view sits somewhat uneasily with his view that it is ultimately a desire, factual or counterfactual, that is needed to ground a claim about what I might have a *reason* to do, or—as I have extended his claim—about what might be *good* for me to do. His position is by no means inconsistent. What puzzles is his confidence about the objective purport of *any* claim about what is good for one.

The motivation for insisting on the existence of brute desire—namely, desire the object of which is not desired as being good—might stem from an unwillingness to admit that the concept of good may be so basic that it goes all the way down. One may be reluctant to admit that, parallel to my simply desiring something here and now for myself here and now, there might also be such a thing as something simply appearing good to me here and now—where "simply appearing" refers to the sort of appearing that does not imply a reflective value judgement or a reasoned evaluative stance of any sort. (One could call this "simple" or "brute appearance.") If one grants the existence of simple appearances of goodness, one also has to grant that there is a concept of good which is as basic as that of desire.

At a pretheoretical level, people are quite happy to speak of goods, or of things being good, at this very basic level, as for instance, when they say that something "feels good." Although the expression "feels" indicates subjectivity and immediacy, the term "good" should not on that account be considered misused. It would be quite misguided to suggest to the person who "feels good" that he is really only having a desire for something, or that he finds something pleasant or agreeable. If this is how things are at a pretheoretical level, why should a theorist be reluctant to grant the existence of simple seemings of goodness? Perhaps the reason is the following: if one takes desires, wants and the like—as Williams does—along with factual beliefs, as the basic items we use to explain actions, one may want to exclude concepts that might easily become competitors. Observe that nothing detrimental to the view that takes desires to be basic explanatory items would *follow* from admitting the existence of simple appearances of goodness. Rather, what could be worrisome here is the use to which these "appearances" might be put in a competing theory of action.[11] Aristotle's theory of action is such a competing theory. The aim of my argument here has been a plea—an argued plea—that the theory get a more sympathetic hearing.

---

[11] Insisting on the existence of brute desire might be due to an attempt to keep the line between facts and value nice and clean. I do not want to go into a general discussion of how nice and clean that line should be.

9.   One might think that a sharp line between desiring and valuing will come in handy when we turn to cases of akrasia, weakness of the will, or at least *some* such cases. In some cases of akrasia—let me call them *elementary akrasia*—desiring and valuing seem to fall entirely apart. The akratic person is thought to go for something that is an object of an immediate desire, in spite of his commitment to a value judgement that speaks against the desire. Such an akratic does not, we are told, place any value on what he desires. (Aristotle would approach the case designated as *elementary akrasia* in terms of some variety of non-rational desire, whether appetitive or spirited, rather than in terms of "immediate" desires. Many appetitive desires are on his view very basic and urgent. Appetites are said to be for food, drink, sex and "the like." He might then grant that the akratic agent of this sort acts against his value judgement, but not that he acts against any valuation whatsoever.)

   Consider now an entirely different sort of case. We are sometimes led to think that what might at first look like an akratic action is not akratic after all, since the agent does not in fact have an appropriate degree of commitment to the value judgement against which he appears to be acting. What I have in mind here is the sort of suspicion we might have of a person's "akratic" weakness for chocolate, if the person displays too much of it too often. Sometimes, when we look more closely into the matter, we come to think that the allegedly akratic action accords all too well with the agent's "principles." If something is to be properly described as an akratic episode, this sort of *quasi-akrasia* has to be ruled out.

   If the sharp line between desiring and valuing appears especially well suited to accommodate elementary akrasia, the Aristotelian view according to which there is a continuity between the less reflective and the more reflective kinds of desiring—and, in fact, a continuity between the entirely non-reasoned and the reasoned sort of desiring—is especially well suited to accommodate quasi-akrasia. Given that the correct description of an action as akratic rules out quasi-akrasia, it seems that the Aristotelian view might provide a different, but not necessarily less sensitive, framework within which to handle akrasia.[12]

   By ruling out quasi-akrasia, I do not mean that before classifying something as a case of akrasia one has to prove that the case is not one of quasi-akrasia. Rather, in any case of what appears to be akrasia, there is a real question whether the agent acts against his considered judgement of what is better, or rather acts against a judgement the commitment to which is too tenuous to render the action akratic.

   Whereas the view that drives a wedge between desiring and valuing derives some support from our everyday experience of cases in which it seems clear that the agents desire something but it is not so clear whether they value it, the

---

[12] This leaves untouched the question of which approach is ultimately more promising for a satisfactory account of akrasia.

Aristotelian view draws support from some of our well-entrenched everyday evaluative practices. We say, for instance, that actions speak louder than words. Literally, we mean that a person's professed purpose may be different from the purpose that in fact guides his action. Less literally, we take it that the lives people lead provide some measure of evidence for the valuations to which they are committed regardless of how reflective their valuations are, and regardless of the role reasoning might have played in their arriving at such valuations.[13]

IV. Socrates, Protagoras, and Apparent Goods

10.   One might worry that the spectre of relativism is lurking behind Aristotle's notion of an apparent good. I cannot fully dispel that worry here, but a few words on the concept of an apparent good are in order. Aristotle introduces this concept aware of its relativist connotations, and, I believe, precisely as a part of an attempt to turn the concept of an apparent good against relativism. One can catch a glimpse of this by looking at his discussion of the concept of wish, *boulêsis*, in Book III of the *Nicomachean Ethics*.

The puzzle raised in *EN* III. 4 is whether the object of a wish is the good (*to agathon*), or rather the apparent good (*to phainomenon agathon*). Aristotle seems to be referring here to a standing debate between two camps. On one side are those who say that what is wished for is *the good* (1113a 16–19); on the other those who maintain that it is *the apparent good* (a 20–22). The outline of the debate is sketchy, but it appears that to the second camp belong people like Protagoras. On the view of those belonging to this camp, "what each person wishes (*to boulêton*) is what he takes to be good (*hekastô(i) to dokoun*)." However, Aristotle himself observes, "different things, indeed opposite things, if it so happens, appear good to different people" (a 20–21). On the Protagorean view, which Aristotle seems to have in mind here, whatever appears good to a person is good for him. There is no room here for any talk about goods, or the good, as such, apart from what appears good to particular people in particular circumstances.

Aristotle does not want to side with either camp. In fact, he seems to think that the question itself, as formulated—"Is what is wished for the good or the apparent good?"—is not well posed. It forces those who do not want to side with Protagoras to accept the absurd consequence that what is wished for by a person who does not choose or desire correctly is not wished at all, since it is not the good (1113a 17–19). On the Protagorean view, on the other hand, there is no room at all for the possibility of someone making a wrong choice or wishing for the wrong sort of thing. Aristotle finds both consequences unacceptable.

---

[13] A rational desire or wish, *boulêsis*, is not necessarily formed by reflection, although some exercise of practical reason is involved in the formation of a wish.

Socrates must be the person Aristotle is thinking of as the main proponent of the view that the good is what is wished for. Socrates embraces the view that all wanting is for something he calls "the good." He starts from the plausible thought that we all want to do well for ourselves. In different circumstances, he thinks, we identify what is good for us with different things, and very often we are wrong. Nonetheless, however misguided our conceptions might be of what is good for us, what we are after in all our actions is that which in fact is good for us. If we knew what that is, we would attain the good, and live well. The absurd consequence Aristotle mentions at 1113a 17–19 as entailed by this view—namely, the consequence that what is wished for by a person who does not choose correctly is not wished at all—is embraced by Socrates. It is this line of thought that stands behind his declaration in the *Gorgias* that orators and tyrants do not do what they want to do (*ha boulontai*) (*Gorgias* 467a 8ff.). In the *Protagoras*, Socrates is represented as saying that it is not "in human nature to want (*ethelein*) to go toward what one believes to be bad instead of the good (*anti tôn agathôn*)," and that "no one goes willingly (*hekôn*) toward the bad (*ta kaka*) or what he believes to be bad" (*Protagoras* 358c 6–d 4).[14] Although Aristotle ultimately rejected the Socratic view, it undoubtedly left a deep impression on him.

What perhaps is not so obvious is the impression Protagoras left on Aristotle. Aristotle is hardly tempted by Protagorean relativism. He clearly rejects the view that whatever appears good *to each person* is good *for that person*. One gets the feeling, moreover, that he believes there is something complacent about this brand of relativism. In settling too quickly for appearances, it refuses to look more deeply into the matter of what could be wrong with some of them. However, Aristotle also believes that Protagoras got something right, something no other philosophical theory he knew of—or perhaps as he knew it—did get right. In the domain of ethics at least, there is some truth to Protagoras' claim[15] that the individual human being is the measure of all things. We cannot be entirely wrong about what is good for us, since there is some connection between things appearing good to us and their being good for us. Witness Aristotle's irritation with those who claim that a person who is broken on the wheel or in other great misfortunes is happy, provided only that he is good (*EN* VII. 13 1153b 19–21), as well as with those who reject a certain hedonist argument by maintaining that what everybody goes for (*ephietai*) is not good (*EN* X. 2 1172b 35–36). In both cases, Aristotle declares that the people who put forward these claims are "talking nonsense" (*ouden/outhen legousin*).

What he has in mind in the latter passage seems to be the following: if indeed it were true that everybody goes for pleasure, a philosophical position

---

[14] I provide a philosophical reading of these claims in "No One Errs Willingly: The Meaning of Socratic Intellectualism," chap. 3 above.

[15] Diels/Kranz 80 B 1.

that simply dismissed this fact would be irresponsible. Things that are taken (*dokei*) to be good by all, Aristotle goes on to say, are (*einai*) good; someone who undermines confidence (*pistis*) in such things can hardly himself propose something that inspires more confidence, *pistotera* (1172b 36–1173a 2). It is noteworthy that both passages occur in the context of a discussion of pleasure. Pleasure strikes most people as good, and very few would accept that a thoroughly unpleasant life can be happy. Such widely shared appearances, Aristotle insists, must receive the weight they deserve.[16] Even if the theory according to which pleasure is the ultimate human good is rejected, seemings of goodness that are almost universally shared should not be shortchanged.

Aristotle thinks that what we should do cannot lie too far apart from what we in fact do. For him, the appearances of goodness embodied in our actions and our everyday value judgements are not the end of the story concerning the question of how one should live, but they ought to be the beginning. They should also be something one repeatedly comes back to as one is conducting an ethical inquiry. If, in the end, one comes to think that such appearances are wrong, one must give an adequate account of why they are wrong.

11.   Let me now return to the aporia about the good and the apparent good (*EN* III. 4 1113a 15ff) with which I started the present section. Having rejected the dilemma whether the object of a wish is the good or the apparent good, Aristotle at 1113a 25–1113b 2 gives what I take to be his own reply to Protagoras: the good person is the standard and measure (*kanôn kai metron*) in matters having to do with "what is fine and pleasant" (these being ethical affairs in general) and, "in each sort of case, what is true appears to him" (*en hekastois talêthes autô(i) phainetai*, 1113a 29–31).

Aristotle's use of the Protagorean idiom[17] in formulating his response to Protagoras' challenge to the objectivity of ethical judgement is, I believe, not only deliberate, but also of some philosophical importance. He makes a point of retaining the idiom of things "appearing" good or bad to a person while affirming, in fact precisely when affirming, his commitment to objective ethical judgement.

In addition to the passage quoted, we should also note *EN* VI. 12 1144a 34–36: "This [sc. the telos and the best] appears (*phainetai*) only to the good person; for vice perverts us and leads us to be deceived about the starting

---

[16] More on what kind of appearance Aristotle has in mind here in § 12.

[17] We know Protagoras' position only through second-hand reports by Plato and Sextus, but it is not adventurous to assume that Protagoras did, as reported, refer to the individual human being as the measure (*metron*) of all things, and that he made the point that what *appears* to each person *is* so for that person. See Diels/Kranz 80 B 1. I would venture a guess that he used the term "apparent goods" himself, or at any rate spoke of things appearing good or bad to people.

points of action." At X. 5 1176a 15–19, Aristotle says: "But in all such cases it seems that what is [so] is what appears [so] (*to phainomenon*) to the good person. If this is correct, as it seems to be, and virtue, or the good person insofar as he is good, is the measure of each thing (*hekastou metron*), then pleasures are what appear to be pleasures to him, and what is pleasant is what he enjoys." The good and practically wise person is an embodiment of the objectivity of ethical judgement. Aristotle's message—or rather, the part of the message that interests me at the moment—is that the concept of an apparent good as something at which human action aims need not, and should not, be rejected in order to make room for the objectivity of ethical judgement. This concept is not something to be dispensed with once we get over the relativist challenge. It is needed for a proper understanding of what motivates action: virtuous and vicious, well-directed and ill-directed alike.

Consequently, Aristotle's concept of an apparent good is different from what we can presume the corresponding Protagorean concept would have been. Note Aristotle's claim in *De motu animalium*, at 700b 28–29: "And we must suppose that the apparent good occupies the same position as the good, and so does the pleasant, since it is an apparent good." The issue discussed here is the explanation of the "movement of animals," a category that includes human action. Restricting our attention for the moment to human beings, his point is that the notion of the good and that of the apparent good play the same role in the explanation of human conduct. This is so because nothing could motivate human action that did not appear good to the agent himself, regardless of whether what appears good to him is actually good. His view is that the good—namely, that which actually is good for the agent—motivates human conduct, but it does so by being represented as a good.

Aristotle's claim that the apparent good occupies the same position as the good, indicates something important about his notion of the apparent good. The apparent good, as he understands it, does not lie on the other side of what is objectively good—as its Protagorean counterpart presumably does. Aristotle does not think that we are locked into our own perceptions or conceptions of goodness without the possibility of ever hitting upon what is in fact good or correct. To apply a remark he makes in a different context, we are not at the mercy of *phantasia*, with the ends of action, what we aim at, being simply given to us in our perceptions or conceptions.[18] A person who is favourably situated, and has appropriate dispositions and ethical outlook, can attain the truth in practical matters.

---

[18] *EN* III. 5 1114a 31–1114b 1, "Now one may say that everyone aims at the apparent good, and has no control over the appearance (*tês de phantasias ou kyrioi*), but as each person is, so the end appears to him [. . .]." The issue discussed here is not relativism, but the agent's responsibility for his own states of character. Aristotle clearly rejects the view that we do not have any control over appearances.

V. *Phantasia* Proper

12. I drew a rough distinction in § 4 between things striking a person as good, and things being taken or considered to be good by a person. This distinction runs parallel to Aristotle's division of desires into non-rational and rational ones. When a person has a non-rational desire for something—whether an appetitive one, *epithymia*, or a spirited one, *thymos*—Aristotle takes it that the object of the desire appears good to the person. He sometimes uses the term "apparent good" specifically to designate something that appears good non-rationally, for instance, to someone who has a non-rational desire or passion.

I shall refer to this as apparent good in the strict sense, or apparent good proper. *EE* vii. 2 1235b 26–29 is relevant here: "That is why the pleasant is desired; for it is an apparent good of some sort. Some take it (or believe it, *tois men dokei*) [sc. to be good], to others it appears (*tois de phainetai*) [sc. good] although they do not take (or believe, *dokei*) it [to be good]. For appearance (*phantasia*) and belief (*doxa*) are not in the same part of the soul."[19] *Phainetai* is here contrasted with *dokei*, and *phantasia* with *doxa*. Thus this sort of *phantasia* is confined to the part of the soul which is not *doxastikon*, namely, which itself is not a source of belief, *doxa*.[20] The home of *doxa* is, of course, reason.

I refer to what appears to the non-rational part of the soul as the apparent good *proper* because I surmise that Aristotle intended his talk of "appearances" as a corrective to something he saw as a Socratic error. He strongly disagrees with the Socratic position which refuses to recognize the existence of non-rational desires and passions. He might well have adopted the terminology of "appearances" of goodness in order to underscore his view that the evaluative stance involved in non-rational desires and passions need not amount to a rational belief or judgement, *doxa*. *Doxa* is the word Socrates uses to characterize desire and passion. Aristotle, rightly or wrongly, gives a narrow intellectualist interpretation to the Socratic *doxa*, and hence needs a different term to express his position. This might account for the contrast between *phantasia* and *doxa* that he draws in the *Eudemian Ethics* passage.[21]

Aristotle's anti-Socratic stance, however, puts him under new theoretical pressures. He now needs to provide a unified account of motivation, and

---

[19] For the text, see note 23.

[20] Aristotle on occasion restricts the expression *to phainomenon agathon* even further, applying it to something that mistakenly appears as good. Thus at *EE* ii. 10 1227a 18–22 we read: "The end is naturally always good [. . .], but contrary to nature and through perversion, not the good but the apparent good." Compare a few lines further down: "Likewise too, wish is naturally of the good, but contrary to nature and through perversion, also the bad" (1227a 28–30). The use of the expression *to phainomenon agathon* to designate an illusory good is special, and I shall leave it on one side here.

[21] Cf. *De anima* III. 3.

especially so in the case of actions that reflect virtue of character. It is in particular here that he needs the broad sense of *to phainomenon agathon*, and the related broad use of the verb *phainesthai*, to appear.

The fact that the broad reading of appearance is very much in evidence in the ethical writings may in part be due to this. When he speaks of an object of a rational wish, *boulêsis*, as something that *appears* good to the person who has such a wish—notably so in the *Nicomachean Ethics* III. 4, the chapter on the object of *boulêsis*—and when he describes the good person as the one to whom what is ethically true "appears (*phainetai*) in each case" (1113a 29–31), Aristotle is clearly not confining his attention to what appears to the non-rational part of the soul. The broad sense of "appearance" is also striking in Book Ten, at X. 6 1176b 23–24: "It is reasonable then that, just as different things appear (*phainetai*) honourable to boys and to men, different things appear honourable to base and to decent people." Something similar happens in the *Eudemian Ethics*. In *EE* i. 3—a chapter which deals with the method to be adopted in ethical inquiry—we find *doxa* included among things that *appear* to people: "It would be superfluous to examine all the beliefs (*doxai*) which people have about it [sc. happiness]. For many things appear (*phainetai*) to children and the diseased and the deranged, and no sensible person would concern himself with puzzles about them [. . .]" (1214b 28–31).

The complexities in Aristotle's use of the term "apparent good" stem from his desire to strike a balance between the Socratic and the Protagorean position on truth and appearance in ethical matters. When he comes to formulate his own understanding of virtue, he will repeatedly rely on the two main strands in the concept of the apparent good which he has developed, as I have argued, in the context of his polemics with Socrates and Protagoras. The notion of something that appears good to the non-rational part of the soul— especially when a person has a non-rational desire or passion—will be useful in explaining certain types of akrasia. However, on Aristotle's view there is a continuity between the ways in which the world strikes us as a result of our having non-rational desires and the ways in which the world appears to us in the context of our rational desires. This continuity accounts for the very possibility of ethical upbringing. What above all characterizes an Aristotelian virtuous character is a perfect fit between his non-rational appearances of goodness and his reasoned and reflective judgements about goodness.

Comparing the account of appearance in the ethical works, on the one hand, and the remarks on *phantasia* in *De anima* and *De motu animalium* raises a number of difficulties. For my purposes, what is significant is simply that the relaxed use of "apparent good" which we have identified in the Ethics is matched by the broad scope given to *phantasia* in some passages of *De anima* and *De motu*. At *De motu* 702a 19, we read that *phantasia* "comes about either through thought (*noêsis*) or through perception (*aisthêsis*)." In either case, *phantasia* is "critical"— that is to say, it has to do with *discerning* or *discriminating* activities of the soul.

Here is how the point is made at *De motu* 700b 19–22: "Both appearance (*phantasia*) and perception (*aisthêsis*) occupy the same position as understanding (*nous*); for they are all discerning (*kritika*), though they differ from each other in ways discussed elsewhere." At *De anima* III. 9 432a 15–16 as well, discernment or discrimination is imputed both to thought, *dianoia*, and to perception, *aisthêsis*. In the subsequent chapter, *De anima* III. 10, we find appearance divided into that connected with reasoning or calculation (*phantasia logistikê*) and that connected with perception (*aisthêtikê*) (433b 29); further down at 434a 5–7, perceptual appearance is mentioned along with deliberative appearance (*bouleutikê*).[22]

We have found that the restricted and the relaxed use of *to phainomenon agathon* are roughly matched by the restricted and the relaxed use of *phantasia*.[23] Whereas *phantasia* proper is restricted to the non-rational part of the soul, *phantasia* in the broad sense has to do with how human beings represent the world quite generally.

13. Appearances play an important role in Aristotle's understanding of dialectical procedure. The fact that "apparent goods" figure prominently in his ethics has something to do, I would like to suggest, with the dialectical procedure he follows there. A dialectical procedure starts with *ta phainomena*: "appearances," or more precisely, "things that appear to be the case." Prominent among such appearances are commonly held opinions, and the so-called *endoxa*, rendered accurately even if somewhat clumsily as "reputable opinions." These are often philosophical positions on the issue under consideration.[24] Among the "appearances" one starts with in an ethical theory are opinions and judgements. These will include highly reflective, and especially well-regarded, opinions and judgements. I would like to urge, however, that the relevant appearances also include prereflective or unreflective seemings and judgements.

[22] On the view presented in *De anima* III. 10, *phantasia* is *not* restricted to a separate part of the soul, unlike in the *Eudemian Ethics* vii. 2 1235b 28–29, the passage mentioned in the beginning of this subsection. When Aristotle in the *EE* passage says that appearance (*phantasia*) and belief (*doxa*) are not in the same part of the soul, this non-doxastic *phantasia* could—but need not—correspond to what in *De anima* III. 10 he calls *aisthêtikê phantasia*, perceptual appearance. It cannot, however, correspond to *phantasia bouleutikê* or *logistikê*, deliberative or calculative appearance (433b 29–30 and 434a 5–7), whatever this may turn out to be.

[23] Recall *EE* vii. 2 1235b 26–29: διὸ καὶ τὸ ἡδὺ ὀρεκτόν· φαινόμενον γάρ τι ἀγαθόν τοῖς μὲν γὰρ δοκεῖ τοῖς δὲ φαίνεται κἂν μὴ δοκῇ· οὐ γὰρ ταρ ἐν ταὐτῷ τῆς ψυχῆς ἡ φαντασία καὶ ἡ δόξα. It is not only "apparent good" (φαινόμενον[. . .] ἀγαθόν) that has narrow scope here; the related verb "to appear" (φαίνεται) and the noun "appearance" (φαντασία) have a correspondingly narrow scope as well.

[24] See Aristotle's description of dialectical procedure as dealing with *ta phainomena*, at *EN* VII. 11145b 2–7. On the role of *ta phainomena* in Aristotle's dialectics, see G.E.L. Owen's "*Tithenai ta phainomena*," in *Logic, Science and Dialectic, Collected Papers in Greek Philosophy*, pp. 239–251. On *ta endoxa* as "reputable" opinions, see Jonathan Barnes, "Aristotle and the Methods of Ethics," *Revue Internationale de Philosophie* 34, 1980, pp. 490–511.

We should observe that the expression *ta phainomena* sometimes refers not to what is said, thought, or believed about the matter under consideration, but to observed facts. In *EE* i. 6—another important methodological chapter in the *Eudemian Ethics*, in addition to i. 3, mentioned in § 12—we read: "[. . .] we should not in all cases pay attention to what emerges from arguments (*tois dia tôn logôn*) but often rather to what appears to be the case (*tois phainome-nois*); as things are, whenever they cannot solve a problem, they are forced to put their trust in (*pisteuein*) what has been said (*tois eirêmenois*) [. . .]" (1217a 12–14). The phrase *ta phainomena*, "what appears to be the case", is here contrasted with words or arguments (*hoi logoi*) and with what has been said (*ta eirêmena*), and is best understood as referring to the observed facts of the matter in question.

One can see how this sense of *ta phainomena* might have emerged from *ta phainomena* in what I have above called the restricted sense, namely, from *ta phainomena* as those things which appears to the perceptive part of the soul, when these are contrasted with *ta dokounta*, things that are held or considered to be the case. The emergence of the notion of paying attention to observed facts, as opposed to the arguments advanced by various people, will be of significance in the future development of thought about the proper method of scientific inquiry.

The remarks made thus far about the role of *ta phainomena* in explaining human conduct hold good of *ta phainomena agatha*. An apparent good can be something that is taken or considered to be good. In fact, it can be something that is considered to be good by someone who has spent a great deal of time considering it. However, Aristotle takes the view that all desire is for something that seems good to the person who desires it; hence he takes the objects of both rational and non-rational desires to be *phainomena agatha*.

The appearances relevant for dialectical procedure in ethics go beyond *ta legomena or ta eirêmena*, what has been said on this issue of goodness, or more generally, on the issue of value in action. As we have seen, all goal-oriented actions embody valuations. Such valuations should be among the ethical starting points. In order to find out about values in action, we shall have to turn to observation. Although some of the appearances of goodness embodied in our actions are predoxastic, the results of our observation will not be. The observation we have to carry out will not exclude, but rather especially require, interpretive efforts on the part of the observer.

14.   A non-rational desire carries with it a certain way of seeing the world. An experience of something as good is part of this way of seeing the world. This is not yet for Aristotle objective or unconditional goodness,[25] but it is at

---

[25] On unconditional goods, *ta haplôs agatha*, see *De anima* III. 10 433b 8–10; *EE* vii. 2 1235b 31–1236a 9–10, 1237a 26–27 and 31–33, *EE* viii. 3 (=vii. 15) 1249a 12.

the very least something appealing or attractive. Having the power to attract is an important part of what it is for something to be (non-instrumentally) good. In Aristotle's view, something that had no such power could not possibly be good. Both practical and non-practical goods have such appeal. (See *Metaphysics* XII, especially chapter 7).

Once the notion of an objective good is reached, it is easy to see how something that attracts us need not be good. Pondering about the attraction then comes to be seen as the central component of what it is for something to be good. Desire falls to the side of mere attraction. The view Aristotle takes, however, is that ponderings come after the fact. We find ourselves drawn to things, and we do so because they strike us in a certain way. However much pondering we end up doing, we cannot get around this fact. Primitive seemings of goodness are ineliminable, and reveal something very basic about the way we relate to the world and the world to us.

When Aristotle argues in the *Nicomachean Ethics* that we should not dismiss the view that pleasure is a good, what he relies on is not only that most people believe pleasure to be a good. Another reason why he thinks we should not dismiss this view is that most people *find* what is pleasant good. We all go for pleasure. The respect for appearances that guides Aristotle in his ethics is thus a respect for non-rational seemings as well as for theoretical pronouncements.

For pleasure as an apparent good, we should look at *EE* vii. 2 1235b 18–30. This passage is a discussion of an aporia about what is loved (*to philoumenon*). Is what is loved the pleasant or the good? The broader context here is Aristotle's discussion of different kinds of friendship (*philia*): one kind of friendship is directed at what is pleasant, another at what is good. He designates what is pleasant (*to hedy*) as the object of an appetitive sort of desire: "appetite is of the pleasant" (*EE* vii. 2 1235b 22). (The point is also made at *De anima* III. 3 414b 5–6, *EE* ii. 7 1223a 34 and ii. 8 1224a 37). A few lines down, at *EE* vii. 2 1235b 25–27, we read: "For what is desired and wished for is either the good or the apparent good. That is why the pleasant is desired; for it is some sort of an apparent good (*phainomenon ti agathon*)." The same claim, that the pleasant is an apparent good, is put more straightforwardly at *De motu* 700b 28–29: "And we must suppose that the apparent good occupies the same position as the good, and so does the pleasant, since it is an apparent good."

The appearances of goodness that go along with appetitive desires have, Aristotle believes, a particularly strong hold over us. The fact that we need to remind ourselves that what appears good because pleasant may not in each case be good is testimony to the power which this kind of *phantasia* wields over us. As he observes, "In the many, however, deception (*apatê*) seems to arise because of pleasure, for it appears good when it is not.[26] At any rate, they choose the pleasant as (*hôs*) good, and avoid pain as (*hôs*) bad" (*EN* III. 4

---

[26] Hence the relevance of the use of *to phainomenon agathon* mentioned and set aside in note 20.

1113a 33–1113b 2). The *hôs* construction is often used to express an implicit conception with which one acts. In other words, then, people choose what is pleasant and avoid what is painful implicitly assuming that pleasure is something good, and pain something bad.

In the absence of deliberative excellence, *phantasia* proper carries a considerable potential for deception. Nonetheless, Aristotle's desire to preserve appearances, which ultimately stems from his determination to link his ethics in some way to human nature, enjoins respect for non-rational seemings of goodness and badness.

In embracing the view that non-rational desire is as much a source of human motivation as rational desire, Aristotle rejected the Socratic position on human motivation, following Plato instead. However, Aristotle follows Plato up to a point. Having accepted the Platonic view that there are non-rational sources of motivation as well as rational ones, Aristotle sides with Socrates in holding that everything that is desired is desired as being something good.[27] Socrates took the fact that some things attract us as evidence that we have a positive evaluative judgement or belief—*doxa*—about them. On Aristotle's view, some things have a power to attract us quite independently from reason. The things that so attract us are represented by us in a certain way, and this representation, even if not a judgement, *doxa*, is nonetheless a result of some discernment or discrimination.[28] Representation that is due to such discrimination is what I have called *phantasia* proper. This concept of appearance and the corresponding concept of an apparent good are distinctly Aristotelian. Aristotle thus takes a new line on motivation, different from the positions of both Socrates and Plato.

VI. Telos as the Mover

15.   On Aristotle's view, the telos of an action itself is "the mover" (*to kinoun*). The goal we aim at in action motivates us to act as we do. At *De motu* 700b 23–28, he says: "Hence what moves in the first place is the object of desire and the object of thought (*to orekton kai to dianoêton*); not, however, every object of thought, but the end of things done in action (*to tôn praktôn telos*). So the mover

---

[27] I am assuming here what I take to be the standard reading of Plato's argument for the existence of non-rational desires in Book Four of the *Republic*. On this reading, he argues that non-rational desires as such are not directed at what is good. The argument is notoriously difficult, and I am in fact not convinced that the standard reading is correct. The material outside Book Four of the *Republic* points in a different direction. However, if Plato did think that some kind of valuation is involved in non-rational desire, I find no indication that this would be a *phainomenon agathon* as Aristotle understands this term.

[28] The origin of the motivational pull of the desire and the source of the representation of the object of desire may to some extent be independent.

(*to kinoun*) is a good of this sort,[29] not everything fine (*kalon*). For insofar as something else is done for the sake of this, and insofar as it is an end of things that are for the sake of something else, thus far it moves (*kinei*)."

Aristotle claims here that what moves "in the first place" is the object of desire and the object of thought. He gets to this claim by reducing, at 700b 17–19, the original list of five movers—thought, appearance, choice, wish and appetite: *dianoia, phantasia, prohairesis, boulêsis* and *epithymia*[30]—to two: *nous* and *orexis*, thought and desire. We should recall here his view that thought and desire are "moved movers," whereas the object of thought and the object of desire are "unmoved movers," and that unmoved movers are "prior" to moved movers (*De motu* 700b 35–701a 1; *Met.* XII. 7 1072a 26–27). That is why Aristotle says that what moves "in the first place" is the object of thought or the object of desire.[31] He had already stated, at 700b 18–19, what moves in the second place—namely, thought (*nous*: synonymous with *dianoia*, which was mentioned in the original list) and desire (*orexis*).

We are used to thinking that agents are moved by desire. Aristotle for some reason takes the *object* of desire to be the mover in the primary sense, and desire itself to be a mover only in the second instance. What could be the reason for this?

He seems to start from the interaction one can observe between animals and the environment they live in. Animals move themselves primarily because there is something external to them that they need. When they discern what they need, they tend to go for it. The animal is a self-mover of a sort. It sets itself in motion, however, because of something outside it, which it needs. The object needed is an *unmoved mover.* It is a *mover*, since it is responsible for there being a movement on the part of the animal; it is *unmoved*, since the onset of this movement toward it is not something that affects it. The animal, by contrast, is a moved mover.

Another puzzle is why thought, *nous*, is listed separately from desire, *orexis*, in spite of the fact that the object of thought on Aristotle's view moves only when it is aimed at, thus when it is an object of desire as well as the object of thought.

One reason why Aristotle might be listing thought separately is that he has in mind animal movement, on the one hand, and human action, on the other. A standard case of animal movement occurs when an actual object attracts the animal as something that can satisfy its need, and causes it to set itself in motion. When an external object is absent, and the animal is merely imagining something, the same mechanism appears to be in place. The animal goes for the imagined object, which it feels attracted to. Imagination takes the

---

[29] Omitting τό after διό, with YVb₁P, at line 25.

[30] The list is longer in some manuscripts.

[31] For a discussion of Aristotle's view that the object of desire is the mover of animals, see David Furley's classic essay "Self-Movers," in *Essays on Aristotle's Ethics*, ed. A. O. Rorty, pp. 55–7.

place of perception. With creatures that have a capacity for thought, however, an entirely different mechanism of self-movement comes into being. A human animal can aim at a state of affairs it has thought up, and set in motion a long chain of events in order to bring about what it has thought up. Something new seems to be going on here. Something new also seems to be happening with regard to the goodness of the objects of thought which human beings aim at in action. The goodness of human goals is ultimately not entirely independent of the conception which they have of their goals.

However, Aristotle still considers the object—namely, the noetic object the human being aims at—to be the mover in the primary sense, and *nous*, or thought, the mover in the secondary sense. The object aimed at is still seen as responsible for there being a movement on the part of the human animal. The conceived object is not itself affected by the origination of the movement. It, too, is an unmoved mover.

Aristotle's view seems to be that an object (or state of affairs) moves *by being perceived, imagined, or thought of* in a certain way. It is aimed at and desired *as such*. The fact that something is desired is always connected with how the object is being represented in *phantasia* broadly understood.

De anima III. 10 433b 11–12 supports the view that the object moves by being represented in a certain way: "the most primary mover is the object of desire (*to orekton*); for this moves without itself being moved, by being thought or represented in appearance (*tô(i) noêthênai ê phantasthênai*)." *Phantasthênai* here refers either to perception or to perception-based imagination.

Now Aristotle thinks that the perceived, imagined, or recognized *goodness* of the object desired is causally responsible for self-movement. Given our previous discussion of desire, we shall not find this surprising. Nor shall we find it surprising that the *De motu* passage with which I started this subsection continues (at 700b 28–29) with a statement about the apparent good: "And we must suppose that the apparent good occupies the same position as the good, and so does the pleasant, since it is an apparent good." The animal tends to be drawn to what is in fact good for it without ever having *considered* its goodness; it would not, however, move if it did not represent the thing in question as good. However different thought might be from perception, the same principle holds. An object of thought attracts only when it is represented by *nous* as good.

16.   At *EN* VI. 2 1139a 35–1139b 4, Aristotle says: "But thought as such (*dianoia d' autê*) moves (*kinei*) nothing; what moves is thought that is for the sake of something (*hê heneka tou*) and practical; [. . .] what is *prakton* [as opposed to what is *poiêton*] is the unconditional end, for acting well (*eupraxia*) is the end, and desire is for the end." Leaving aside here the reference to *eupraxia* and to the unconditional end, we can put Aristotle's point in the following way: thought moves by being directed at an end. Only thought that aims at a *telos* is practical, and moves.

When the conception involved in the agent's aiming at a telos is a rational conception, Aristotle can describe that state of affairs in two ways. He can say that the object of thought moves the agent—which amounts to saying that the end moves him, rationally conceived as a good—or, he can say that practical thought (*praktikê dianoia*) moves him. For Aristotle, the two descriptions express two aspects of the same situation. Thought moves insofar as it is involved in a rational conception of the end at which the agent aims. When practical thought or practical reason is said to move the agent, this is not to be understood as saying that reason, *as opposed to desire*, moves him. On Aristotle's view, when the agent is moved by practical reason, he is moved by a desire that has its origin in reason.

Aristotle finds it important to maintain that thought itself is a mover. There would not be much point to saying that thought itself moves if what moved the agent was desire for an object that also happened to be an object of thought. By calling the thought itself a mover, Aristotle emphasizes the causal efficacy of thought. Thought itself moves an agent when it has a certain directionality, namely, when it aims at something. Since thought has the power to move the agent—not in an absence of a desire, but also not in a way that is dependent on a prior existence of a desire—it is counted as a mover in its own right.

VII. Goals, Dispositions, Actualizations

17.   When actions are seen as involving a projection of human purposes into the world, they are seen as instances of *praxis*. The same items are often referred to by Aristotle as *energeiai*, activities. When he speaks of the same things sometimes as *praxeis* and sometimes as *energeiai*, he views them from somewhat different perspectives.

Both *praxis* and *energeia* have their internal, subjective component, but the subjectivity of *energeia* is different from the subjectivity of *praxis*. As instances of *praxis*,[32] actions are linked to some telos, and hence to an appearance involved

---

[32] The scope of this word, and of the related verb *prattein*, to act, exhibits a nesting pattern. Broadly speaking, *praxis* is every goal-directed activity (*EN* I. 1 1094a 5–6), including not only voluntary action from an appetitive or spirited desire (*EN* III. 1 1110b 6–15, and esp. 1111a 24–1111b 3), but clearly also involuntary action (*EN* 1110b 30–1111a 2, and esp. 1111a 15–21). Sometimes, however, *praxis* is restricted to actions stemming from *prohairesis*, choice. This sort of action Aristotle takes to be specifically human, since on his view other animals are not capable of choice (*EN* VI. 2 1139a 17–20, a 31; *EE* ii. 6 1222b 18–20). Third, *praxis* can be used to refer to ethical activity (*EN* VI. 2 1139a 33–35), as opposed to *poiêsis*, productive activity (see *EN* VI. 4, esp. 1140a 1–6, a 16–17, *EN* VI. 5, esp. 1140b 3–4, 6–7; *Politics*, I. 4 1254a 5–7). This is close to the second usage, except that choice here is ethical choice. (It is clear from *EN* VI. 2 1139a 33–34 that the term *prohairesis*, choice, is itself sometimes used to refer to ethical choice.)

in having that telos. As *energeiai*, actions are exercises, and in some sense expressions, of one's capacities (*dynameis*) and of one's states or dispositions (*hexeis*).

In distinguishing *dynameis* and *hexeis* here, I follow the *Nicomachean Ethics* (II. 5 1105b 23–28 and 1106a 6–13) as well as the *Eudemian* (ii. 2 1220b 7–20). The distinction made in the Ethics supplements the general theory of capacities presented in *De anima*. *De anima* II. 5 distinguishes between what might be called bare capacities, namely, capacities one has as a living thing of a certain sort, and developed capacities, which are actualizations of bare capacities, and hence called *first actualizations* (*entelecheiai*). Activities (*energeiai*) are actualizations of developed capacities, and hence *second actualizations*. Since first actualizations involve such things as knowledge (*epistêmê*), which consists of fairly complex dispositions, it is not surprising that ethical *hexeis*, or states of character, count as first actualizations on the scheme one finds in *De anima*. In the ethical writings Aristotle seems to introduce a subdivision within the first actualizations, or developed capacities, of *De anima* into capacities proper— simply called *dynameis* in the *EN* and *EE*—and dispositions or states, *hexeis*. Among the states are the complex dispositions to act and feel in certain characteristic ways which constitute one's character (*êthos*). These are naturally of special interest to ethics.

The immediate point of contact between Aristotle's concept of telos and the *hexis/energeia* pair lies in the fact that dispositions that go to define a person's character are dispositions to pursue ends of a particular kind. At *EE* ii. 11 1228a 2–3, a person's character, which is a set of *hexeis*, is expressly linked with the ends the person pursues: "[. . .] it is from his choice that we judge what sort of person he is; that is, from that-for-the-sake-of-which he does something, not from what he does." People of different character have different ends, and are distinguished precisely by the sorts of ends they tend to pursue in life. Since an end is identified through the conception the agent has when he aims at it, and such a conception presupposes that he sees the circumstances of his action in a certain way, the virtuous and the vicious will be distinguished as much by their goals as by their distinctive vision of the world.

18.   A question comes to mind here concerning the purpose of Aristotle's concept of *hexis*. If we are interested in understanding and explaining actions, why bother with *hexeis*, states or dispositions, at all? If we grasp clearly what the telos of an action is, including the relevant background information— how the agent sees the circumstances of the action, what feelings the situation brings forth in him, in general, what motivates him to act as he does on the particular occasion—why ask in addition how he *tends* to see things, feel or act, or how he *habitually* perceives things, feels or acts? In dwelling on the dispositions that are supposed to be "exercised" or "expressed" in actions, are we not just getting some more of the same?

It would seem that by bringing into the picture the *hexis* a given action expresses, in addition to its telos, one particularizes the action. By learning more about the agent's dispositions that bear on the action, one can often distinguish that action from other actions similar to it either externally or with regard to its telos. Yet the concept of *hexis* also brings in an element of generality on a different side. The generality involved concerns the subjectivity of the agent. By looking into those of the person's states that are relevant to his action, we can learn, for instance, how the person responds to difficult or demanding situations, what the scope is of his interests or passions, how certain affects pervade his life and influence his actions. Having placed the action in a broader context of this sort, we might come to see the action in a new and more revealing light.

Clearly, this sort of explanation is not called for by every "Why did he do it?" question. It is not necessary to explain, usually, why a man took an umbrella with him on a rainy day. What is interesting about Aristotle's approach to action lies precisely in the fact that he attempts to define a standpoint from which the need for the explanation of actions in terms of the states of the sort described arises. This standpoint, which he labels "ethical," pushes the desire to explain actions in a new direction.

The ethical interest in action is not exhausted when the telos of an action is identified. A preliminary identification of the telos sets the stage for further questions, such as: what motivates the agent's interest in that particular telos? what other ends does the given telos serve? what role does the telos play in the agent's life? Thus, an interest in states of character does not stem from a desire to explain φ-ing by a disposition to φ. The operative concern here is to place the telos of an action into a larger motivational structure, with a view ultimately to understanding what kind of life the action in question is a part of. Socrates' question looms behind it: our concern with how people live is driven in part by our interest in the question how it is best for us to live.

19.   That each human being has a life to live is, on Aristotle's view, the hardest metaphysical and ethical fact about human beings. Since life itself is activity, *energeia* (see, for instance, *EN* X. 4 1175a 12), activity is essential to the human condition. Moreover, there is a sense in which it is appropriate to say that for Aristotle the human being *is* the life he leads. Human beings are, of course, living *things*. They are a certain kind of substance: bodily substances that are, necessarily, ensouled. But the human being is in some sense his form, and his form is fully what it is when it is actuality and activity rather than potentiality. In this sense, human beings *are* the life they live.

The emphasis that Socrates put on the soul as the person's most precious possession is, Aristotle believes, misplaced. This is so not only, or not primarily, because in Aristotle's view the soul is essentially related to the body; the emphasis on the soul as the most prizeworthy possession is misplaced because the point of the capacities and dispositions which in large part make up a person's soul is their exercise.

This thought—although there is some difficulty in identifying its precise status[33]—intuitively makes sense. A capacity for seeing would be wasted if for some reason it was never exercised. Virtue, as a *hexis*, would be wasted if it never led to a virtuous action. (The same, of course, holds of vice.) Aristotle expresses this thought by saying that actualizations are prior to potentialities.[34] He also claims that actualizations are better than potentialities, which in this instance means that, if the point of the soul is to make us live (*EE* ii. 1 1219a 24), then in some sense life matters more than the soul. Likewise for the relationship between the good life and that which, when exercised, leads to it, namely, virtue: the point of virtue is its exercise (see, for instance, *EE* ii. 1 1218b 37–1219a 9 and ii. 11 1228a 13–14). Hence, contrary to Socrates— or perhaps, contrary to Socrates as Aristotle understood him—human life matters more, and is a more prizeworthy possession, than the human soul alone.

Someone who thinks that the soul is the person's most precious possession would probably not agree with Aristotle that the whole point of the soul is to make us live, even if he agrees that the soul is that which makes us live. Plato's Socrates does appear to take the extreme view, at times at least, that the condition of the soul is the only thing that matters. If this were so, it would follow that a person cannot be harmed by any hostile action or any adverse external circumstances as long as he preserves the good condition of his soul. (Recall Socrates' claim in the *Apology* that his accusers cannot harm him in any way—*Apol.*, 30c.)

It is highly unlikely that Socrates failed to realize what the commonly held view on the matter was, although Aristotle may be right in thinking that he failed to appreciate it. If, however, the commonly held beliefs should be taken seriously,[35] Aristotle's view that life matters more than the soul comes off better than the view that attributes pre-eminent importance to the condition of the soul as such. Whether this view is truly Socratic is a question I shall leave on one side. Aristotle no doubt took Socrates to be ascribing pre-eminent importance simply to the internal condition of one's soul, regardless of whether this state gives rise to any actions.

---

[33] The difficulty is the following. Aristotle's claim that actualizations are "prior to" and "better than" potentialities is both a metaphysical and an ethical claim. As an ethical claim, it is supported by certain commonly held views and, Aristotle argues, some common evaluative practices. See *EN* I. 12 1101b 31–34, *EE* ii. 1 1219b 8–16 and ii. 11 1228a 11–18. As a metaphysical claim, this statement needs further explication and support. For the texts, see next note.

[34] He may also express other thoughts by saying this. For different senses in which actualization or actuality (ἐνέργεια) is said to be prior to potentiality (δύναμις), see *Met.* IX. 8. For the claim that actuality is better than potentiality, see *Met.* IX. 9.

[35] A point Socrates himself would not grant.

20. The importance Aristotle attaches to *energeia* in his ethics might give the impression that for him the condition of being active, of exercising one's capacities and dispositions, is what matters in life. However, looking at his overall position, it seems clear that he wants to strike a balance between two different views of what makes for the good life. On the first view, being active in the right way, by aiming at the correct ends, is what matters. On the competing view, whether a person lives well or not is a function of what he accomplishes in life. If one's properly directed actions yield no accomplishment, they do not contribute to the good life. Both views have a strong Aristotelian flavour. The former view emphasizes Aristotle's concept of *energeia*, and telos seen as a projected goal. The latter lays heavy weight on the accomplished end rather than a merely projected end of action.

There can be no doubt that Aristotle is attracted to both positions, and wants to strike a balance between them. The interesting question is how precisely he achieves the balance. When he says of eudaimonia: *zôê gar poia tis estin*, "it is a certain sort of life" (*Met.* IX. 8 1050b 1–2), how is this *poia tis*— "a certain sort of"—to be understood? Which aspects of life matter for that felicitous form of living Aristotle calls eudaimonia?

In order to outline the solution he gives to the dilemma just sketched, I shall help myself to a notion he did not himself articulate. On his view a full-blown activity that misses its mark—does not attain its telos—counts as an actualization of the relevant capacities and dispositions just as much as the corresponding activity which does hit the mark. On the *De anima* scheme, both activities are second actualizations. By a "full-blown" activity, I mean one that is not aborted from the outset, thus one that involves aiming in a definite direction, and also goes some way toward attaining its goal, whether or not it ultimately attains it. An activity that is not only full-blown, but also achieves its goal, is what I shall refer to as a *third actualization* or *third entelechy*.

If human life is *praxis*, as Aristotle claims,[36] and *praxis* is fully successful only when it achieves its telos, successful living requires that a reasonable number of the ends one pursues in action be achieved. Aristotle does not simply rely on the assumption that under normal circumstances ethically correct aiming will tend to be realized. In his view, successful ethical life requires achievement.

---

[36] *Politics*, I. 4 1254a 7–8: "But life is action (πρᾶξις), not production (ποίησις), hence the slave is a minister of things that contribute to action (ὑπηρέτης τῶν πρὸς τὴν πρᾶξιν)." The passage discusses what sort of instrument the slave is—the allegedly natural sort of slave. The point seems to be that although human life contains productive activities, on an overall view of what human life is, it is more properly described as action, πρᾶξις. Perhaps the comforting thought here is that the "natural slave" is an instrument in the mode of life that is most specifically human.

The terminology I have adopted here is in keeping with his general under-standing of *entelecheia* as something that involves a realization of a telos. The whole point of aiming is to hit the target one is aiming at. An activity that is essentially directed at the achievement of something cannot hit its mark un-less that achievement is reached.

This understanding of what is required for the good life fits well with an in-teresting picture Aristotle paints of human activities in *Nicomachean Ethics* X. 4 (1174b 14–1175a 2). While discussing pleasure, he introduces the concept of a complete activity. A complete activity (*teleia energeia*) is an exercise of the subject in the best condition directed at the best sort of object relative to the capacity exercised (1174b 18–19). The object referred to can be either an object of perception or an object of thought, so the activity could be either perceptive or intellectual (1174b 34). The term *teleia*, as used here, carries a strong connotation of perfection. These complete or perfect activities, Aris-totle says, are accompanied by pleasure, in fact by such pleasure as one would expect to find only in a fully happy, *eudaimôn*, life (1174b 20 and 21–22).

If a complete activity involves third actualization, we can see why Aristo-tle assumes that at least those complete or perfect activities that are actions, *praxeis*, are accompanied by pleasure. The telos of a person's action is an ob-ject of desire. Attaining the telos normally involves a satisfaction of the desire that motivates the action, and such a satisfaction usually involves pleasure.

Activities of perception, *aisthêsis*, and of thinking or "intellection," *noêsis*, have to be related in an appropriate way to actual, existing objects or states of affairs, to count as perception or intellection at all. A successful completion of these activities requires that they reveal something about the world. That the successful completion of such activities is accompanied by pleasure is some-thing that Aristotle seems to think depends on our being animals of a certain sort. A human being is such as to exercise perception and intellection, and to find pleasure in that exercise. Although pleasure in any given goal-directed action, and in any given perceptive or intellectual activity, may prove elusive, on the whole human beings will find pleasure in the successful exercise of ca-pacities and dispositions that characterize their kind.

The picture that emerges from *EN* X. 4 is that human beings aim at some sort of alignment with the world. The world of subjectivity, of *phantasia*, is an attempt to make out what the world is like, and to get attuned to it. The plea-sure that accompanies the properly attuned activities could be regarded as ev-idence that this alignment is what human beings by nature strive for.[37]

[37] If *EN* X. 4 can be seen as offering a model of the happy life, such a life is certainly understood very broadly. Complete or perfect activities are not restricted to actions of the ethical sort. Ex-cellent exercises of both practical and theoretical intellect matter for eudaimonia. Perceiving is a part of the good life as well. Just as it matters to us to hit upon the truth in theoretical and practical activities, so it matters to us that our perceptions relate in an appropriate way to an

21.   In the broad sense of *praxis* discussed thus far, *theôria*, contemplation or speculation, is an instance of *praxis* (cp. *Politics* VII. 3). When the focus of *praxis* is narrowed down to such realizations of human purposes as involve an actual change in the spatio-temporal world (*kinêsis*) brought about by the agent, the concept of *praxis* becomes opposed to that of *theôria*. It is at this level, which we may call the level of *praxis* proper, that we encounter the specifically ethical interest in human beings seen not only as essentially embodied but also as essentially leading some kind of social existence.[38]

Theôria, contemplation or speculation, is also an activity, although an activity of the sort that does not in itself involve kinetic change. The structure of aiming characteristic of *praxis* in the broad sense is present in theoretical activity as well. *Theôria* is concerned with the world no less than *praxis* is; the main difference between the two does not so much lie in the segment of the world that is the proper concern of each of them (although *theôria* may be concerned with the part of the world not accessible to *praxis*, as astronomy was), but in the sort of interest in the world which each of the two types of activity takes.

When the most abstract of theoretical disciplines, metaphysics, comes to be concerned with something that is no longer a part of the world in the proper sense—namely, when it comes to be concerned with the prime mover—it is driven there by its understanding of the world, namely, an understanding that the world could not be what it is without such a "point" outside it.[39] Thus, *theôria* is ultimately distinguished from *praxis* proper by

---

actual, existing, object. I shall leave it open here whether this is Aristotle's last word on the content of the good human life. Book X of the *Nicomachean Ethics* is itself apparently in tension, presenting in places the theoretical type of life as the best possible life, and relegating other "perfect" activities to a secondary place. A tendency toward giving a very broad picture of what is involved in human happiness is certainly one strand in Aristotle's ethical thinking.

[38] The sense of "essentially" in the two occurrences may not be the same. The first sense is metaphysical; the second depends on how one interprets the famous description of human beings as "political animals" in the *History of Animals* (I. 1 488a 7–10), *Nicomachean Ethics* (I. 2 1097b 6–11, VIII. 12 1162a 16–19, and IX. 9 1169b 16–19) and *Politics* (I. 2 1253a 1–9).

[39] It is instructive to compare Aristotle's position on what is outside the world with that of Kant. The crucial difference between the two is that the Kantian point-outside-the-world, the noumenon, is a precondition of our understanding of the world, while the prime mover is a precondition of the world itself, as we understand it. However, Aristotle's conception of the prime mover seems to me to be in one important respect more similar to Kant's understanding of the noumenal than one might think. Precisely because the noumenal for Kant is a precondition of our knowledge of anything that can be known, it is in principle something that cannot be known. Aristotle is not driven to this harsh consequence. The prime mover is not in principle unknowable, but what is known about it is in fact very limited, since there is no readily available point of view from which one can gain informative knowledge of the prime mover. The prime mover is grasped by the faculty for abstract reasoning, *nous*; thus the prime mover is a

the nature of the aims that guide it, and by a distinctive conception of its own goals.

22. Ethical correctness requires that the agent aim at the right sorts of ends, and that his actions express the right kind of dispositions. In committing himself to this view, Aristotle took Socrates' lead. In deploying, implicitly, the notion of third actualization, Aristotle took a new step. The notion of third actualization is a notion of success of a particular sort. To think that third actualization is required for the goodness of life is to think that realizing one's objectives in action, whether practically or theoretically oriented, is an essential part of the happy life.

In the jargon of our time, Aristotle's ethics is a "virtue ethics." However, what is distinctive about his own position, when seen in the context of ancient ethical theorizing, is not so much the emphasis he placed on moral character, as the emphasis he placed on accomplishment. It is quite likely that the almost unprecedented role Aristotle assigned to the achievement of one's goals in his ethics[40] is linked both to his acknowledgment of widely shared Greek views about this matter, and to the powerful hold he thought the other

---

noêton, an object of abstract reasoning (a noumenon in fact, although that is not what Aristotle calls it). What Aristotle takes to be known about it is reached mostly by negative reasoning: since it has to be a source of movement without being moved itself, the unmoved mover has to move in the way an object of thought (*to noêton*) moves, and this moves by being aimed at. However exactly the conclusion is reached that the prime mover is the noetic activity directed at itself, *noêsis* which is a *noêsis noêseôs*, our grasp of what this is is derived from our ability, as beings who have *nous*, abstractly and reflectively to grasp what our own noetic activity involves. Anything more specific than this—and perhaps even this—forces one to rely on an analogy with our own noetic activity, and has no good claim to being knowledge. Thus with regard to the issue of the limits on our knowledge of what is outside the world, Aristotle and Kant stand closer to one another than one might think; they both think that our knowledge is limited because of a lack of a point of view from which the pure noumenon or *noêton*, the object of pure thinking, can be accessed. However, with regard to the relationship our practical activity bears to that which is outside the world, the difference between the two is profound. As Aristotelian ethical agents, we originate kinetic change in the world. The fact that for Aristotle our causal intervention in the world is guided by our goal-directed activity, and that human activity essentially involves rational self-determination of some sort, is not to be construed as involving the claim that we, as ethical agents, belong to the noumenal world. On his view, if we do get close to that which is outside the world, it is as theoretical, not practical, agents. Kant's position on this is precisely the opposite. However, if my observations above about the relationship of our own noetic activity and (that of) the prime mover in Aristotle are correct, we might in our theoretical activity get close to the prime mover, but we are hardly in touch with it. When engaging in theoretic activity we might be like the god—this is one of the points strongly conveyed by Book X of the *Nicomachean Ethics*—but what we know of the god is severely limited.

[40] Unprecedented in Greek philosophical thought (see, however, next paragraph), while quite common in Greek popular thinking.

type of non-rational desire—*thymos*, or spirit—has over us. This type of desire strives after honour or glory, in the sense of being highly regarded by others. It also strives after accomplishment.

I have argued that Aristotle thought we should start in ethics not only with views and opinions of experts and common folk on values, but also with the values embodied in action. Some of the values in action represent the standpoint of our non-rational strivings and passions. Aristotle gave these strivings and passions theoretical authority. His view was not simply that we should give sufficient room to the satisfaction of non-rational desires and passions within the framework imposed by reason. When he came to consider the question of what shape human life as a whole should take, the answer he gave itself reflected the standpoint of appetite and spirit.

Accordingly honour and glory—banned by Socrates—return to the stage in Aristotle's ethics. Although he considers the respect of others too "superficial" to count as the human good all by itself (*EN* I. 5 1095b 22–26), Aristotle acknowledges its claim on human happiness. If he inherited a respect for what others think about matters of value, and about us, from anyone, it is most likely Protagoras. We know too little about Protagoras' views to be certain that Aristotle is following him here,[41] but what we do know points strongly in his direction. It was left to Aristotle to embed Protagorean insights into a metaphysical framework of his own.

---

[41] The picture we get of Protagoras from the Platonic dialogue named after him is of an ethics that gave pride of place to accomplishment and the respect of others.

Six ～

Deliberation and Choice in Aristotle

There was no obvious questioning, nor figurings, nor diagrams. There was, apparently, no considered loopholes. It appeared that the swift wings of their desires would have shattered against the iron gates of the impossible.
—Stephen Crane, *The Red Badge of Courage*, London & Glasgow: Collins Clear-Type Press, nd, p. 222–3

1. What Is Deliberation?

Our understanding of what deliberation (*bouleusis*) is for Aristotle should start from his remarks about *euboulia*, the virtue of deliberating well. For that is deliberation at its best.

At *EN* VI. 7 1141b 12–14 he characterizes the unconditionally good deliberator, *ho haplôs euboulos,* as "the person who is capable of aiming (*stochastikos*) in accordance with calculation (*kata ton logismon*) at what is the best for a human being of things pursued in action."[1] This characterization very nearly sums up Aristotle's understanding of practical wisdom, *phronêsis,* the overarching virtue of practical intellect. He makes the point himself, by way of preface to the characterization of the good deliberator just quoted. He says: "we say that deliberating well (*to eu bouleuesthai*) is above all the *ergon* of the practically wise person" (1141b 9–10). An account of some things is to be sought in the work they do. Aristotle uses the term *ergon* to capture the kind of activity that defines a thing of this sort. (Thus he attempts to specify what makes human beings the beings they are in his *ergon* argument at *EN* I. 7.) The *ergon* of a thing is best characterized as what the thing does that makes it what it is. Accordingly, to specify the practically wise person's *ergon* is to spell out precisely what makes him practically wise. To say that deliberating well is above all the *ergon* of the practically wise person is to say that what makes a person practically wise is, beyond all else, the person's *euboulia,* deliberative excellence.

---

[1] *Logismos,* calculation, as Aristotle uses it here, looks to be a near synonym for *bouleusis,* deliberation. See *EN* VI. 1 1139a 12–3: "Deliberation (*to bouleuesthai*) and calculation (*logizesthai*) are the same."

That deliberative excellence is a defining feature of practical wisdom is a point Aristotle makes more than once. At *EN* VI. 5 1140a 25–8, he notes: "It is thought to be a mark of a person of practical wisdom to be able to deliberate well about what is good and expedient for himself, not in some particular respect, e.g. about what sorts of thing conduce to health or to strength, but about what sorts of thing conduce to the good life in general." And a little bit further on, at 1140a 30–1: "It follows that in general the person who is good at deliberating (*ho bouleutikos*) is practically wise."[2]

A virtue for Aristotle is always something *idion*, specific or proper to the activity of which it is a virtue. *Euboulia* is what makes one good at deliberation—it is that activity's "proper" virtue. If *bouleusis*, deliberation, were thought of as a process of reasoning in the narrow sense—going through the steps of an argument, whether deductive or inductive, or working out by which means to attain a goal—then *euboulia*, as its proper virtue, could not consist in aiming at the right goal, or a tendency to aim at the right goal,[3] in accordance with reasoning or calculation. Rather, it would consist in being good at reasoning or calculating in a narrower sense. A good deliberator would be someone who produces good inferences, which can serve him well in the pursuit of whatever goal he has.

The characterization of the good deliberator given at *EN* VI. 7 is reinforced by the account of deliberative excellence at *EN* VI. 9, the chapter that specifically deals with this virtue. At VI. 9 1142b 21–22 *euboulia* is described, and in fact defined, as correctness of deliberation (*boulê*) which achieves a good (*hê agathou teuktikê*), or which tends to achieve a good ("tending to achieve" is a possible, and, I think, the intended meaning of *teuktikê*). A reliable tendency to achieve the end requires aiming in the right direction, and more. One's conception of the end has to be correct, and the steps one takes in an attempt to attain the end must be the right steps. The characterization of *euboulia* in terms of a tendency to achieve the end is therefore more demanding than the characterization given at 1141b 12–14, where this virtue is taken to be responsible only for the correct aiming.

Given the account of deliberative excellence in VI. 9, it is not surprising that this excellence is regarded as a definitive mark of practical wisdom. Someone whose use of his reason reliably enables him to aim at, and attain, the best life for a human being is someone who uses his reason as well as reason can be used for practical purposes. The two characterizations together make it clear that correctness of deliberation demands directedness at the right goal, not just formally correct reasoning in pursuit of an independently given goal.[4]

---

[2] See also VI. 9 1142b 31–32: "since, then, deliberating well is a mark of people of practical wisdom [. . .]."

[3] *Stochastikos* can have either meaning.

[4] A widely used translation of the *Nicomachean Ethics* renders the first two passages quoted above on deliberative excellence in a way that entirely obscures the point I have been attempting to

The characterization of *euboulia* as a tendency to achieve the right goal appears in the context of a very careful examination of what sort of correctness is involved in deliberative excellence (1142b 8ff.). A good deliberator could not be someone who tends to achieve the goal if he were not good at reasoning, especially of the means-end sort. At 1142b 22–26 Aristotle mentions the need to reach the right goal through a correct inference, noting that reaching the right end through a wrong inference (*pseudê syllogismô(i)*) is "not yet" *euboulia*. The remark shows that Aristotle, even as he makes the point that producing correct inferences is necessary for deliberative excellence, is not tempted to identify this virtue with an inferential skill.

The good deliberator, as someone who aims at, and tends to attain, the right goal by making correct choices, is someone who is good at effectively directing his desiring, and more specifically his aiming in action, toward goals that he chooses as ways of living a good life. What he is good at—deliberation—is not simply reasoning in the service of a practical goal, but an effective determination of desire toward the right goal by means of reasoning.

bring out. In Terence Irwin's translation, 1141b 9–10 reads: "deliberating well is the function of the intelligent [i.e. practically wise] person more than anyone else." However, *malista*, "above all," undoubtedly modifies *ergon*, "the function." The meaning is that deliberating well characterizes the practically wise person more than anything else does [characterize him]. It would be extremely awkward for Aristotle to point out that deliberating well is a function of the practically wise person *more than of anyone else*. ("Anyone else" is not in the Greek; it is added by Irwin.) The practically wise person is an embodiment of the ideal practical use of reason, so it goes without saying that he is a better deliberator than anyone else. What does not go without saying is that excellence in deliberation is more than anything else a definitive mark of a practically wise person, namely, that it defines the excellent use of practical reason which makes for practical wisdom. As I already pointed out, this reading is supported elsewhere, for instance, by 1140a 25–8. The characterization of the unconditional *euboulos* at 1141b 12–14 reads in Irwin's rendition as follows: "the unconditionally good deliberator is the one whose aim expresses rational calculation in pursuit of the best good for a human being that is achievable in action." The central claim that the good deliberator is *ho stochastikos*—the one who is *capable of aiming*, or the one who *aims* at the best goal for human beings—has been lost here. Irwin's translation steers us toward the view that the excellent use of reason consists in calculation. This fits Irwin's rather narrow understanding of deliberation in Aristotle. See his *Aristotle's First Principles*, Clarendon Press, Oxford 1988, and especially "Some Rational Aspects of Incontinence," *The Southern Journal of Philosophy*, vol. XXVII, 1989, Supplement, pp. 49–88. Both translations, however, are far from the Greek. (The translation of 1141b 12–14 is otherwise not felicitous: it is not a prerogative of a good deliberator that his aim expresses rational calculation in pursuit of eudamonia. The bad deliberator's aim might be expressive of his (bad) rational calculation in pursuit of eudaimonia just as well.)

A puzzle concerning the relationship between deliberation and virtue of character points toward the same understanding of deliberation. The puzzle is the following. All virtuous actions are in Aristotle's view chosen, and therefore result from deliberation. (He defines choice as what is determined by deliberation at *EN* III. 2 1112a 15). Yet if by "deliberation" we understand a process of explicit reasoning or calculation, of the means-end or some other sort, it is simply not reasonable to claim that all virtuous actions are done after deliberation. This is so even if we allow for the possibility that the relevant piece of reasoning was carried out quite some time before the action.[5] Many virtuous actions are not deliberated in the usual sense of this word. Courageous actions come to mind, but virtue more generally seems not to require, or sometimes even permit, calculation. Aristotle would have recognized this more than anyone else. His insistence that we become, say, just by doing just actions indicates that it is not an excogitated action that counts as virtuous, but one that stems from one's properly formed emotional and desiderative propensities. In some cases immediacy of response may be a distinguishing mark of a courageous, or otherwise virtuous, person. To assume in such cases that deliberation must have been carried through some time before the action seems like an attempt to save at any cost Aristotle's view that virtuous actions are chosen.

The view that virtuous actions involve choice, and therefore deliberation, is not detachable from Aristotle's understanding of virtue. He builds it into the definition of virtue. On one reading, the famous definition of virtue of character at *EN* II. 6 1106b 36–1107a 2 states: "Virtue, then, is a state having to do with choice (*hexis prohairetikê*), lying in the mean which is relative to us and which is determined by reason, such reason by which the practically wise person would determine it."[6] This definition has been variously interpreted. The precise sense in which the ethical *hexis* is related to choice has been a matter of debate. Virtue could be a state concerned with choice, a state which chooses, a state formed as a result of choice, etc. Virtue of character is in fact connected with choice in more than one way, and the difficulty lies in determining which connection Aristotle has in mind when he defines virtue of character. It seems most likely that virtue is defined as a prohairetic state in the sense that it is a disposition to make correct choices. These choices are determined by reason, and the determination is of the sort the person of practical wisdom would make.

---

[5] As John M. Cooper has plausibly argued. See his *Reason and Human Good in Aristotle*, Harvard University Press, Cambridge, Mass. & London 1975 (repr. Hackett, Indianapolis 1986), especially pp. 7–8.

[6] Reading Bywater's text: ὡρισμένῃ λόγῳ καὶ ᾧ ἂν ὁ φρόνιμος ὁρίσειεν at 1107a 1–2. ᾧ is Aspasius' reading; the manuscripts have ὡς.

The practically wise person—defined as he is above all by his deliberative use of reason—figures in the very definition of virtue of character.[7] The reason for this is that ethical virtues—courage, moderation, or gentleness, for instance—are all without exception deliberative virtues. Each involves a capacity to use reason to reach the right choice in a certain well-defined range of circumstances—too well defined, perhaps, for Aristotle seems anxious to combat the Socratic tendency to construe particular virtues in the broadest terms possible. Socrates wanted each virtue to expand to fill the whole field of virtuous action, since he was convinced that there was only one thing properly called virtue.[8] For Aristotle, the well-delimited circumstances pertaining to each particular virtue naturally provoke a definite range of desiderative or emotional responses: fear, appetitive desire, or anger, in the case of the three virtues mentioned. An agent's response to such specific circumstances is virtuous only if the resultant action is motivated by desires and passions that not only are moderate, but whose moderateness has been shaped by their reasoned outlook on life. The training of emotions that qualifies one as a brave, temperate, or gentle person essentially involves a training of the intellect. The standard of what counts as moderate is set by reason. Aristotle was therefore firmly convinced that all ethical virtue involves rational judgment. Virtue of character not only requires, but—being a disposition to choose correctly—directly embodies the excellence in deliberation that is the defining characteristic of the practically wise person.

The admitted difficulties, however, in reconciling Aristotle's view that all virtuous action is chosen, and therefore deliberated, with the fact that many virtuous actions are not excogitated have prompted the suggestion that deliberation in some cases be regarded hypothetically—not as an actual process of arriving at a choice, but rather as a theoretical device deployed for the purpose of explaining or justifying actions. Even when a moral choice has not been reached by explicit calculation—as so often seems to happen—we can, it is suggested, *regard* it as deliberated, since the person's reasons for acting will, when produced, constitute a deliberative argument in favor of the choice made. Deliberation could be said to lie behind every virtuous action in a hypothetical guise. If the agent acted on *reasons*, it is *as if* he had deliberated in accordance with a practical argument that spells out those reasons.[9]

As a view about application of practical arguments to actions, the hypothetical approach is a highly reasonable. Yet it cannot be the correct view of

---

[7] Some of Aristotle's thinking behind the view that the practically wise person is the standard of correctness of ethical judgement is discussed in Section 5 below.

[8] See Plato's *Laches* and *Protagoras* for a Socratic analysis of courage, the *Charmides* for an analysis of moderation, and the *Protagoras* for the view that virtue is one and indivisible.

[9] Cooper, pp. 9–10.

Aristotelian deliberation. The remarks that follow are meant to show that we need to draw a clear line between practical arguments and deliberation.

Actions resulting from deliberation are not the only ones that can be represented by practical arguments. A person motivated by a non-rational desire, either appetitive or spirited,[10] acts for reasons. These reasons can be set out in a form of a practical argument. Aristotle does so himself. In his account of weakness of will in *EN* VII. 3, he mentions two practical arguments, which result in a weak-willed action of eating something sweet. The premisses of one of these arguments are: "Everything sweet is pleasant," and "This is sweet" (1147a 32–3). The other argument's universal premiss, which goes unheeded, "forbids tasting" (1147a 32). Aristotle does not want us to imagine that the weak-willed agent is assailed by the thought expressed in his conveniently provided universal premiss, "Everything sweet is pleasant." The akratic need not have reasoned from this thought, combining it with the observation that the piece of cake in front of him is sweet to reach the conclusion that this piece of cake is pleasant, and should therefore be tasted (see the other helpfully provided premiss "Everything sweet should be tasted," at 1147a 29). The premisses "Everything sweet is pleasant" and "This is sweet" (as well as "Everything sweet should be tasted") are simply a way of expressing in words the standpoint of the appetitive desire that here motivates the weak-willed action. The awkwardness of the verbal expression of the appetitive impulse comes as no surprise.

Since on Aristotle's view a non-rational desire carries with it an appearance of goodness—namely, a valuation of the object of desire as good—the premiss of a practical argument representing the desired object as good (or more specifically, pleasant, in the case of an appetitive desire) can be used with full propriety to represent the non-rational desiderative motivation that prompted the action. None the less, the akratic actions so represented by practical arguments typically do not stem from deliberation. Even someone who did not make the assumption that desire involves valuation could quite legitimately use practical arguments to represent in quasi-deliberative form the agent's reasons for action.

If one therefore permits deliberation in a hypothetical guise in order to secure the link Aristotle envisages between deliberation and virtue, one will have permitted too much. Weak-willed actions, which stem from a breakdown of practical rationality, will count as deliberated. The point of linking virtue with deliberation and choice will have been lost.

A practical argument is a theoretical device for explaining or justifying actions; deliberation is not. Aristotle defines deliberation as a *zêtêsis*, a search or an inquiry (with considerable insistence: *EN* VI. 9 1142a 31–32, a 34, b 2,

---

[10] Appetite (*epithymia*) and spirit (*thymos*) are for Aristotle two types of non-rational desire. In recognizing these desires, he follows Plato, and especially the *Republic*.

b 14, b 15), or a *skepsis*,[11] an investigation, of some sort—which, when successfully completed, results in a choice (*prohairesis*). He takes this characterization of deliberation seriously. The difficult task of course (valiantly tackled in VI. 9) is to explain what kind of search or inquiry deliberation is. But whatever kind of inquiry or search it should turn out to be, it is an actual process of arriving at a choice.[12] It is, moreover, part of Aristotle's account of choice that it is a desire of some sort which is causally explained by deliberation.[13] This could not be so if deliberation were not something actual—an actual process, or activity, of some sort. Deliberation must therefore be understood straightforwardly as the process of arriving at a choice, and not be regarded in a hypothetical guise.

In the light of this, we must distinguish between practical arguments and deliberation. When an action is deliberated, and a practical argument is used to explain it, the two will of course be closely linked. The premises of the argument should in some form capture the content of the reasoning, whether implicit or explicit, that motivates the agent to act as he does. This should be so at any rate if the practical argument is accurately to reflect the considerations that move the agent to act as he does. However, practical arguments extend further than deliberation and choice. Actions that are not chosen—in the sense of stemming from *prohairesis*—are no less susceptible than chosen actions to representation by a practical argument.

Scholarly discussion about practical reason in Aristotle was for a long time focused on the so-called "practical syllogism." Even a cursory reading of Aristotle's ethical treatises, however, strongly indicates that his discussion of practical reason centers on deliberation rather than practical argument.[14] The expression "practical syllogisms" occurs at most once. As used by Aristotle, the term *syllogismos* does not refer to a syllogism, but more broadly to a deductive

[11] *Skepsis*, which means primarily looking into some matter, is used in this context especially in the *Eudemian Ethics*. For *skepsis*, see *EE* ii. 10 1226b 8, 1227a 12. For the relevant usages of the related verb *skopein*, see *EE* ii. 10 1226b1 and ii. 11 1227b26; also *EN* III. 3 1112b 16.

[12] Cooper is well aware that deliberation is described by Aristotle as an actual process of arriving at a choice, and he often treats it as such. In taking it sometimes as a hypothetical device, he offers a reasonable solution to the conflict created by Aristotle's insistence that virtuous action is chosen and his considered views about virtuous action as not requiring explicit calculation. However, deliberation is never regarded by Aristotle hypothetically. Whereas Cooper's solution works for practical arguments, it does not help us to understand *bouleusis*.

[13] See *EE* ii. 10 1226b 19–20, and the discussion of choice in Section 4 below.

[14] The centrality of deliberation in Aristotle's ethics has been fully recognized by David Wiggins: see "Deliberation and Practical Reason" in his *Needs, Values, Truth*, 2nd edition, Blackwell, Oxford and Cambridge, Mass. 1991, pp. 215–237 [originally in a different form in *Proceedings of the Aristotelian Society*, 76 (1975–76), pp. 29–51], and "Weakness of Will, Commensurability and the Objects of Deliberation and Desire," in *Needs, Values, Truth*, pp. 239–267 [originally in *Proceedings of the Aristotelian Society*, 79 (1978–79), pp. 251–277].

inference. In the practical context, *syllogismos* may well be used in a non-technical sense, as a counterpart to the verb *syllogizesthai*, which can refer broadly to putting things together, or reaching a conclusion, by means of reason, but not necessarily by deductive inference. Moreover, in the passage that allegedly uses the term "practical syllogisms," the words corresponding to "practical" probably do not modify the term translated as "syllogisms."

The sentence reads: *hoi gar syllogismoi tôn praktôn archên echontes eisin, [epeidê toionde to telos kai to ariston, hotidêpote on—estô gar logou charin to tychon], EN* VI. 12 1144a 31–33. On one reading *tôn praktôn* goes with *hoi syllogismoi*: "For the inferences which deal with acts to be done are things which involve a starting point, [viz. 'since the end, i.e. what is best, is of such and such a nature,' whatever it may be—let it for the sake of the argument be what we please]" (in Ross's translation, substituting "inferences" for "syllogisms"). On an alternative, and far more plausible reading, *tôn praktôn* goes with *archên*: "For the inferences which contain the starting point of things done in action run as follows: ['since the end, i.e. what is best, is of such and such a nature,' etc.]" That *ta prakta*, things done in action, have a starting point, *archê*, which is the goal of action, is something Aristotle points out repeatedly. The phrase itself, *archê tôn praktôn*, is an established part of his ethical discourse. See, for instance, his explanation at *EN* VI. 5 1140b 16–7: *hai men gar archai tôn praktôn to hou heneka ta prakta*, "the starting points of things done in action are that for the sake of which things are done in action." By contrast, *tôn praktôn* as modifying *syllogismoi* is odd and unprecedented. Moreover, what in this case remains of the clause, *archên echontes eisin*, is syntactically extremely awkward.[15] The alternative reading is much to be preferred.

Aristotle's interpreters have tried to impose a common form on the notoriously varied kinds of argument-type structures he supplies when describing actions. However, even if there is something he would call a "practical syllogism," there is reason to doubt that it would be an argument of a special sort, governed by distinctive rules of inference in the way deductive arguments are governed by the rules of deductive inference. Some of the arguments Aristotle produces are deductive in nature, others not; some are not even valid. It would be misguided to expect every argument he uses for illustrative purposes to exhibit a single canonical form.

This does not mean that practical arguments are not important theoretical tools. When our concern is to explain or justify an action, as it often might be, it is well worth our while to try to cast the considerations that motivated the agent in a rationally assessable form. Since the activity of figuring out what to do sometimes does take the form of explicit calculation, a

---

[15] Stewart, who wonders if ἔχοντές εἰσιν is sound, proposes that it be taken as equivalent to ἔχουσιν(J. A. Stewart, *Notes on the Nicomachean Ethics of Aristotle*, Clarendon Press, Oxford 1892, *ad loc.*).

practical argument will not explain the action in an adequate way unless it captures the central elements of the reasoning that led the agent to his action. Some approximation to the agent's reasoning must therefore be sought if the explanation is to be a good one. Yet most explanations do their job quite well without being true to life in capturing the deliberative process. Moreover, a single action, even one that is motivationally not especially complex, can be adequately represented by *ex post facto* arguments of different logical forms.

Explicit calculation is only the limiting instance of a range of shapes that the process of figuring out what to do might take. But Aristotle's determination to regard all virtuous action as deliberated is not sheer obstinacy. It is an expression of his considered view of the extent to which reason is engaged in moral action. It is also based on a recognition of what the process of arriving at a choice—which it is natural to call "deliberation"—is actually like. There is no reason to expect the process of arriving at a choice to much resemble going through steps of a rational argument, even if the considerations that guided the agent can *ex post facto* be captured in the form of an argument. The deliberative process is not necessarily explicitly calculative; where it does involve explicit calculation, this hardly resembles going through steps of "practical arguments" as they occur in philosophy textbooks.

Aristotle's construal of deliberation, allowing as it does ways of arriving at a choice that are not marked by explicit reasoning, is broader than what is termed "deliberation" in English, and probably similarly broader than *bouleusis* in its ordinary uses. Yet it is a natural enough extension of the term. Aristotle may sometimes have spoken of "deliberation" in a way that comes closer to the narrow, more calculative, construal. He helps himself to a more conversational usage, for instance, when he distinguishes between two types of akrasia, impetuosity (*propeteia*) and weakness (*astheneia*). The weak person, Aristotle says, deliberates but does not abide by the result of his deliberation "because of his affect" (*pathos*), whereas the impetuous person is driven by his affect "because he has not deliberated" (*EN* VII. 7 1150b 19–22). In particular, Aristotle observes, quick-tempered people (*oxeis*) and ardent people (*melancholikoi*) tend to be impetuous akratics; they "do not wait for reason, since they tend to follow appearance"—the quick-tempered because of the urgency (*tachytês*) of their impulses, and the ardent because of the intensity of their impulses (*EN* VII. 7 1150b 25–28).

In saying that the quick-tempered and the ardent fail to "wait for reason," Aristotle probably wants to say that they do not pause to reflect on their action, or to calculate its consequences. However, the quick-tempered and the ardent who are described as driven by their affect "because they have not deliberated" also fail to deliberate in the sense that they do not, on the occasion on which they yield to impetuousness, act on their choice. Both the impetuous and the weak akratics have exercised their deliberative abilities well enough to be credited with having the right choice; when weak-willed, they do not act on the deliverances of their deliberative effort.

Seen as a process of arriving at a choice, deliberation is an activity that modifies an initial set of desires and concerns which the agent brings to bear to his action into another set of desires which are wants or willings. This activity is deliberative only if the modification of desires can be regarded as a result of an exercise of reason.[16] Deliberation, as Aristotle understands it, is not simply reasoning that serves a practical purpose, but an effective direction, or redirection, of one's will by means of reasoning.

2. Deliberation "Is Not of the End": The Practical Starting Points

Aristotle repeatedly states that deliberation is not of the end, telos, but of *ta pros to telos*—things that are toward the end, or, as this phrase used to be translated, the means toward the end[17] (*EN* III. 3 1112b 11–12 and 1112b 33–34; *EE* ii. 10 1226a 7–17 and 1226b 9–12; *EE* ii. 11 1227b 25ff; see also *Rhet.* I. 6 1362a 18–19). Thus, for instance, Aristotle says, a doctor does not deliberate whether his patient should be healthy or not, but whether, say, he should take walks or not (*EE* ii. 11 1227b 25–26; *EN* III. 3 1112b 12–13).

The claim that deliberation is not about the end has suggested to some that ethical deliberation is only about means, and not about ends. However, this view clashes with the picture that emerges with clarity elsewhere in the Ethics, in particular, in *EN* Books VI and VII. There Aristotle claims, among other things, that choice—which is a product of deliberation—reveals character better than actions do. Instrumental reasoning is hardly indicative of character. Moreover, the overall picture of ethical deliberation and choice provided in Books VI and VII does not support the view that ethical deliberation is of the means only. To rely only on the few passages already quoted, if ethical deliberation were only of the means, its excellence could not consist in aiming at, and tending to achieve, the right goal.

The debate whether Aristotle in *EN* Book III argues that ethical deliberation is always about instrumental means and never about ends appears,

---

[16] A transition from one set of desires to another can in some sense be a result of an exercise of reason, yet not be deliberation. An activity of designing computer programs might lead to a person's desire to give up his present occupation and do computer programming instead. Yet this desire need not be a result of deliberation. If the desire to do computer programming is a result of deliberation in Aristotle's sense, the relevant exercise of reason is not just that involved in designing computer programs. The point of calling the relevant employment of reason "practical" is to call attention to the fact that reason in this employment specifically focuses on desires and their content, and does something with them or about them.

[17] *Ta pros to telos* means roughly "[things] with reference to the end."

however, to be settled. There seems to be an agreement among the more recent interpreters of Aristotle that as a result of ethical deliberation we choose not only the means to happiness, but also the ends, in particular, the constitutive parts of happiness. What settled the debate was in part the recognition that the phrase *ta pros to telos* refers not just to instrumental means, but also to the constitutive parts of an end.[18]

However, even if this is granted, problems remain. If on Aristotle's view we deliberate about the constituents of happiness, then we do, in an important sense, deliberate about happiness as well; hence one needs to explain what he has in mind when he insists that deliberation and choice are not "of the end" or "about the end." Furthermore, since the examples Aristotle gives at *EE* ii. 10–11 and *EN* III. 3 are restricted to deliberation in the technical domains, a doubt may still linger in some minds that Aristotle models ethical deliberation, at least in *EN* III. and *EE* ii., after technical deliberation.

A closer look at several passages from the *Nicomachean* and the *Eudemian Ethics* shows, I believe, what point Aristotle is trying to make by saying that deliberation is not of the end. *Eudemian Ethics* Book ii is especially useful here:

> We deliberate not about the ends, but about what is toward the ends (*tôn pros ta telê*). For the doctor does not deliberate whether he shall heal, nor the orator whether he shall persuade, nor the statesman whether he shall produce law and order (*eunomia*), nor does any other practitioner of art deliberate about the end. Rather they lay down the end (*themenoi to telos*), and then examine how and by which means to bring it about [. . .] For a deliberator seems to search and analyze in the way described, as though analyzing a diagram. (*EN* III. 3 1112b 11–21)

> Since the deliberator always deliberates for the sake of something, and there is always some goal (*skopos*) with reference to which he investigates what is useful, nobody deliberates about the end, this [sc. the end] being a starting-point and a hypothesis (*archê kai hypothesis*), like hypotheses in the theoretical sciences [. . .], but everyone's investigation is about what contributes to the end (*tôn pros to telos pherontôn*). (*EE* ii. 10 1227a 5–12)

---

[18] Cooper, John M. *op. cit.*, p. 19ff; W.F.R. Hardie, *Aristotle's Ethical Theory*, 2nd edition, Clarendon Press, Oxford 1980, p. 256; cp. also L.H.G. Greenwood, *Nicomachean Ethics, Book Six*, 1909, Cambridge U.P., Cambridge 1909 (reprint Arno Press, New York 1973), pp. 46–47. Note that this wider interpretation should not be restricted to the phrase *ta pros to telos*. This phrase is in any case equivalent to *ta tou telous heneka* or *ta tou telous charin*, "things which are for the sake of the end"—see, for instance, *EE* ii. 10 1226a 7–11. That the expressions *heneka* or *charin* ("for the sake of") covers constituents as well as instrumental means is suggested already by the following passage: "[. . .] we choose honor, pleasure, intelligence and every sort of virtue both because of themselves [. . .], but we also choose them for the sake of happiness (*tês eudaimonias charin*), thinking that through them we shall be happy" (*EN* I. 7 1097b 2–5). Honor, pleasure and intelligence are not represented here as instrumental means to happiness. Virtue, in fact, cannot on Aristotle's view of happiness (*EN* I. 7) be such a means.

For the doctor does not look into whether his patient should be healthy or not, but rather whether he should walk about or not; nor does the physical trainer look into whether one should be fit or not, but whether one should wrestle. In the same way, no other [science or art] is about the end. Just as in the theoretical sciences, the hypotheses are starting-points, so in the productive [sciences or arts] the end is the starting point and hypothesis (*archê kai hypothesis*). Given that this thing needs to be healthy, if that is to come about, such-and-such must be the case, as, in the other area, if a triangle contains two right angles, such-and-such must be the case. (*EE* ii. 11 1227b 2–32)

Nobody deliberates about the end, but that is presupposed (*keitai*) by everybody. (*EE* ii. 10 1226b 9–10 (Walzer/Mingay; 10–11 in Susemihl)

Those who do not lay down some end (*hois mêtheis keitai skopos*) are not deliberators. (*EE* ii. 10 1226b 29–30)

In the *Nicomachean* passage deliberation, as a search (*zêtêsis*) or investigation (*skepsis*), is compared with geometrical analysis, in particular, with the attempt to solve a geometrical problem by recognizing that the figure in question can be analyzed as containing, for instance, a certain kind of triangle. Now if by pointing out that deliberation is not about the ends, Aristotle were at pains to stress that deliberation is always concerned with instrumental means, it would be rather peculiar for him to invoke the example of geometrical analysis, which has nothing to do with means-end reasoning. But it would be equally wrong to assume that the reference to geometrical analysis indicates that Aristotle intends to present theoretical reasoning, or more specifically the sort of reasoning involved in solving geometrical problems, as a paradigm for practical reasoning. The point Aristotle wants to make in the passages quoted is quite different. The *Eudemian Ethics* goes some ways toward spelling it out.

The reason why deliberation is not about the end, according to the first two *Eudemian* passages quoted, is that the end plays a different role. It is a *hypothesis*—something laid down or posited. The end is what in the practical sphere corresponds to a hypothesis proper, that is, a hypothesis in theoretical sciences. The Greek term *hypothesis* refers to something that is laid down, posited or presupposed—provisionally perhaps, but not necessarily in a tentative way. When Aristotle says that the end is a hypothesis, or that we lay down or posit the end (in the remaining three passages), he invites us to think of the end in deliberation as something taken as a fixed point. In order to deliberate, the deliberator has to hold something constant; there can be no reasoning or deliberation without presuppositions. In the third *Eudemian* passage quoted, *EE* ii. 10 1226b 9–10, Aristotle directly links the claim we are interested in here, that we do not deliberate about the end, with this point about presupposition: "Nobody deliberates about the end, but that is presupposed (*keitai*) by everybody" (or, "laid down by everyone"—*not*, as Woods translates it: "that is there for everyone"[19]). The line of thought begun at 1226b 9 ends at 1226b 29–30 with the claim (quoted last): "Those who do not lay down some end are not deliberators."

The reasoning involved in deliberation is not in fact hypothetical in our sense of the word. Deliberation does not consist in figuring out what would have to be done *if* the deliberator had such and such an aim in view. A mere opinion that something ought or ought not to be done is put aside at 1226b 23–24, shortly before the last of the passages quoted, as a potential candidate for the starting point of deliberation. To say that deliberation is not of the end, but that the end is laid down in deliberation, is to affirm that deliberation starts from an actual practical commitment to some end. Without such a commitment there is no deliberation—those who do not lay down some end are not deliberators.

Deliberation starts with a state of aiming at a particular telos, and this involves having a desire for the object at which one aims. As the practical counterpart to the theoretical hypothesis—what we might call the "practical hypothesis"—the end which the deliberator is committed to, the desire for which guides his deliberation, is an integral part of the deliberation. If the deliberation is spelled out as a practical argument, the desire for the end may be formulated as the first, universal, premiss.[20]

What is laid down by the deliberator, however, is not simply an end, but a certain conception of the end. One cannot deliberate how to bring about health without having some conception as to what health involves and what sorts of things might bring it about (cf. *Metaphysics* VII. 7 1032b 15–1033a 1). A person is not a technical deliberator unless he is both committed to the end that defines his *technê*, craft, and guided in his deliberation by his expert conception of that end. Likewise, a person is not an ethical deliberator without having eudaimonia as the end in his deliberation and without having some (non-expert) conception of eudaimonia, which is presupposed in deliberation.

In Book III of the *Nicomachean Ethics*, as well as Book ii of the *Eudemian*, Aristotle focuses mostly on the likeness between technical and ethical sorts of deliberation, but the likeness he wants to draw our attention to is not the concern with instrumental means. Rather, he is trying to explain what makes the reasoning involved in deliberation *practical*. What makes both technical and

---

[19] See Aristotle, *Eudemian Ethics*, Books I, II and VIII, translation and commentary by M. Woods, 2nd edition, Clarendon Press, Oxford 1992. κεῖται does the job here of the perfect passive of τιθέναι, meaning to "lay down" or "posit"—the very verb from which the word *hypothesis* is derived. This is a standard usage of the verb κεῖσθαι. Note that κεῖται is used in the same way in the passage cited just below: διὸ οἷς μηθεὶς κεῖται σκοπός, οὐ βουλευτικοί (1226b 29–30).

[20] This does not mean that the deliberator reasons from that premiss. The practical argument merely spells out in some form the content of the considerations that bring about the action.

ethical deliberation practical is (in part) that deliberation presupposes aiming at a particular goal, and starts with a certain conception of the goal.

The differences between ethical and technical deliberation emerge when some issues are discussed that are not broached in the *EN* III. or *EE* ii. The most striking differences are due to the role the conception of the end plays in each type of deliberation, and especially the sort of guidance that each conception provides. Once Aristotle has explored these differences, ethical deliberation will be seen to lie far apart from technical deliberation. (I will mention some of the differences in Section 5 below.) The fact that Aristotle in *EN* III. 3 and *EE* ii. 10 and 11 discusses ethical and technical deliberation in one breath is due to the evidently introductory purpose of these chapters.[21] He is working his way toward an account of the use of reason in ethical deliberation by comparing and contrasting this use of reason with other uses of reason: solving mathematical problems, figuring out what cure to apply to make a man healthy. These comparisons do not lead to the view either that theoretical problem-solving or that technical deliberations are paradigms for the practical use of reason.

3. Ethical Deliberation and Reflection

When discussing courage, Aristotle makes the following observation:

> Hence also it is thought the mark of a more courageous man to be fearless and undisturbed in sudden alarms (*en tois aiphnidiois phobois*) than to be so in those that are foreseen; for it must have proceeded more from the state of character (*apo hexeôs*), because less from preparation (*ek paraskeuês*); foreseen acts may be chosen by calculation and reason (*ek logismou kai logou*), but sudden acts (*ta exaiphnês*) in accordance with one's state of character (*kata tên hexin*). (*EN* III. 8 1117a 17–22)

On the other hand, we have seen that, according to Aristotle, virtuous action is chosen, and therefore deliberated. Moreover, ethical deliberation, in Aristotle's view, always involves a conception of the final end, the good life. At *EN* VI. 12 1144a 31–33, he says that "the inferences which contain the starting point of things done in action run as follows: 'since the end, i.e. what is best (*to telos kai to ariston*), is of such and such a nature.'" A virtuous person's deliberation, one might think, also has to start from such a premiss.

The thought that the virtuous person's action ensues on deliberation the first premiss of which states a conception of the good life may well seem to conflict with the quoted description of an unpremeditated courageous action which Aristotle presents as a sign of greater courage than a premeditated and

---

[21] This is independent of the question of the order of composition of, say, Book III of the *Nicomachean Ethics* vis-à-vis Books VI and VII.

calculated one. Some have sought a way out of the conflict by assuming that *to telos kai to ariston*, the end that figures as the premiss of deliberation, is a more specific end than the good life. Hardie, for instance, claims that the end referred to by the phrase *to telos kai to ariston* is not the ultimate good, "but the kind of end a soldier has in view when he sets himself to behave well in a battle [. . .]."[22]

However, this cannot be right. *To telos kai to ariston* is Aristotle's standard expression for the ultimate end (*kai* is clearly epexegetical here). And in any case, Aristotle believes that if ethical deliberation—whether narrowly or broadly construed—is to be carried out properly, it is of importance that the agent's overall conception of eudaimonia be available at every point during the deliberative process. It is not his view that one explicitly consults one's whole conception of the good life. Not all of it is explicit or available for scrutiny. Aristotle does not seem to impute a fully explicit conception of eudaimonia even to the practically wise and virtuous person. His thought rather is that one's overall evaluative outlook on the conduct of life should be on call in every situation of action.

Coming to a deliberative situation equipped with a conception of eudaimonia is not to be understood as starting with a large premiss containing one's whole conception of the good life—"Eudaimonia is. . . ."—and deducing from that premiss what one is to do here and now. If deliberation *generally* speaking does not consist in deductive argument, there is no reason to assume that *ethical* deliberation starts from a grand premiss specifying the person's general ethical outlook. The way in which deliberation involves the deliberator's whole conception of eudaimonia is best described by starting from an incisive remark by David Wiggins: "few situations come already inscribed with the names of all the concerns which they touch or impinge upon."[23]

Human life involves facing situations in which it is not immediately, or even upon reflection, clear what is at stake, from the point of view of the person involved. A given situation will typically not activate a virtuous person's whole conception of the good life; it will activate only a part of it. However, which part is activated depends on what the whole conception is. A virtuous person's overall evaluative outlook is responsible both for bringing forth those features of the situation that he perceives as practically relevant in his initial scanning of the situation, and also for bringing about his specific response to the situation thus perceived.

If this is a fair interpretation of Aristotle—as I believe it is—there is no reason to worry whether he represents ethical deliberation as starting from a

---

[22] W.F.R. Hardie, *Aristotle's Ethical Theory*, Clarendon Press, Oxford 1968, p. 252.

[23] "Deliberation and Practical Reason", *op. cit.* (n. 14 above), p. 231. The lines of thought I briefly mention in this paragraph are discussed insightfully, and at length, by Wiggins and by John Mc-Dowell, "The Role of *Eudaimonia* in Aristotle's Ethics", in Amélie Oksenberg Rorty ed., *Essays on Aristotle's Ethics* (University of California Press 1980), 359–376.

"grand premiss" stating the agent's overall conception of the good life. He is not arguing that in acting virtuously, for instance, we *reason* from such a premiss. If we are in the business of explaining an action by citing a practical argument, we may start with the grand premisses—or not, depending on what our explanatory purpose is. In most cases, we are interested in what made the agent respond to this situation in the way he did; the story of how he came to analyze the situation as involving this or that salient concern is not to the point.

If one looks at a situation which has already aroused some deliberative response in the agent, then one can say—with Hardie—that "the end and the best" is something less general than the agent's whole conception of eudaimonia. However, if one thinks of an agent who has just faced, or is about to face, a new situation, "the end and the best" must be taken to refer to the ultimate good. But even in the first case, on Aristotle's view, the whole conception of eudaimonia is involved among what he calls the deliberative starting points.

A conception of the good life, which is the starting point of ethical deliberation, is a set of evaluative attitudes—from simple desires to more complex evaluative attitudes which involve a desiderative component, such as choices, practical concerns, commitments, etc.[24]—which, if their content were fully spelled out, would jointly amount to some specific picture of how one should live one's life. An ordinary person's conception of eudaimonia is to a large degree implicit; it is also usually vague and gappy in parts, not well-integrated, and, more often than not, not fully consistent. Nonetheless, it is Aristotle's view that most human adults have evaluative attitudes which involve such substantive valuations and which jointly amount to an evaluative outlook on the manner in which they should conduct their life.

Deliberation is ethical if the agent's overall moral outlook guides his perception of the situation in which he acts, activating this or that part of it. The concerns or interests that are activated by the situation are always specific. Yet Aristotle—following in the steps of Socrates—has a holistic conception of the exercise of reason that backs virtuous action. Moderation, justice and courage are to some extent independent motivational propensities. Yet no single action of any kind is fully virtuous unless it is backed by an integral view of how one ought to go about things in life.

The person of practical wisdom is in many ways not unlike the ordinary moral agent. He would not of course be practically *wise* if his conception of the good were inconsistent, or his conception misguided. But he is like the rest of us in that his conception of the good life is largely embodied in his dispositions to view particular situations, and respond to them, in certain ways.

---

[24] No claim is made here that these more complex evaluative attitudes cannot be analyzed into beliefs, on the one hand, and desires, on the other. That level of analysis is in any case typically too fine-grained for ethical purposes.

He does not reach his decisions from a carefully worked out scheme of values, which he simply applies to particular situations; his insight, Aristotle insists, is bound up with recognition of particulars. In some cases, a virtuous response demands an action that is unpremeditated and uncalculated, like the courageous action Aristotle speaks of at *EN* III. 8 1117a 17–22.

Yet for Aristotle the practically wise person is a far more reflective character than some recent interpretations have made him out to be. Aristotle attributes the correctness of the virtuous person's choice to reason, not merely to the appropriate direction of desire and emotion, if this is seen as not mediated by reason. Virtuous action requires a width of perspective, and articulateness, that is easily lost sight of when we get too focussed on the picture of the virtuous person responding to particular features of situations as they present themselves to him in his own life. The sort of perceptiveness Aristotle has in mind when he speaks of practical wisdom as 'this eye of the soul' (*EN* VI. 12 1144a 30) can only exist in someone whose dispositions to act are shaped by a use of reason that is reflective and critical. Aristotle describes such a use of reason in a way that lays stress on its social element. His discussion of two special virtues of the intellect bring this out.

The first virtue is *synesis* or *eusynesia*, comprehension or good comprehension (*EN* VI. 10). A person who has *synesis* understands and assesses well what other people have to say about their deliberation and reflection on practical matters. Unlike practical wisdom, *synesis* is not prescriptive (*epitaktikê*), but rather critical, or concerned with judgement (*kritikê*) (1143a 8–10). In exercising comprehension, one develops one's interpretive skills and skills of critical assessment which are necessary for conducting one's own deliberation well. Through exercising comprehension, one also gains access to other people's conceptions of the ends they pursue. These provide material, and sometimes the motivation, for one's own deliberation. Aristotle believes that, when beginning our ethical development, a reliance on other people's judgement is indispensable in order to get us going at all; it is indispensable, in other words, if we are eventually to come up with a conception of eudaimonia that is our own. *Synesis* as a virtue, however, is not represented as relevant only to moral development. Someone who is capable of attaining what is best for the human being of things pursued in action has the ability to judge well the things others say about ethical conduct.

Aristotle's emphasis on the ethical relevance of *synesis* throws some light on an issue to which he gives little direct discussion. This is the issue of the role ethical reflection plays both in the acquisition of one's conception of the good life and in deliberation. Deliberation is an exercise of reason which is practical strictly speaking; it is a process, or rather an activity, which directly affects desires and volitions. But one does not modify desires for the sake of modifying desires. The impetus for changing desires comes from a person's evaluative outlook. This outlook is not acquired only through deliberation.

People think about practical issues in a manner that is not strictly practical in Aristotle's sense of the word; they reflect on their past actions, the content of the ends they tend to go for, the relationship among the particular ends they go for. The direction of their deliberation is often affected by such reflection. It seems then that Aristotle needs to introduce here a distinction between the exercises of reason that are practical strictly speaking, and the exercises of reason the point of which is action as well, ultimately—but not necessarily directly or immediately. Although *synesis* itself is restricted to thinking of, and judging about, what *other* people have to say about ethical issues, in attaching importance to this virtue, Aristotle implicitly recognizes the practical significance of ethical reflection. For that exercise of intellect which is concerned with the conduct of life, but is not practical in the strict sense—being, as he puts it, merely critical—is or involves what we usually call practical reflection.

Aristotle appears to address the issue of ethical reflection in one passage in the *Eudemian Ethics*. At *EE* ii. 10 1226b 25–26; he ascribes to the deliberative part of the soul an ability to contemplate the ends of human action. He says: "that part of the soul is deliberative which contemplates (*to theôretikon*) the cause of a certain sort; for that-for-the-sake-of-which is one of the causes." Apart from this passage, we know that he regards his own ethical theory, as developed in the *Ethics*, as practical. This seems to indicate, first, that ethical inquiry on his view includes both deliberation, which is directly or properly speaking practical, and ethical reflection, which is practical in an indirect sense.

The virtue of *synesis* or *eusynesia* conspicuously displays a social element. It shows Aristotle concerned, as he is throughout the *Ethics*, with other people's appearances of goodness. The desirability of some virtuous actions is often revealed only to those whose vision has been shaped by what others have to say on the matters of human life. The kind of practical insight that Aristotle thinks characteristic of practical wisdom is also shaped by an understanding of others, as another virtue of practical reason—consideration or *syggnômê* (*EN* VI. 11)—reveals.

What is peculiar from our own point of view is that the virtue of being considerate and forgiving is classified by Aristotle as an intellectual virtue. There is no talk here about the emotion of compassion, but rather about a correct discrimination (*krisis orthê*) of what is decent or equitable (*tou epieikous*), 1143a 20. Understanding the other person and the willingness to extend forgiveness are ascribed to a discriminatory insight of some sort (1143a 19–20). This does not mean that the insight is based on some abstract principle of fairness; rather decency in dealing with other people, which is a characteristic of all good people, seems to be a matter of insight into particulars (1143a 31–2). It is the sharpening of one's insight into the circumstances of the other people's actions, and into what moves them to act as they do, that leads to a considerateness which tends to forgive. Yet the forgiveness is not

162   CHAPTER 6

unbounded: it is guided by a proper grasp of the other person, and a sense of
fairness (which is another way to translate *to epieikon*, what is decent or equitable).

Synesis and *syggnômê* are attitudes of mind distinct from practical wisdom.
They each display a certain other-oriented understanding, and are not immediately bent on action. Yet even if different in account, comprehension and
forgiveness are found in the practically wise (1143a 25–31). When we think of
the practically wise person as someone who makes right choices, we have also
to think of him as someone whose choices result directly from the kind of reflective and discriminatory insight that forms the core of *synesis* and *syggnômê*.

4. Choice

Deliberation is a process which, if successfully carried through, leads to a *prohairesis*, a choice or decision. Aristotle's notion of choice is the most original
part of his ethics.[25] Choice, on this view, is a psychological attitude that involves both a belief and a desiderative state.

At *EE* ii. 10 1227a 3–5, Aristotle says: "It is clear that choice is neither
simply wish (*boulêsis*) nor belief (*doxa*), but belief and desire (*orexis*) together
when as a result of deliberation they are brought to a conclusion." The claim
made here is apparently only that choice involves desire and belief, not that it
is an attitude of some third, distinct, kind.[26] However, at *EN* VI. 2 1139b 4–5,
choice is characterized as "deliberative understanding" (*orektikos nous*) or
"rational desire" (*orexis dianoetikê*), which comes closer to suggesting that
choice is a state of the soul that is *sui generis*, and not merely a combination of
a desire and a belief.

The following, preliminary, characterization of choice, or rather of a chosen action, is suggested by the passages I cite below. A chosen action, on
Aristotle's view, is caused by a certain kind of wish (*boulêsis*), which we may
call a (rational) wanting or willing.[27] My wish to φ is a wanting or willing to
φ just in case the wish to φ involves a belief that my wishing to φ will bring it
about that I φ. My action (of φ-ing) is chosen just in case: (a) it is caused by
my willing to φ, and (b) this willing to φ is caused by deliberation.

---

[25] The term *prohairesis* is used only once in Plato, at *Parmenides* 143c. Deliberation might well
have been of interest to the Sophists (in Plato's *Protagoras* 318e 5–319a 2 Protagoras claims to
teach his pupils *euboulia*), but we have no evidence that they developed anything like the conceptual analysis of deliberation and choice that Aristotle offers.

[26] A similar claim is made at *De motu animalium* 6 700b 23: "choice shares both in intellect (*dianoia*) and in desire (*orexis*)." See also *De anima* III. 10 433a 22–30.

[27] I take it that "wish" is an appropriate translation for *boulêsis*—as, for instance, when we say that
we wish to be immortal, or to rule over mankind—but the most interesting kind of wish, that
involved in choosing, is in fact more appropriately called "willing" or "wanting."

Let me first provide the grounds on which I attribute this preliminary characterization of a chosen action to Aristotle. With regard to (b), see *EE* ii. 10 1226b 16–20: "[. . .] choice is deliberative (*bouleutikê*) desire (*orexis*) for those things which are up to us [. . .] By deliberative desire, I mean desire whose origin (*archê*) and cause (*aitia*) is deliberation (*bouleusis*). For (a), see *EN* VI. 2 1139a 31–33: "Now the origin of action is choice—[the origin in the sense of] the source of motion, not that for the sake of which—while the origin of choice is desire (*orexis*) together with reason which is for the sake of something [i.e. which aims at some end]." The origin in the sense of "the source of motion" is what later came to be called an efficient cause, or simply, cause.

Conditions (a) and (b) are well-attested; how about the claim that a wish involved in a choice is a willing or wanting, as characterized above? For this, we should look at the discussion of choice at *EE* ii. 10 1226a 17ff and *EN* III. 2 1111b 19ff, where Aristotle argues that choice is a wish, but not just any kind of wish. Choice is said to be a wish for what is possible (not, for instance, a wish to square a circle, or a wish for immortality); for what can be otherwise; for what is in human power to do or not to do; for what is in the power of the agent to do or not to do (thus not, for instance, a wish concerning affairs in India—on the assumption that one has no connection whatsoever with India). Aristotle appears to be saying that a choice is a wish for what the agent believes is possible; what he believes is in human power, etc. See *EN* III. 2 1111b 23–26: "Further, wish is also for things that are not achievable through one's own agency, for instance, a victory for some actor or athlete; but nobody chooses anything of that sort, but what one thinks (*oietai*) can come about through one's own agency." The relevant kind of wish to φ involves a belief on the part of the deliberator that what he wants to attain by φ-ing is the sort of thing he can achieve by his own agency. Why is a wish that is involved in a choice restricted in this way? We should first recall here Aristotle's concept of telos: I can wish for a victory for a particular athlete, but I cannot aim at it. In addition, Aristotle believes that chosen actions are caused by their choices. A part of his concept of human agency is that we in some sense know, or believe, that we are—through our choices—causes of our actions. Through a choice or decision we knowingly make ourselves into causes of our actions. Thus, when I choose to take a walk, my choice involves an awareness that my determination to take a walk will bring it about that I take a walk.

The preliminary characterization of a chosen action, as it stands, does not specify a sufficient condition for an action to be chosen. Suppose that I want to speed through an intersection against the red light, as a result of deliberation. Suppose further that, being suddenly seized with fear, I change my mind about this, still in time safely to stop before the intersection. However, in panic, I press the gas pedal, and indeed race through the intersection against the red light. How would Aristotle deal with this sort of case? Observe that choice on his view is not just any combination of belief and desire (or perhaps, is not a combination of just any sort of belief and desire), but a combination that involves aiming at some goal. As Aristotle puts it at *EN* VI. 2 1139a 32–33, the origin of choice is desire together with "reason which is for the sake of something" (*logos ho heneka tinos*). On his view, both the aiming to φ and the action of φ-ing are caused by deliberation, and if the action itself is chosen, the same causal process must be involved in both the aiming to φ and the action of φ-ing.

A more precise Aristotelian characterization of a chosen action might therefore run somewhat like this: An agent's action of φ-ing is chosen if: (i) it is caused by the agent's willing to φ; (ii) it involves the same state of aiming as that which is involved in the agent's willing to φ, and (iii) the agent's willing to φ is caused by deliberation. The fact that Aristotle's account of a chosen action involves a two-step causal story is not, I think, problematic. A willing caused by deliberation—a choice—need not result in an action. If the choice does lead to an action, he takes it that the deliberation which causes the choice also causes the action. The state of aiming involved in the agent's willing to φ and that involved in his φ-ing are assigned to the same deliberative process. The causal story behind an action is unitary. The conception of the end that is the starting point of deliberation and leads to a chosen action is the same as, or is a direct causal ancestor of, the conception that is involved in the willing to φ that causes the action.

I have used the term "wanting" or "willing" to bring out an aspect of choice which is separate from the causal origin of choice in deliberation. The willing is a desiderative state of some sort; unlike mere desire, however, it involves a preparedness to bring about a definite state of affairs in the world through one's own effort. Aristotle's restriction of choice to such changes as can be brought about through human action, and through one's own action, has to be seen in this light. One cannot be bent on bringing about a state of affairs through action without implicitly believing that the state of affairs in question is of the sort that can be brought about through that very action (and therefore, through one's own action, and through human action). The question of the causal origin of this sort of desiderative state, which corresponds fairly closely to what we might call willing, is logically separate from the account of the state in question.

Why then does Aristotle not separate the notion of willing, which is implicit in his concept of choice, from the causal origin of choice in deliberation? The reason for this is probably that he regards the two as more than accidentally conjoined. We should recall here that deliberation for him is not necessarily a process of explicit figuring out what to do in a particular situation. Deliberation is a process that leads through an exercise of reason to a preparedness to act. The fact that Aristotle never considers the possibility that there could be a willing, or a choice, without deliberation, seems to indicate that he thought of the state I have called willing as essentially having its source in reason. If he did think of deliberation as a process of deliberative reasoning in the more ordinary sense, he would have been drawn to accept the instances of nondeliberated volition. However, explicity working out what to do is merely one way in which reason can be exercised in determining what to do in a particular situation. Aristotelian deliberation covers this broader range of cases.

Aristotle does not ascribe what I have called willing or wanting to a separate faculty, the will. He does not speak of anything that could naturally be translated as "the will."[28] He does take it that reason in its practical employment gives rise to something we have good reason to call willings or volitions. That reason can do this is what makes it in Aristotle's view practical. If we do not think of the will as a separate faculty, but as an ability of reason to effectively determine action, we can say that the will in this sense is implicit in Aristotle's account of deliberation and choice. To this extent Aristotle is indeed a precursor of modern conceptions of the will.

5. The Person of Practical Wisdom as the Standard of Ethical Judgement

The claim that the *phronimos*, the practically wise person, is the standard of ethical correctness, is one of the central claims of Aristotle's ethics. I shall conclude my discussion of his conception of practical reason by looking into some of the reasons he has for making this claim.

Phronêsis, practical wisdom, can be described as a virtue of practical judgement. Whereas reasoning, in the strict sense of this word, does not aim at truth itself, but at the preservation of truth from premises to conclusion, judgement aims at truth itself. When Aristotle describes the *euboulos*, good deliberator, as "the person who is capable of aiming in accordance with calculation (*logismos*) at what is best for a human being of things pursued in action"

---

[28] Anthony Kenny, in *Aristotle's Theory of the Will*, Yale U.P., New Haven 1979, translates *boulêsis* as "will." However, *boulêsis* is simply a wish. One may wish for the impossible. Aristotle's own examples are a wish for immortality, and a wish to have a kingly power over the whole of mankind (see *EE* ii. 10 1225b 32–34 and *EN* III. 2 1111b 22–23). A different kind of example comprises wishes for what is possible but not (normally) attainable by one's own agency, such as a wish that one's favorite team win a competition (cp. *EN* III. 2 1111b 23–24). These desires are not practical in any sense, and certainly do not amount to wanting or willing of any kind. Eventually, the word *boulêsis* will be used in the sense that warrants its translation as "will," but it is not so used in Aristotle. As I argued in "No One Errs Willingly: The Meaning of Socratic Intellectualism" (chap. 3 above), the term *boulêsis* was used by Plato's Socrates in the *Gorgias* in a way that picks out certain strands of the concept of the will. Aristotle, however, contrasts *boulêsis* with choice, *prohairesis*. It is in his account of choice that an implicit notion of willing is to be found.

(*EN* VI. 7 1141b 12–14), he characterizes the *euboulos* as someone who, in addition to being able to reason well in the formal sense, has the virtue of good judgement about practical affairs.[29]

Yet practical wisdom is not just the virtue of having good judgement *about* practical affairs; the excellent use of reason that characterizes the practically wise person is itself practical in nature. An employment of reason is practical only if it directly affects a desire, or a complex psychological attitude which involves a desire, and thus has an impact on the person's motivation to act. The *phronimos* is someone who is as good as one can be at using his reason in modifying his desires, and in arriving at choices to act, with a view to living the best possible life.

To say that a person who has the virtue of practical judgement is the standard of ethical correctness may appear to be trivial. The *phronimos* is understood to begin with as someone who makes the right choices as the result of his excellent use of practical reason. But by making this claim, Aristotle himself clearly intends to make a non-trivial point. He defines virtue of character as a mean of some sort which is determined by reason, namely, "the reason by which the practically wise person would determine it" (*EN* II. 6 1107a 1–2). His response to Protagorean relativism is formulated in the claim that things which appear good to the *phronimos* are, as a matter of fact, good (*EN* III. 4 1113a 25–1113b 2). Aristotle's response to Protagoras indicates that he wanted to make his understanding of ethical objectivity depend on his account of practical reason. However exactly he wanted to do this, he could not defeat Protagoras by the mere notion that the person of practical wisdom is by definition an embodiment of ethical correctness.

Here are some considerations that motivate Aristotle's characterization of the practically wise person as the standard of ethical correctness.

(1) There is an element of irreducible subjectivity in Aristotle's account of what the good life for a human being consists in. This might seem at first surprising. One might think that Aristotle, as a staunch ethical objectivist, might have been tempted by the following two (broadly Aristotelian) lines of thought. First, the extent to which a person does well in life depends on how many of his worthwhile ends he realizes, and perhaps also on which combination of these ends he realizes. According to the second Aristotelian strand of thought, a human being, as a natural creature of some sort, endowed with the capacities characteristic of his species, does well in life to the extent that he

---

[29] The term *logismos* is intended here widely. A *logismos* in the narrow sense is calculation, especially of the arithmetical sort, but more broadly it is any activity of figuring things out by reason, *logos*, thus also an activity of finding out the truth in practical affairs insofar as this activity is a reasoned process. In particular, *logismos* should not be understood as restricted to means-end reasoning.

develops and exercises such capacities in a way typical of the well-functioning mature specimens of his species.

These two lines of thought both draw on Aristotle's reflections about eudaimonia. However, on his view the good life for a human being is not a simple function of either sort. What is missing in these characterizations of the good human life is Aristotle's thought that a human being does not do well in life unless he lives in accordance with his own conception of what doing well in life consists in. This conception has to be one's own, in the sense of being to a large degree a result of one's own deliberation. It has also to be one's own in the sense that it is not a picture of the good life one merely speculates or fantasizes about, but is rather a conception that is operative in what one aims at in life. If one is to give an ideal representation of the human good, as Aristotle understands it, it will not do to provide an impersonal list of worthwhile human ends (perhaps along with some description of the deliberative priorities that attach to these ends in specific contexts). Nor will a list of the specifically human capacities do (accompanied perhaps by a description of the typical ways these capacities are exercised by mature human beings). What Aristotle needs is an ideal representation that embodies the agent's aiming at eudaimonia, and doing so under a conception which is a cumulative result of the agent's own previous deliberation. An appropriate device of representation for an ideal human life is someone who does these things well, and that is the Aristotelian *phronimos*.

(2) Aristotle's characterization of the *phronimos* as the standard of ethical correctness has to do with the sort of thing a conception of eudaimonia is, and also with the sort of guidance a such a conception provides in ethical deliberation. Two features essentially belong to ethical deliberation. Firstly, ethical deliberation is a procedure which is not guided by genuinely independent standards, and secondly, the conception of eudaimonia any agent—including the practically wise one—is guided by is incomplete.

Whereas the final end of various technical competences plays a constructive role in technical deliberation, such a constructive role seems to be lacking in ethical deliberation. We have some independent standards for judging whether the final end which defines a given craft (e.g. health or safety in navigation, seen as defining medicine and the art of navigation) is reached in particular cases. These standards are independent in the sense that they do not depend on technical conceptions of what health or safety in navigation involve, and how they are best produced or secured. We can judge whether people are healthy or ill to some degree independently of the conception of health which is involved in medicine as a technical expertise. Hence, in arts or crafts we can adjust our activities to the effects these activities tend to produce. These effects can serve as our reference point, since we have some independent ways of judging whether they are produced or not. By contrast,

practical wisdom in some sense "refers" everything to the ultimate good, but
there are no fully independent ways of judging the sort of success in the conduct of life which eudaimonia amounts to.[30]

We do derive some independent evidence for the soundness of our valuations concerning the conduct of life by observing, for instance, what sorts of
actions tend to wreck other people's lives, or make their lives successful. But
we take such evidence to be limited in significance because it involves an external point of view, in other words, precisely because it is independent. Although Aristotelian "eudaimonia" is considerably more objective a term than
"happiness" is, it shares with happiness the fact that it cannot be adequately
judged independently of the agent's own perspective.

In addition, as ethical agents, we do not have anything resembling an effective procedure for deciding how to act in a satisfactory way in the light of
the variety of valuations that make for our conception of the good life.[31] In
ethical deliberation, we have to work from both ends. Ethical deliberation is
guided by the deliberator's general ethical outlook; this outlook may be regarded as that which is laid down or posited in a particular deliberative situation. However, the general ethical outlook may in a given situation point in
different directions, or in no particular direction. In such cases some work on
the valuations that go into one's ethical outlook may be necessary.

The agent's conception of eudaimonia contains valuations of unequal
weight. Some parts of his ethical outlook are more important to him than
others. Thus, deliberation may lead him to abandon a part of his ethical outlook in favor of another part, one which he is more committed to and less
willing to give up. Conflicts in the agent's conception of eudaimonia are typically revealed and resolved in particular deliberative situations. Solutions to
such conflicts can sometimes be reached without articulating the conflicting
concerns and explicitly working on a solution to the problem. But some practical difficulties are sufficiently tough to require such an articulation, and may
not be resolved even when a person's most carefully thought out evaluative
judgements and their best deliberative skills are employed in an attempt to
solve them.

---

[30] For the Aristotelian idea that the ultimate good is a reference point of some sort, see *EN* I.
12, and especially the following: "By not praising pleasure although it is a good we indicate,
he [Eudoxus] thought, that pleasure is better than the things which are praised; and god and
the good are of this [better] sort, since the other things are referred to them (πρὸς ταῦτα
γὰρ καὶ τἆλλα ἀναφέρεσθαι" (1101b 28–31)). (Cp. *EE* ii. 1 1219b 11–13.) Although
Aristotle does not say so, the thought that the good is a reference point of some sort is also
Platonic: see *Phaedo* 76de, *Republic* 484c, and my "Aristotle on the Varieties of Goodness",
chap. 4 above.

[31] When Eudoxus speaks of "referring" things to the ultimate good, pleasure, he might have in
mind such an effective procedure. On Aristotle's view, such a procedure is not available to us.

In some cases, the agent's general ethical outlook will not point in any particular direction. The cases I have in mind are not of the sort in which the agent does not have any clue as to what is going on in the situation from the ethical point of view. I am assuming that the agent can recognize some of the ethical considerations that are of relevance to the case at hand, yet these considerations are not sufficient either for him to adopt a conclusive interpretation of the situation, or to move him to act in any particular way. On occasion, one has to make a stab in the dark in the hope that the implications of one's action will be apparent at a later point. Sometimes this is the only way in which one can acquire the valuations one needs in order to deal with the new circumstances.

Yet another situation arises when the agent finds that the concerns he took himself to be firmly committed to lead unambiguously to a solution to the practical difficulty that in the given circumstances strikes him as a wrong thing to do. Pondering over the grounds for this disparity may lead to a revision of the original commitment.

These remarks are meant to explicate the kind of indeterminacy which Aristotle believes is inherent in ethical deliberation. This indeterminacy is not something that only the agents who are not fully virtuous and practically wise have to face. The practically wise person is not someone who does not have to make a stab in the dark, or to revise his commitments; rather, he is someone who is good at judging when it is appropriate, or permissible, to make a stab in the dark, or to make an appropriate revision.

This brings me to the incompleteness of the conception of eudaimonia. The practically wise person does not have at his disposal all the valuations he would need in order to reach a correct choice as to how to act in all the situations he might face. We should not be misled here, again, by the fact that the *phronimos* represents a certain ideal. The *phronimos* can only be in possession of whatever knowledge his specific excellences—above all, *euboulia*, the general deliberative excellence—involve, since he is nothing but an embodiment of these excellences. *Euboulia* does not consist in one's being equipped with a full body of practical knowledge which would enable one to arrive at a correct choice in any given situation. Aristotle's conception of the good deliberator is primarily a conception of someone who, in addition to having some body of practical knowledge, has the ability to acquire the further knowledge he needs in order to deal with the new circumstances he finds himself in. Thus, Aristotle thinks of practical wisdom as, among other things, an excellence of learning.

This leads us to another reason why Aristotle chooses to describe the *phronimos* as the standard of the correctness of ethical judgement. If he thought that possessing a definitive body of practical knowledge were involved in being practically wise, he could refer to that knowledge as the standard of ethical correctness. However, he believes that the virtue of good practical judgement essentially involves the ability to revise and expand the necessarily incomplete conception of eudaimonia which the agent has acquired to a large degree as the result of his deliberations in the very specific circumstances of his own life. Thus, it makes better sense for Aristotle to refer to the person of practical wisdom himself as the model of ethical correctness rather than the necessarily incomplete knowledge this person has at any point in time.

Aristotle thinks of his conception of the good practical judgement as standing in sharp contrast to the Platonic position on the excellent use of reason in practical affairs. Aristotle complained that the Platonic form of the good is not something that can guide human action (see *EN* I. 6 and *EE* i. 8). But Aristotle must have been aware of the fact that Plato intended the form of goodness to be something that is *prakton* in the sense of providing guidance for action. Plato took the form of goodness to be a *paradeigma* of some sort, a pattern or model, not only in the ontological sense, but also in the sense of being some sort of guide or reference point for our actions. He seemed to believe that if we knew the form of goodness, or the good-itself, we would be able to recognize what is good in all its guises, and thus would be able to attain fully reliable practical guidance.[32] His view might even have been that the good-itself—that which he describes as truly good—cannot be understood independently of the ability to recognize what is good or bad in the particular circumstances of one's life.

However closely Plato might have connected knowledge of the good-itself with choosing the right courses of action, Aristotle would regard the very notion of such a kind of knowledge as misguided. Complete and exact knowledge concerning practical affairs is not—in the language of *EN* I. 6—*ktêton* for human beings: it cannot be "had" or possessed by us. What we can have, ideally, is a procedure for dealing with practical problems which rests on some knowledge, and which helps expand that knowledge to cope with the new circumstances we encounter.

Ethical deliberation, on Aristotle's view, is distinct both from the theoretical and from the technical employment of reason. Whereas the theoretical use of reason does not involve a modification of one's desires, the technical use of reason, as Aristotle thinks of it, does. However, a technical expert has the benefit of having some standards of successful practice in his area that are independent of his own expert conception of successful practice.[33] If this is

---

[32] This view is suggested by Plato's *Republic*. Socrates in the early Platonic dialogues makes a similar assumption. When he proposes the view that virtue is knowledge, he seems to have in mind an all-comprehensive body of knowledge which provides an effective practical guidance in all circumstances of action. However, Socrates does not make it clear whether he thinks that such a knowledge could be attained. He certainly denies that he himself has the knowledge in question.

[33] For an insightful examination of the similarities and differences between the practical and the technical use of reason, see Sarah Broadie, *Ethics with Aristotle*, Oxford U.P., Oxford, New York 1991, esp. pp. 190–198 and 202–212. This examination reveals, among other things, that our grasp of what is involved in a technical expertise is in many ways not adequate enough to provide a firm basis for the comparison between technical expertise and practical wisdom.

so, then there is on Aristotle's view no *technê*, art or craft, of living well. Nonetheless, Aristotle believes that with regard to practical affairs, there is something he would describe as a sound procedure, *methodos*.[34] On his view, there is a way of going about things in life which, although it does not amount to an exact or complete procedure, does reliably lead to a considerable measure of success in the conduct of life.

---

[34] Compare the opening sentence of the *Nicomachean Ethics*: "Every craft (τέχνη) and every μέθοδος, and likewise every action (πρᾶξις) and choice (προαίρεσις) is thought to aim at some good [. . .]." A *methodos* is usually understood by Aristotle's interpreters as an approach followed in a science, *epistêmê*, or a craft, *technê*, or sometimes even as the science or the craft itself. See for instance, J. Burnet, *The Ethics of Aristotle*, Methuen & Co, London 1900, *ad loc.*, and Stewart, *ad loc.* However, Aspasius already made an attempt to construe the term broadly. See Aspasius, *In Ethica Nicomachea quae supersunt commentaria*, ed. G. Heylbut, *Commentaria in Aristotelem Graeca*, The Royal Prussian Academy, vol. 19, Berlin 1889. A *methodos*, I believe, is no more than a procedure, or a way of going about things, that is sound and to some degree systematic. This is precisely what, on Aristotle's view, the practically wise person has, although the procedure he follows is neither scientific nor technical.

Part Three

Seven ~

Review of Roger Crisp, Translation of Aristotle's *Nicomachean Ethics* (New York, Cambridge University Press, 2000)

Aristotle's great ethical work, the *Nicomachean Ethics*, has fared well in its English incarnations. Among them two stand out: W. D. Ross's translation, which appeared in 1925 as volume IX of the Oxford Translation of Aristotle, and Terence Irwin's 1985 translation for Hackett, revised by Irwin in 1999 for the second edition. The unrevised Ross is out of print, but the translation is available as revised by Urmson in the Revised Oxford Translation of Aristotle, and as revised by Ackrill and Urmson in Oxford's 'World's Classics' series. Other available English translations are Ostwald's for Bobbs-Merrill, Thompson's for Penguin, and Rackham's for Wordsworth.

The translations of Ross and Irwin, both distinguished scholars of Aristotle, have been widely used. Yet the need for a different kind of translation has been felt for some time, above all by those whose task it is to present Aristotle's ethics to non-professional readers. Roger Crisp's new translation, in the series 'Cambridge Texts in the History of Philosophy', is a noteworthy new competitor to Ross and Irwin, though it needs improvement in certain respects. Before I turn to Crisp, a few words concerning Ross and Irwin.

Ross's translation is marvellously crafted, unsurpassed in linguistic elegance, and guided throughout by his nuanced philosophical understanding of Aristotle. The translation is so much a work of art in its own right that the revisions by other hands, while improving upon his renditions in places, somewhat spoil Ross's unique achievement. One wishes Oxford would reprint the unrevised Ross. However, although always enlightening, this translation is not ideal as an instructional tool, mostly because Ross does not stay close to Aristotle's own idiom. Irwin, by contrast, attempts to do just that. He aims at giving a translation which is linguistically and philosophically more rigorous than Ross's. The translator's plain and occasionally clipped idiom follows Aristotle's own. He stays syntactically close to the Greek, and pays special attention to Aristotle's technical terminology. Irwin is often successful in attaining the precision he seeks. He also provides a wealth of valuable material in his notes and glossary.

Yet the precision attained by Irwin is often a precision away from Aristotle. The thoughts expressed by his translation are more circumscribed than the

original. This precludes the possibility of understanding the text in ways
which the Greek clearly allows. The translator's hand is throughout strongly
guided by his own understanding of the text. Even in the second edition,
where he has somewhat reduced his editorial interventions into Aristotle's
text, Irwin retains an iron grip on his reader. The supplementary material has
been greatly expanded. Along with the translation, which it now exceeds in
length, it steers the reader almost ineluctably toward Irwin's own understanding of Aristotle.

What, then, is needed is a translation that is rigorous enough and yet allows for the play of different interpretations. But a translator who undertakes
to turn the *Nicomachean Ethics* into English afresh has a difficult task. A new
translation has to contend with Ross's insight, sensitivity and great linguistic
gifts, on the one hand, and with the interpretive rigour of Irwin, on the other.

Crisp goes a long way toward satisfying these desiderata. He makes room
for different textual and philosophical interpretations while turning Aristotle's Greek into a lively and readable English. The economy of expression he
achieves is almost startling. One typically needs much longer English sen-
tences to render accurately their Greek counterparts. Crisp discovers in English the economy which we may well have come to think was not there. His
rendition of many interpretively difficult and much discussed passages
achieves a remarkable combination of precision and flexibility, which is just
what we have been hoping for in a new translation. The linguistic tact and fe-
licity of expression often goes beyond what we could have hoped for. Especially successful are the translation of the function argument in Book I and
the passages about deliberation and practical wisdom in Books III and VI.

However, to establish itself as the translation of choice, this translation
needs to be revised in places. Passages that strikingly stand in need of improvement are the methodological ones. For instance:

> Accepting from a mathematician claims that are mere probabilities seems rather
> like demanding logical proofs from a rhetorician. (p. 5, *EN* I. 3 1094b 25–7)

The term 'logical proof' is at best unclear. An *apodeixis* is not merely a proof
that deserves to be called 'logical" in some sense of the word. In an *apodeixis*, the
premisses and the conclusion must express necessary truths, and the premisses
must be 'better known' than, or epistemologically prior to, the conclusion.
Apodeixeis at 1094b 26 is thus better rendered as 'demonstrations'. Aristotle
turns to the practical and theoretical use of intellect in Book VI, and stresses
there the demonstrative nature of scientific knowledge, *epistêmê*. To make the
required connections with the later parts of the *Nicomachean Ethics* (where
Crisp uses the word 'demonstration', 108, *EN* VI. 6), as well as with Aristotle's
other works, it is important that terms like this be rendered precisely.

Whether the expression *mathêmatikou pithanologountos* at 1094b 26 refers to
probabilities is highly debatable. It is fairly certain, however, given the

contrast with *apodeixeis* at b 27, that Aristotle refers here to *arguments* being made by a mathematician rather than *claims*. The somewhat unusual verb *pithanologein* is clearly connected with the adjective *pithanon*, meaning 'persuasive'. Thus the passage would be better rendered as: 'Accepting persuasive arguments from a mathematician . . .'.

Crisp seems to follow the unrevised Ross in this and other methodological passages. However, in such passages Ross is the least reliable translator. Much work has been done on these issues since the time he published his translation. Urmson appropriately substitutes 'demonstrative proofs' in the passage discussed for Ross's 'scientific proofs' to render *apodeixeis*. Irwin for his part gets all the important terms in this passage right.

The tone of Aristotle's remark as translated by Crisp is also slightly off. The breezy 'seems rather like' does not capture well the force of *phainetai* at 1194b 26. Ross took *phainetai* here to amount to 'evidently'. One is not bound to follow him here. Instead of opting for a weightier word, one might, for instance, simply say 'accepting persuasive arguments from a mathematician *is like* . . .'. Some change in the wording, however, is desirable.

The same tone recurs in other methodological remarks as translated by Crisp, and elsewhere. This tone gives a note of levity to the remarkably smooth flow of this translation, thus turning one of the translator's strengths into a weakness.

Here is another methodological passage in Crisp's translation:

> Nor should we demand an explanation in the same way in all cases. A sound proof that something *is* the case will suffice in some instances, as with first principles, where the fact itself is a starting point, that is, a first principle. (p. 13, *EN* I. 7 1098a 33–1098b 3)

Several interpretations of this important passage are possible. Ross's informal 'to establish well' for *deichthênai kalôs* seems to me to be preferable to Irwin's 'to prove rightly'. It is very likely that nothing like a proof in the strict sense is meant here, but simply a showing of some sort *that* something is the case. However, both Ross's and Irwin's translations of *deichthênai kalôs* have enough latitude to allow for alternative readings of the passage. By opting for 'sound proof', Crisp inappropriately chooses a term that has a definite technical meaning in English. At best, this closes off the interpretative issue; at worst, it gets Aristotle wrong.

Aristotle's remarks on method, though brief, are extremely important, making it well worth the translator's while to try to convey as accurately as possible both their substance and their weight. Minor revisions would go a long way here.

One can always quarrel about a translator's choice of key terms. On the whole, Crisp's choices compare well with those of his competitors. I would like to take issue, however, with his rendition of one central term. 'Skill' seems to me to be a very poor way to render Aristotle's *technê*. Admittedly, none of the customary translations—'art', craft', or 'expertise'—is ideal. Each of them is, however, preferable to 'skill'. In *EN* I. 7 Aristotle, after presenting the famous function argument, says that one should first give an outline of the good and fill in the details later, and that advances in the arts were made in such a way (1098a 20–6). For 'arts' Crisp has 'skills'. However, the claim that '[t]his is how skills have come to advance' (p. 12) may well puzzle the reader. The skill of a surgeon or carpenter is increased above all by repeated practice. What develops in the way Aristotle describes is not a skill, but the whole body of practical knowledge that constitutes, for instance, the art of medicine or the art of warfare.

Similarly, a reader encountering the first chapter of Aristotle's treatise in Crisp's translation might easily fail to recognize that medicine, shipbuilding and household management are themselves prime instances of what Crisp labels 'skills'. He supplies 'science' here—such as 'military science' and 'science of horsemanship'—but the reader would hardly guess that *technê* would be supplied just as readily, and that in this context *technê*, art, and *epistêmê*, science, are interchangeable. Medicine and the art of warfare involve skills, but are themselves not mere skills.

Crisp would do well to revise and expand his glossary. Entries for such central terms as *hexis*, *nous* (especially in view of the fact that it is translated as 'intellect'), and *technê*, and a separate entry for *ergon*, should have their place in the glossary. Something ought to be done about the peculiar translation of *daimôn* as 'fortune', under the entry 'eudaimonia'.

The Introduction merits some reworking as well. In designating Aristotelian greatness of soul, *megalopsuchia*, as 'unmodern and pre-Christian' (p. xviii), Crisp misses the modernity of the virtue that combines robust self-respect with the appreciation of the importance of being recognized by others.

Bernard Williams observed—in the course of some biting critical remarks about John McDowell—that kindness is 'not an Aristotelian virtue' (*Ethics and the Limits of Philosophy*, 218, n. 8). Apparently following this line of thought, Crisp maintains that '[t]he virtue of kindness or beneficence . . . is almost entirely absent from Aristotle's account, though he does allow that human beings do feel some common bonds with one another on the basis of their shared humanity (*EN* VIII. 1 1155a)' (pp. xvii–xviii). The great-souled person, Crisp further claims, is 'unlikely to stir himself to help the vulnerable' (p. xviii).

The question of kindness in Aristotle's ethics is an exciting topic, well worth broaching in the introduction. Yet Crisp's comments are contestable. The great-souled person is undoubtedly a thoroughly decent, *epieikês*, character, who would regard his fellow citizens with *eunoia*, good will, and be moved to help a person in need. He could be counted upon to exercise *euergesia*, beneficence, on a scale that is as great as his means allow. As Aristotle portrays him, the great-souled person is neither cold-hearted nor unwilling to help.

One passage where Crisp missed the opportunity to appreciate how kindness may be involved in Aristotelian decency is *EN* VI. 11. Here is his translation of 1143a 19–22:

> What is called discernment (*gnômê*), in virtue of which we say that people are discerning (*suggnômonas*) and have discernment (*gnômên*), is correct judgement of what is equitable (*tou epieikous*). This is indicated by the fact that we say that the equitable person is especially discerning (*suggnômonikon*), and that it is equitable (*epieikes*) to be discerning in certain circumstances (*to echein peri enia suggnômên*). (p. 114)

Crisp opts for 'discernment' for both *gnômê* and *suggnômê*. These two words are indeed nearly synonymous here, but they do not amount to mere 'discernment'. What 'we', which is to say, the Greeks of Aristotle's time, say is that a decent person, *epieikês*, is especially forgiving, *suggnômonikos*, and that it is decent to have forgiveness about certain things. The important philosophical implications of this claim are lost if one translates the sentence in the way Crisp does.

That forgiveness should count as a virtue of practical *intellect* may well seem peculiar to a modern reader. This fact, however, fits very well with Aristotle's understanding of practical reason. A person who is forgiving in the right circumstances is indeed on Aristotle's view more discerning than an unforgiving person. He sees more than an unforgiving person does. The way in which the meaning of the terms *gnômê* and *suggnômê* glides from the intellectual 'discernment' or 'consideration' to the moral 'considerateness' or 'forgiveness', and back, is indicative of Aristotle's understanding of practical rationality, and of this particular virtue of practical reason.

None the less, kindness is not an Aristotelian virtue. This is true in the sense that a propensity to help the needy is not the touchstone of the correct ethical disposition as Aristotle understands it. Nor is Aristotelian *philia*, friendship, which is discussed at such a length in the *Nicomachean Ethics*, anything like Christian *caritas*. A sensitive discussion of the relationship between the two types of ethics would be most welcome. However, to condemn Aristotelian virtue from a Christian standpoint, as Crisp in effect does in his Introduction, is no service to a reader of Aristotle's ethics.

Finally, here is what Crisp says about using Aristotle today:

> [Aristotle] was writing two and a half millennia ago, for noblemen in a city-state of tens of thousands. He believed such a city to be the best form of human society, and might well have thought it absurd even to attempt carrying across his conclusions about happiness in such a polity to what he would have seen as highly degenerate nation-states. It is not, in other words, a good idea to claim Aristotle as an ally in a modern debate the very assumptions of which he might have questioned. (pp. xviii–xix)

It is reasonable for Crisp to sound a note of caution against context-insensitive use of Aristotle. However, his wording gives the impression of an attempt to insulate Aristotle from contemporary ethical and political debates. I do not think that Crisp intended this. Yet that is what his formulation conveys. His success in letting Aristotle speak to a contemporary reader in a way that is strikingly relevant to current ethical concerns makes this apparent lapse into a hands-off stance seem entirely out of place.

A teacher looking for a single translation of the *Nicomachean Ethics* to use as a textbook, and a general reader who wishes to rely on a single translation of this work, will do well to choose Crisp. However, Crisp will serve his reader even better if he undertakes some of the revisions suggested.

Eight

Two or Three Things We Know about Socrates

Socrates is without doubt the most enigmatic and most influential intellectual figure in antiquity. He has been credited, by his admirers and detractors alike, with decisively shaping the Western intellectual outlook. My aim here is to give a brief outline of the enigma that attaches to the historical Socrates. I shall also mention some of the Socratic views that have cast such a long shadow on the Western intellectual tradition.

Socrates was an object of intense fascination and controversy during his lifetime and upon his death. He provoked much ridicule, attack, and admiration. The ridicule came from fifth-century BC comic playwrights, his contemporaries, whose portrayal of Socrates was anything but flattering. The only comical portrayal of Socrates made during his lifetime that has survived intact is Aristophanes' *Clouds*. Several passages from other fifth-century comedies have also been preserved. These comical portrayals could hardly have been found funny by Socrates' contemporaries had they not borne some resemblance to the man himself. Attacks on Socrates led to his trial, condemnation, and death in 399 BC. Shortly after his death, a new literary genre emerged—*Sokratikoi logoi*, Socratic discussions or discourses. The Socratic writings of Plato and Xenophon have come down to us intact. But these two authors were not the only ones who practised the new genre. Socratic discourses appear to have been quite popular in the fourth century BC. We possess remains of the Socratic writings of Antisthenes, Aeschines of Sphettos, Phaedo, and Eucleides of Megara, and some information regarding the views of Aristippus (collected in Giannantoni 1991). Another fourth-century ancient author often regarded as providing brief but significant information about Socrates is Aristotle.

There are two main reasons why Socrates has been, and is likely to remain, an enigmatic figure: first, he left no writings of his own, and second, the writings on which we have to rely for our information about him have received radically different assessments regarding their character, veracity, and accuracy. Whereas some regard Plato's and Xenophon's Socratic writings as instances of imaginative fiction, the aim of which is not historical portrayal of any kind, others take the two authors, or at least one of the two, as providing reliable information about the historical Socrates.

Hardly anyone thinks that Plato and other fourth-century Socratics intended their Socratic conversations as accurate transcripts of the conversations the man Socrates actually held. It is equally naive to think that Plato and others aimed at anything like the sort of accuracy we would nowadays expect of historical reports. We must bear in mind that all Socratic works—including Plato's early dialogues, his *Apology of Socrates*, Xenophon's *Memorabilia*, and *Symposium*—are literary creations. They appear to bear some relationship to the historical Socrates; what is at issue is the nature of this relationship.

From the fact that Socratic discourses are literary creations, we must not, I think, conclude that they are entirely fictional and were never aimed at representing actual views of the people they depict. For comparison, much of our knowledge about various post-Aristotelian schools of thought derives from second-hand sources, and some of the material is to be found in fictitious dialogues (see, for instance, Cicero's *Academica*, or *De finibus*). But it would be wrong to assume that we know nothing about the views of the authors whose work has been represented to us in this way. Coming back to Socrates, the intention of those who wrote Socratic dialogues is either not stated, or, where the intention is stated, we might have reason to disbelieve it (as some have argued we ought to in the case of Xenophon). It will not, however, do to declare, as has been done recently by Charles Kahn, that the Socratic discourses as a whole are a genre of imaginative fiction, never intended to have any relation to historical facts, and that hence we should not use them as sources for the views of Socrates himself (Kahn 1996). It seems to me that the way Aeschines might have thought of his Socratic discourses need not have been the same as the way Plato thought of his. The existence of a genre does not determine the use that particular authors make of it. In addition, although the remains of the Socratic discourses other than those written by Plato are invaluable, still we are in a better position to judge Plato's intentions by looking at his own work than by making generalizations about a genre which seems to have given birth to very disparate progeny. The genre of *Sokratikoi logoi* was in any case new: those who practised it, were inventing and practising it at the same time. Plato in particular succeeded in transforming the genre into something quite unique and unparalleled.

I think that we must also keep in mind that if Socratic dialogues were a literary genre, so were courtroom speeches. I thus do not agree with Kahn in excepting Plato's *Apology* from the category of imaginative fiction. Whereas I agree that the *Apology*, when used critically, provides useful information about the historical Socrates, I do not think that our licence to use it in this way derives from its purportedly radically different status when compared with the dialogues. The conversations we find in Plato's dialogues are probably fictitious, and so is Socrates' defence speech as given in Plato's *Apology*. However, literary works can provide useful historical and doxographical information, when read in a way that is responsive to the form, structure, and purport of the work in question.

There is only one of more than twenty-five works written by Plato in which Socrates does not appear—his last and unfinished work, the *Laws*. In most of the dialogues, Socrates is a principal interlocutor. The role of Socrates, however, changes. In the early dialogues, the larger metaphysical and epistemological concerns of Plato's later dialogues seem to be absent, and so is his Theory of Forms. In the early works, Socrates is a questioner and examiner who ultimately professes ignorance about the only issues he is keenly interested in—the issues of human virtue and the good human life. The early dialogues have traditionally been called Socratic, on the assumption that the views expressed by Socrates there bear a close resemblance to the views of the man Socrates himself. This traditional view of the early dialogues relies in part on the testimony of Aristotle, who distinguishes the views of Socrates from the views of Plato, and unambiguously assigns the Theory of Forms to Plato. The philosophical concerns, activities, and views that Aristotle assigns to Socrates are consistent with the Socrates that is depicted in Plato's early dialogues. But should we take it that the Socrates of the early dialogues does indeed tell us something about the man Socrates? I believe that to some limited extent, we should. We can rely on the general picture of Socrates that emerges from these dialogues, especially when it overlaps with the picture we get from Xenophon and other Socratic writers and with the testimony of Aristotle, although it would be wrong to assume that *any* particular bit of dialogue is a record of an actual conversation.

It is sometimes argued that the consistency between the picture of Socrates we get from Xenophon and Aristotle and what we find in the early dialogues of Plato cannot be taken as any kind of evidence for the views of the historical Socrates, because the testimony of Xenophon and Aristotle is not independent of Plato's writings. Many think that Xenophon derives some or all of his characterization of Socrates from Plato's dialogues. Some believe that the claims Aristotle makes about Socrates are likewise all or in part based on Plato's dialogues. The latter belief seems to me quite implausible. Aristotle came to Athens in 367, about thirty years after the death of Socrates. Thirty years is a long time. Nonetheless, it is difficult to believe that no oral tradition existed in Plato's Academy, and that all Aristotle had to go by were Plato's dialogues. Aristotle in his writings clearly distinguishes the *dramatis persona* of Plato's dialogues from the man Socrates, and also conveys information about Plato that he could not have gotten from Plato's own writings. It may not be irrelevant to mention that when Aristotle came to Athens, Plato was still alive. Some credence, I think, has to be given to Aristotle as a partially independent source. As for Xenophon, he probably did rely to a considerable extent on Plato's dialogues. However, it has been plausibly argued that he also relied on other Socratic authors, in particular Antisthenes, and that Plato only gradually established himself as a pre-eminent Socratic writer. We should be skeptical of the notion that it is the voice of Plato that we hear in all the fourth-century pronouncements regarding Socrates that have come down to us. The Socratic writers must have exerted influence on one another. It is hardly to be expected that any single one of them is an entirely independent source. But why should that be a condition for their being taken seriously?

When it comes to Socrates' philosophical activity and views, Plato is the most important of our sources. But the enigma of Socrates now becomes compounded by the enigma of Plato. Unlike Socrates, Plato did write; indeed, he was a prolific writer, combining a powerful philosophical mind with amazing literary gifts. But, as W. D. Ross observed, it is a salient feature of these works (Plato's dialogues) that they do not provide a key to their own interpretation (Ross 1933, p. 12). Hard work on the literary (and philosophical) interpretation of Plato's dialogues, including especially the early ones, is needed in order to make any sense at all of the relation between Plato's Socrates and Socrates the man. Controversy and dispute are unavoidable here, and may well be desirable.

What, then, do we know about the philosophical views of Socrates? With certainty, very little. However, if we make criticall use of the available sources I have mentioned, we find good reason to attribute to Socrates certain general concerns and views. Plato's *Apology* suggests the following picture: The most important thing one can do in life is to care for one's soul. This care requires getting to know oneself, and ridding oneself of ignorance, especially ignorance of one's own ignorance. Rational inquiry, which involves cross-examination, contributes to this positive goal. The soul is harmed whenever one does anything that is wrong. Suffering wrong is better for the soul than committing it. Socrates professes ignorance about the ultimate objects of his inquiry: the question of virtue and of the good human life. He denies he is anyone's teacher. Nonetheless, he believes that by cross-examining his fellow citizens, he is performing a very important service to them.

Several philosophical theses are especially associated with Socrates. These theses are paradoxical in the sense that they go against common opinion about the relevant matters (*doxa* is Greek for opinion or belief; *para* means 'against'). A philosophical elaboration of these theses is found in Plato's early dialogues. Further support for ascribing them to Socrates can be derived from Xenophon, Antisthenes, and Aristotle. The theses in question are the following: Virtue is a certain kind of knowledge. Virtue is one and indivisible. In other words, the names for particular virtues, moderation, justice, courage, and so on, all refer to one and the same thing. Finally, there is the most famous (and least well understood) thesis that no one errs willingly. The Socratic claim that akrasia—weakness of the will—does not exist is closely connected to the No-One-Errs-Willingly thesis. These theses jointly define the philosophy of Socrates.

For centuries, the theses just mentioned have being taken as the cornerstones of Socratic intellectualism. Someone who thinks that living well involves living in accordance with a certain kind of knowledge can reasonably be counted an intellectualist of some sort. I tend to think, however, that much of the criticism directed at Socratic intellectualism has been based on a misunderstanding of what sort of an intellectualist Socrates was. The main issue here is what kind of knowledge it is that in his view constitutes human virtue. A reinterpretation and reassessment of Socratic intellectualism is thus called for.

Returning to the issue of the historical Socrates, let me close by accepting the words of Arnaldo Momigliano: The Socratics, including Plato, "moved in that zone between truth and fiction which is so bewildering to the professional historian" (Momigliano 1971, p. 46). The debate that has raged for centuries concerning the problem of the historical Socrates, and which is no doubt likely to continue, might owe some of its force to the discomfort many of us feel when confronted with the ambiguities of this zone. Had the Socratics invented Socrates, their literature would still be of interest. But let us not for fear of ambiguity lose sight of the ambiguous man and philosopher himself.

Bibliography

Giannantoni, Gabriele (1991), *Socratis et Socraticorum reliquiae*. Collegit, disposuit, apparatibus notisque instruxit. 4 vols. Naples: Bibliopolis.

Kahn, Charles (1996), *Plato and the Socratic Dialogue: The Philosophical Use of a Literary Form*. Cambridge: Cambridge University Press.

Momigliano, Arnaldo (1971), *The Development of Greek Biography*. Cambridge, Mass." Harvatd Unibersity Press.

Ross, William D. (1933), "The Problem of Socrates". *Proceedings of the Classical Association* 30, 7–24.

Indices ~

INDEX OF PROPER NAMES, MODERN

Verdenius, W. J., 29n4, 30n
Vlastos, G., 29n2
Von Fritz, Kurt, 13n

Waterfield, Robin, 57n
Weiss, Roslyn, 52n7

White, N., 43n29
Wiggins, 95n, 150n14, 158
Willamowitz–Moellendorf, U. von, 28n1
Williams, B., 119–21, 178
Wolf, Christa, 42n26
Woods, Michael, 92n4, 96–97, 156n19

Subject Index

action: Aristotelian metaphysics of, chap. 5 *passim*; Socratic theory of, 79–85
agency, agent, chap. 5 *passim*
appearances, 112, 121ff.
art, 4, 8; of being a good citizen, 6; of living well, 4, 171

beauty, 38, 41

choice, xiv, 147, 150, 162–65
choiceworthiness, 99–101, 104–5, 107–10
courage, 34, 44–45, 77, 148, 157
craft analogy, 4. *See* art

deliberation, Aristotelian, ix–x, xii–xvi, chap. 6 *passim*
desire (wish), xiii–xvi, 35, 48, 54, 58, 75, 116, 118ff., 123, 162–63; rational *vs.* non-rational, 130–32, 143, 149; second-order, 74, 119

education, chap. 1 *passim*
emotion, 48
eroticism, 30–32, 35–38, 40, 45
expertise. *See* knowledge: practical

fear, Socrates' idea of, 76–77
finality, 107–8
freedom, xiv

goodness, the good, goods, good life, xii–xiii, 4, 48, 54, 64, chap. 4 *passim*, 123ff.

happiness, xii–xiii, xv, 3–4, 104–10, 168
health, 91, 98
honour, 89–91, 104, 106

ignorance, 73
intellectualism, Socratic, ix–xiii, 47, chap. 3 *passim*

kindness, 178–79
knowledge: moral, chap. 3 *passim*; practical, ix; Socrates' conception of, 66–68, 75

language, 40
love. *See* eroticism

magic, magician, 31–32, 42–44
methodology, 176–77
myth, 7–11, 15n13

oratory, orators, 51–54, 59, 80–81

persuasion, 53
pleasure, 89–91, 99–102, 104, 106
poetry, 12–15
power, 51–52, 61–62

reason, practical, ix–x, xv, 120, 150–52
reason, Socrates' conception of, 48, 79–80
relativism, xii n3, xvi, 123

self-sufficiency, 107–8
'Socratic wanting/willing', 51–55, 63, 65–68; defined, 54–55
soul, souls, 4, 38, 48

theory of action, ix
thought (*dianoia, nous*), 132–35
tyrants, 51–54, 59, 80–81

virtue (see also *aretē*), 3–7, 90–91, 97, 101, 104, 145; defined, 166; as knowledge, chap. 3 *passim*; teachability of, 3–7

wealth, 91
will, x, xiii–xiv, 48, 61–62; Socrates' denial of weakness of, chap. 3 *passim*; weakness of, chap. 3 *passim*, 108, 112, 152
wisdom, 35–37, 46, 89–91, 100, 126; practical, 145, 165–171

Index of Greek Terms

aidōs (shame), 8–11
aischros (ugly, disgraceful; opp. *kalos*), 11
akrasia (weakness of will), chap. 3 *passim*, 112, 122, 149
aretē (virtue), 3–4. See also *politikē aretē*

boulēsis (rational desire, wish), xiii, 165n
bouleusis (deliberation), chap. 6 *passim*

dianoia. See thought
dikē (justice), 8–11
doxa (reputation), 25
doxa (opinion, belief), 53, 71–72, 127, 184
dunamis (power, capacity), 7–8, 17, 19, 138n; *dunamis* vs. *hexis*, 136; *dunatos* (powerful), 17; *dunatōtatos* (most powerful), 5, 17–22, 24

entechnos sophia (technical wisdom). See *sophia*
energeia (actuality, activity), 135–37, 138n34, 139–40
epistēmē, 53, 136
ergon (function), 144
euboulia (sound deliberation, good judgement), 5, 25, 144–46
eudaimonia (happiness), *eudaimōn* (happy), 3n, 4, 139–40, 158ff., 168–70, 178
eu prattein (do well), 3

hekōn (willingly), xiv
hexis, 136–38

kalos (beautiful, noble, fine; opp. *aischros*), 11

mathēma (teaching), 4–5, 17, 21n21, 23n24

nous. See thought

ta oikeia (domestic affairs), 5

panourgia (villainy that stops at nothing), 11
pathos, pathēma (affliction), 68–69, 73
phainomenon agathon (apparent good), 112, 117, 121, 123–26, 129
phantasia (appearance), 112, 127, chap. 5 *passim*
phronēsis, phronimos. See wisdom: practical
politēs (citizen), 6
politikē aretē (political virtue), 9–11
politikē technē (political craft, civic art), 22
praxis (action), 135, 139
prohairesis (choice), xiv

sophia (wisdom) (*see* wisdom); *entechnos sophia* (technical wisdom), 8
sōphrosunē (temperance), 9, 23
sōtēria (salvation), 10
synesis, eusynesia (comprehension), 160–62
syngnōmē, 161–62

technē (craft), 4–9, 178; *politikē technē* (political art), 4–6, 16n14
telos (end aimed at in action), telos model of action, 113ff., 132–37, 140, 154
theōria, 141–42
thymos (spirit), 143

Index Locorum

[Aeschylus]
Prometheus Bound
266: 47

Aristophanes
Clouds: 181
254: 34n13
709: 34n13

Aristotle
De Anima: 139

II 5: 136
III 3: 127n21
   3, 414b 5–6: 131
   9, 432a 15–16: 129
   10, 433a22–30: 162
      433b 8–10: 130n
      433b 11–12: 134
      433b 29: 129
      434a 5–7: 129
De Motu Animalium
6, 700b 17–19: 133